THE
GREAT AGE
OF SAIL

CREATED AND PRODUCED
BY
EDITA LAUSANNE

B.W. BATHE · G.B. RUBIN DE CERVIN · E. TAILLEMITE

R.H. BURGESS · R.J. COLLINS · A. FRANZÉN · H. GRUBBE · F. LE BIBOUL · PH. K. LUNDEBERG · E.W. PETREJUS

WITH THE COLLABORATION OF JEAN MERRIEN

THE
GREAT AGE
OF SAIL

EDITED BY JOSEPH JOBÉ

TRANSLATED BY MICHAEL KELLY

Crescent Books   New York

First published in 1967
Smaller, unabridged edition published in 1971
Reprinted in 1977

ISBN 0-517-24 6651
Library of Congress Catalog no. 77-088141

Produced by Edita SA, Lausanne, Switzerland
Published in the USA by Crown Publishers,
Inc., 1 Park Avenue, New York, N.Y. 10016.

Printed in Italy and bound in Switzerland

CONTENTS

FOREWORD

On September 6th, 1522, the *Victoria*, with eighteen exhausted men on board, dropped anchor off the mole at Seville in Spain. Out of the five ships that had set sail from Seville on September 20th, 1519, under the aegis of the emperor Charles V to explore the sea routes to the Far East, she was the only one left. The *Trinidad*, the *San Antonio*, the *Concepcion* and the *Santiago* had all been lost. Out of the 270 men who had sailed under the command of Ferdinand Magellan, only these eighteen survived. The first ship to sail round the world, the *Victoria* returned loaded with exotic woods, drugs, perfumes and spices. In spite of the losses in men and material, this expedition was an unprecedented success and its consequences were to be far-reaching.

This great maritime adventure by men in the west had begun several decades earlier. In 1492, the Spaniards under Columbus had discovered the West Indies and, later, landed on the continental mass known today as the Americas. In 1487, Portuguese sailors at last discovered the long-sought passage to the Indies by way of the Cape of Good Hope, sailing far beyond the southern limits of the then known world.

The significance of these geographical discoveries has not always been fully appreciated. If, for example, instead of the Europeans discovering Asia, Africa and the Americas, seafarers from these continents had discovered Europe, the whole course of western history and civilization would have been inexorably altered for many centuries thereafter. The newly charted sea routes were indeed revealing the full aspects of the globe.

At the beginning of the sixteenth century, Europeans were passing through one of the most enlightened periods in their history. Imbued with the spirit of adventure, they were also adequately, although modestly, equipped to impose their will on communities far away from their homelands. Their sailing-vessels spanned the oceans. Their fire-arms inspired respect and, when necessary, enforced obedience.

This intrusion by Europeans into unknown or hitherto unexplored territories affected not only the discovered countries but also Europe itself. During the Middle Ages, trade from Asia to Europe followed two main routes. The overland "Silk Road" linked China to Europe by way of Central Asia, the Black Sea and Syria, and the Italian town of Genoa had, for a long time, monopolized this traffic. The maritime "Pepper Route" started from Chinese ports and led by way of Ceylon, the Red Sea and overland by caravan through Egypt to the port of Alexandria. This trade was the virtual monopoly of the Venetians. However, in the short space of fifty years, from about 1490 to 1540, mastery of trade in the China Seas and the Indian Ocean hitherto dominated by the Arabs, was snatched from them by the Portuguese and a few thousand seafarers, soldiery and merchants disrupted an economic pattern that had endured for centuries.

In the Americas, the arrival of the Spanish precipitated the collapse of civilizations in the Mexican higher plateaux, the Yucatan Peninsula and in Peru. Simultaneously, the powerful monarchies of Western Europe such as Great Britain, France, Portugal, Spain and the United Provinces of the Netherlands opened up long-distance traffic lanes and, under the influence of new capitalistic ideas, launched themselves on the way towards economic imperialism and the creation of colonial empires.

There is no doubt that this commercial and cultural upheaval was due to many complex causes. Among the most important of these were several technical innovations : the building of sailing-vessels with decks, the use of the compass and the astrolabe — an instrument for measuring the height of the pole-star above the horizon — and, finally, the development of artillery and small-arms. Conversely, sailing-vessels themselves were influenced by the very discoveries they had made possible. Ever larger, faster, more seaworthy and heavily armed vessels were constantly being required to exploit and guard the new sea routes.

Over four centuries, the history of the great sailing-ships was bound up with the political activities of the great maritime powers and their important commercial interests. Concurrently, the very technical developments which enabled sailing-ships to attain the peak of their perfection also doomed them to retirement, through the introduction of steam power which slowly but inexorably supplanted the great clouds of sail. But the history of these great ships is also a powerful, human documentary of captains and crews, creating a legend in the wake of their ships as they sailed through the centuries and over the horizons of time.

Acknowledgements are due to Monsieur G. B. Rubin de Cervin, Monsieur E. Taillemite and Mr. B. W. Bathe for having written a book which, while satisfying those zealots with salt in their veins, will surely fire the imagination of every reader. We are also indebted to our American, Dutch, English, French, German, Italian and Swedish collaborators who contributed the monographs of eight characteristic sailing-ships, thus enhancing the technical and, indeed, the international aspect of our book.

The publishers would also like to thank all the curators of museums and the collectors in Europe and America, who have so ably assisted in compiling such varied and, in many cases, hitherto unpublished illustrations. It only remains for the publishers to hope that readers of this book may relive the epic story of those four centuries of seamanship under sail when the men of Western Europe roamed the seven seas.

Joseph Jobé

G.B. RUBIN DE CERVIN

Curator of the MUSEO STORICO NAVALE, Venice

THE AGE OF DISCOVERY

Before the sixteenth century, only those nations that lay between the Atlantic Ocean and the China Seas, bounded by northern waters and the African shores of the Mediterranean, made history. In the west of this land mass, men dreamed of new territories to conquer, of gold and exotic spices. In reaching out for their dreams, they discovered the world was indeed round. This great step forward in men's knowledge was a triumph for European technical ability and, above all, for the *conquistadores* and the sailors who manned those famous caravels that set their bows to the west, across the ocean.

C. de Gel.

SAILING SHIPS OF THE AGE OF DISCOVERY

Even taking into account the tremendous pace of modern research and progress since the Industrial Revolution, minds usually turn to that historical period, the Renaissance, when discoveries are mentioned. This was the romantic period, when men struggled with Nature to realize their quests. The spirit of the Renaissance had considerable effect on a civilization that was, itself, pushing its horizons further afield. This changed outlook had, *inter alia*, a direct influence on the future design of ships. In a narrow sense, the Renaissance was the revival of Greek learning, a break away from the rigid control and omnipowerful authority of the Medieval Church.

On the other hand, the Renaissance not only influenced art and education, but gave a new impetus to science and invention, the study of geography, and exploration. Names from this age that immediately spring to mind include Columbus, Cabot, Cartier, Cortez, Diaz, Vasco da Gama and Magellan, among others. They discovered the Americas and circumnavigated the world. Seafarers discovered new regions from which exotic tropical produce, precious stones or metals were brought back to enrich national coffers. And they were forced to develop ships with better sailing qualities and increased cargo space. This passionate interest of merchants and sailors

In the foreground of this detail from the "Map of Venice" by Jacob de' Barbari, Venetian ships of 1498 carry four not three masts. A small bonaventure mizzen perched on the taffrail is supplementary to the mizzen lateen, a sail arrangement enabling these ships to beat to windward.

An illustration from "The Great Voyages" by J. Th. De Bry, shows sixteenth century galleons, built up with such tall castles they seem to have an athwart groove cut amidships.

in the exotic products of the east was not entirely romantic or scientific. As root crops for winter cattle feed did not exist in European countries, most livestock were killed off before the winter set in and salted meat had to suffice until the summer months came round and fresh meat was again available. Spices such as cinnamon, cloves, nutmeg and pepper were needed to alleviate the boredom of this mundane diet. Pain-killing drugs, too, were available in the Indies and scarce in Europe. Cheap at the source and so highly-priced in the markets of Antwerp and London, these products provided another financial lure for the intrepid mariners during this period of awakening. There was also another factor. With the conquest of Albania, the Ottoman Empire had spread across the Middle East to the Adriatic, cutting the old caravan routes. Only on the open seas could be found new roads to the old treasure houses.

Although the Italian Renaissance centred on Florence, a great and wealthy city, Rome and Venice also flourished as business centres during this period.

Early in the sixteenth century, Lisbon took over the maritime lead from Venice. Portuguese caravels, built on the Tagus, turned away from the Mediterranean to open up the riches of the New World.

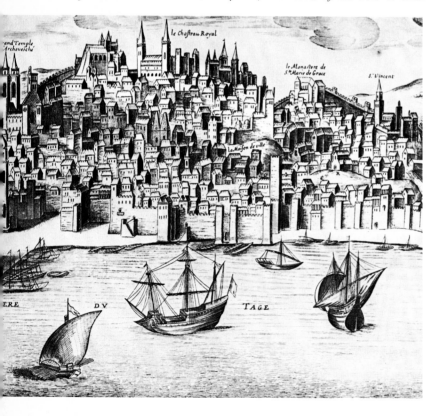

It is from the Christian name of a Florentine, Amerigo Vespucci, that the name "America" is derived. However, the emphasis on trade was shifting and economic conditions were far from stable. Even if competition with Genoa was diminishing in favour of Venice, trade still showed signs of a recession and the city could no longer claim to be the most important commercial centre in the Mediterranean. Certain contemporary illustrations provide graphic evidence of the decline in this city's prosperity.

During 1498, Maître Jacob de' Barbari returned to his native Venice from Bavaria. Although known to be somewhat temperamental in his approach to his work, Barbari brought with him a commission from the Nuremberg publisher, Anton Kolb, to produce the famous *Great Map of Venice*. In the completed engraving by Jacob de' Barbari, a recognized masterpiece in the annals of map-making, merchant ships can be seen lying at anchor the length of the St. Mark dock, from the customs house at the harbour entrance. Oddly enough, they are depicted with no sign of human presence or movement and no trace of cargo on board; each appears to be lying empty and deserted. These boats could have been lying idle as a result of an economic crisis then intensifying in Venice or could have been merely drawn thus by this capricious artist. In view of the close trading relations between Venice and the important northern markets, Kolb, no doubt, believed that his map of this large maritime city would particularly appeal to German buyers with their new interest in the Italian Renaissance.

It was, after all, during this period that the largest warehouses in Venice were built, not far from the Rialto Bridge and known by the name of *Germanicis Domus*. Reserved for German merchants and traders, they were mostly used by the Fugger company which handled a large share of the Venetian metal trade, copper being most important because of the increasing development of artillery in Europe.

The discovery of America in 1492 by Christopher Columbus left Venice businessmen unperturbed. In 1499, however, news spread round the city that alarmed the whole populace. Patrician Girolamo Priuli noted in his *Journal* that "...travellers returning from the Indies have let it be known that three Portuguese caravels have reached Calicut

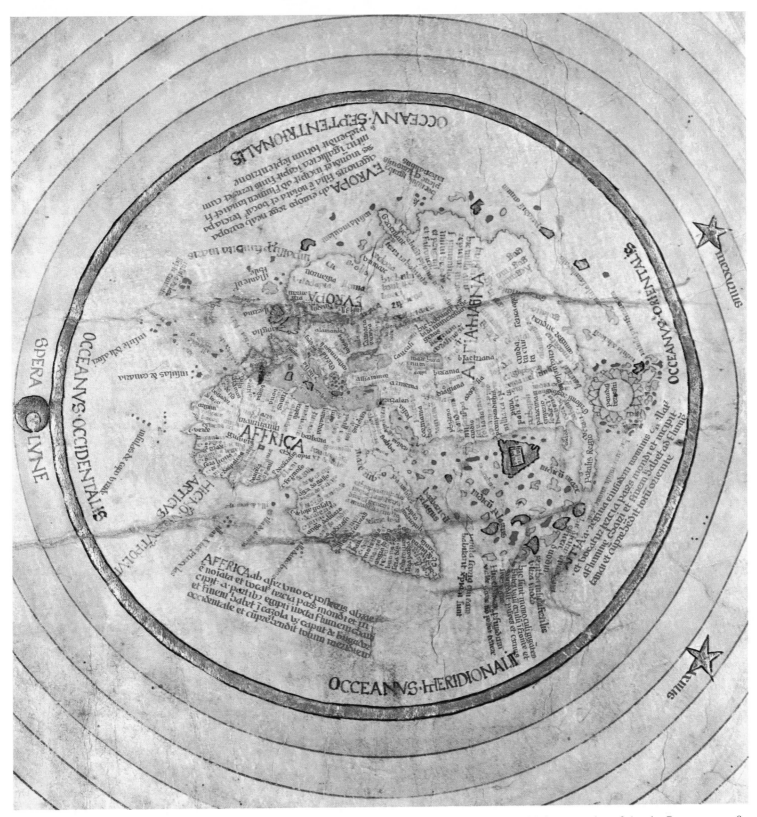

Dated about the end of the fifteenth century, this world map shows the Old World in the process of being transformed by the Portuguese and Spanish discoveries. The west coasts of Africa are quite clearly outlined as is the Cape of Good Hope. As Bartholomew Diaz only succeeded in rounding the Cape in 1488, the map must have been drawn after that date. Farther west in the Atlantic, the cartographer has only indicated the Cape Verde and Canary Islands, and the Azores. America had yet to be discovered. This suggests that the map was drawn up between 1488 and 1493, the date of Columbus' return, and, therefore, can only have been valid for a period of perhaps five years, at the very maximum.

and Aden..." Until then, the Council of Venice had paid little attention to the voyages undertaken by the Portuguese mariners and of the perseverance with which they were drawing ever and inevitably closer to the Indies. This news, however, had immediate repercussions in Venice. There was an overnight slump in spices, particularly pepper prices. Voicing the general pessimism, Girolamo Priuli wrote, " I think this news to be the most calamitous that the Republic has ever received".

From this time onwards Venice lost her privileged position. Inexorably the centre of political and economic activity moved in the direction of Lisbon. Indeed the Portuguese capital was currently enjoying a period of prosperity never known before, and much of this good fortune was the direct result of an increase in shipping and maritime trade. A writer of that time, Fernaos Lopes, recorded that the port of Lisbon boasted more than five hundred ships of a wide variety of flags and types. Whatever these

The Flor De La Mar, *shown in a detail from the " Roteiro de Malaca " in Lisbon, was in fact a galleon, the mightiest warship of her time. Left in Mozambique for repairs by Étienne, the son of Vasco da Gama, the ship was subsequently taken over by Spain.*

claims, the types of ships were not so widely different as, during this period, ships built in the north of Europe and those built on the Mediterranean shores came under reciprocal influence.

Portugal, half way between the north and south, maintained two *frotas* or fleets, one composed of "round" sailing ships employed as merchantmen, the other made up of "long" ships, oared galleys designed expressly as men-of-war and usual to other Mediterranean powers. On the other hand, Venice employed heavy "merchant galleys", a hybrid warship-merchantman, half sail and half oared. Although no documentation on these ships remains, it is understood that they were all built by the State, being chartered for limited periods to private merchant contractors. The ships travelled in regular convoys called *mude*, all the routes and time-tables strictly controlled by the Government of Venice who, preceding the now famous Indian company, exercised a virtual monopoly of all shipping.

Genoese ships trading with the ports of Antwerp and Plymouth, used " round " ships at this time. Masts were raked slightly forward carrying a triangular main sail called a *lateen*, the origins of which are still uncertain although it was probably derived from *a la trina*, in other words, triangular.

While Venetians and Genoese were fiercely wrangling over maritime commerce and sea trade routes in the Mediterranean, to the north, by contrast, a free trade alliance was taking shape, initiated by the Germans. Later called the Hanseatic League, it was subsequently joined by other towns, the principal shipping cities, or *Civitates maritimae*, being Hamburg, Lübeck and Bremen. This association not only developed trade but the Hanseatic ships, as they were called, eventually monopolized the local maritime and river traffic. Also "round" ships, they were rigged with one mast amidships carrying a single large square sail, thought to be derived from the ancient Viking galleys. Here is the beginning of the square-rig, the vital turning point in the development of rigging from which the ocean-going vessel and its familiar silhouette was born.

Hanseatic ships plied between the northern and the Mediterranean ports where shipwrights were quick to appreciate the advantages of this square sail over their lateen. Increasing trade and competition demanded greater hold capacity and, therefore, larger sails. The lateen was becoming increasingly unwieldy on the larger vessels, requiring crews of up to 50 men to handle the outsize yards and to change the sails when the weather blew up. The square-rigged ship had shorter yards and more easily managed sails which could be reefed. Furthermore, smaller crews resulted in lower running costs.

It is not surprising that ships eventually became uniform in shape above the water-line. Below the water-line, there was a marked difference. Ship-wrights on the Mediterranean coasts fixed their planking to the frames edge to edge, giving a smooth surface to the hull, known as "carvel-built". Ships in the north were sturdier, "clinker-built", with each plank overlapping the one below like tiles on a roof, the better to stand up to rougher seas.

The earliest square-rigged ships in the Mediterranean were similar to those in the north, with single masts. Italian shipwrights soon discovered, however, that a ship's sailing qualities and manoeuvrability could be greatly improved by spreading the canvas in the shape of square and lateen sails over three masts. Thus the carrack came into being, the basic design of future ocean-going vessels.

Another important innovation borrowed by the Mediterranean shipwrights from the Hanseatic ships was the single stern rudder, important in the evolution of ships intended for deep sea navigation. Strange as it may seem, this type of helm was not fitted to Mediterranean ships until early in the fourteenth century, noted by Giovanni Villani in his *New Chronicles*. Marco Polo had remarked on the stern rudder on Chinese junks as early as the thirteenth century and was quite surprised, being unaccustomed to this helm in home waters. None of them seemed to have been aware that stern rudders had been common on Hanseatic ships since the beginning of the thirteenth century, as old seals of the maritime cities testify.

The next available evidence to the manifest progress in ship design can be seen in certain Flemish etchings, simply signed "W.A.". Posterity owes "W.A." a debt of gratitude for the wonderfully detailed illustrations of merchant-ships or carracks, called *kraecks* by the artist (see pages 17-18). These are sketched as they appeared to him, sauntering round the Flemish docks and harbours. All these ship illustrations show fore and stern castles, not yet a part of the hull itself but predicting the forecastle and the poop which were to be made much larger in the course of time.

Changes in the rigging can be seen in the available illustrations. The mainmast stepped amidships is shown surrounded by a web of stays. As these run to different points regularly spaced up the mast it can be deduced that the mast is not made from a single tree but built up of sections. Some were simply lashed together while others had the topmast section fitted into a specially prepared socket built round the lower portion and wedged tight. At this joint was built the "top", a semi-circular platform surrounded by a rail and, in many cases, a canvas or wooden screen, intended to provide some protection, at least, against the vagaries of inclement weather.

Sails on the other two masts probably served more to steady the ship and improve her sailing

The heavy armament necessitated by battles in the East Indies brought about a barrel-like appearance to ships such as the Trindade, shown here. Reinforced with longitudinals like barrel hoops and provided with fortified castles, these galleons became very unwieldy under sail.

15

qualities than to increase her drive. Evidence is scarce and although the same characteristics can be seen on ships in the background of paintings by Vittorio Carpaccio about 1490, it is debatable as to whether these ships were truly Venetian and not Hanseatic vessels which just happened to be there.

First mentioned in a Portuguese manuscript dated 1255, the *caravel* was being accepted more widely by mariners. The most famous caravel yards were on the banks of the River Tagus, a place long known as the "shore of ships", near Lisbon (see page 12). At first the name applied to small fishing-boats rigged with two or three lateen sails and not even decked in, and only much later to much larger vessels. Although the name is usually reserved for ships of Portuguese or Catalan origin, it is often used for the nearly identical type of ship that gradually came into service in the Mediterranean, again demonstrating the reciprocal influences that emerged in ship design coupled with new commercial horizons. During the second half of the fifteenth century, the merchant-ship was generally rigged according to a more or less standard pattern, comprizing mizzen, main and fore-mast. Later on, a smaller, rectangular sail was added, high up on the mainmast above the top, called the topsail and handled by the duty watch. Subsequently, another sail was added, this time on the bowsprit. Until the bowsprit was introduced, inclined upwards and reaching out over the bows, the foremast was stepped as far forward as possible. The addition of the bowsprit allowed this mast to be heightened and more firmly stepped aft, as the bow-sprit now carried the forestays. This spritsail was not new, being derived from the *dolon* common to all working ships of the ancient Roman navy.

Slowly and surely a working sail plan was evolving. One of the greatest advances in the history of sailing had been made. At last Man could choose his course independently of the contrary winds. With this more versatile sail plan and greater manoeuvrability the long voyages could begin.

The lateen was carried on the mizzen-mast until the end of the seventeenth century and fitted into the more efficient balance of the new sail plan. From now on, the complete suit of sails could be properly trimmed and a ship could be sailed close-hauled and, by tacking, make headway into wind.

On August 2nd, 1492, Christopher Columbus and his three caravels set sail from Palos harbour and headed out to the west. As is well known, his small fleet was composed of the *Santa Maria*, the *Nina* and the *Pinta*. None of these ships were built for this grandiose undertaking but simply chosen from among those vessels normally coasting off Spain.

Attempts have been made to reproduce these caravels commissioned by Columbus, but the lack of original documentation and positive facts have reduc-ed those experts on naval affairs to basing their research on fragmentary information gathered from outside sources or vague allusions by contemporary diarists. However, on the 400th centenary of the discovery of America, a successful reconstruction of the *Santa Maria*, authentically rigged and equip-ped, sailed across the Atlantic, following the same course as her predecessor, arriving after a voyage of similar duration. At the same time, an Italian com-mittee sponsored the reproduction in miniature of other versions of this famous caravel, based on more recent research. All investigations conducted up to this time had been founded, in essence, on the stand-ards used by the Catalan shipwrights of the fifteenth century, common to all Mediterranean shipyards; the principle for instance of *tres, dos y as* or "three, two and twelve", according to which the depth of the hull should equal half its beam and a third of its length, the only elements common to all the various reproductions. In fact the studies made and the conclusions drawn resulted in models showing as wide a divergence in hull dimensions as in rigging.

In the meantime, it has been possible to arrive at a more accurate conception of these caravels. In 1929, a chance discovery revealed an authentic small-scale model of a merchantman probably dating from just before the time of the ships of Palos. This was an *ex-voto* offering from the sanctuary of Saint Simon de Mataro in Catalonia which, designated by schol-ars under the generic name of *Catalan ship* (see pages 19-24), is housed in the Prins Hendrik Museum at Rotterdam. Although slightly damaged this model can be considered as the most faithful reproduction of a fifteenth century sailing-vessel, resolving certain theories and hypotheses concerning seafaring in those times. Details are clearly seen of projections on the planking; the galleries, triangular at the bows and

This illustration by the Flemish engraver "W.A." is as descriptive of the caravel of Columbus' day as a model.

Woven into the tapestry "Sitio de Rodas" from Barcelona, these ships date from distinctly later than those shown on the right. But they still preserve, multiplied and enlarged, the protective wooden fenders which so greatly hampered manoeuvrability when under sail.

Another sketch by the anonymous Flemish artist "W. A." can be usefully compared to the drawings and the model of the "Catalan ship" itself, now housed in the Prins Hendrik Museum in Rotterdam (pps. 19-24). The strong similarity both overall and in certain details does much to vouch for the authenticity of the model.

rectangular at the stern, and the general arrangements on deck. Assuming that the model was built to a scale of 1 : 24, this ship would have been approximately 80 ft long, 33 ft wide and 20 ft in height, although these dimensions do not truly correspond to those known to have been used by Catalan shipwrights of that period.

Early in the fifteenth century the Portuguese, already active seafarers since the twelfth century, took the lead in maritime exploration, partly because of the development of their sailing-ships but mainly due to the encouragement and crusading spirit of Prince Henry, whose pioneering zeal earned him the name of The Navigator. He launched the navy on a series of voyages destined to open up the coasts of Africa and which ultimately led to the rounding of the dreaded Cape No, the Moroccan promontory now known as Ras Sidi Ouorzek, and with it the hope of opening up the sea route to the Indies.

At Sagres, on the tip of Cape St. Vincent, Prince Henry had built an observatory and a school for navigators. To this *Vila do Infante* came astronomers and mathematicians, chart-makers and cosmographers from Genoa, Pisa and Majorca as well as merchants and master-mariners, among them pilots and Moorish traders, who alone held the secrets of the distant sea routes and hidden harbours. The Prince amassed all their information to piece together his immense *Plan of the Indies* to which he was devoted heart and soul for so many years, and which, one day, was to enable Portuguese ships to reach first the Indies, then the fabulous empire of Cathay, so tantalizingly described by Marco Polo. To finance this undertaking, he envisaged using the vast revenues from the assets of the Order of Christ, of which he himself was the Grand Master. He felt free to dispose of these funds as the goal he had in view was entirely religious, namely to bring under the protection of the Holy Roman Church those pagan nations he would subdue during his crusading

By the same artist as those on the preceding page, numerous details are provided on these fifteenth century ships: the mizzen lateen in its crutch, the newly introduced foremast, the strange barrels on either side of the stern, the sounding-lead, the pear-shaped float, probably used as an anchor-buoy, and a long rod, presumably a log, hung by the cat-holes. The sail (top) still has its "bonnets" laced on.

THE CATALAN SHIP · 15TH CENTURY

BY G. B. RUBIN DE CERVIN

No plans, nor even a rough sketch of the three caravels picked by Columbus for his great adventure across the Atlantic have ever been uncovered. This is quite understandable, as in those early days plans or blue prints were seldom drawn up. Master carpenters in shipyards built up the hulls of their vessels by old rule-of-thumb methods, not only handed down from one generation to the next but often simply by word of mouth. This practice continues, even today, almost six centuries later, among the small shipwrights in the Venetian lagoon.

However, since earliest times, sailors of every nationality have enjoyed modelling the ships in which they weathered the storms and overcame the dangers that were so much a part of their life at sea. Afterwards, these miniature ships were treated as offerings to such madonnas as the churches of their countries were dedicated.

Primitively fashioned as they are, these *ex-votos* often constitute the only valid records for the study of a naval art which evolved from experience rather than theory, and which subsequently vanished. Along the French, Italian and Spanish coasts there were numerous churches dedicated to the Blessed Virgin, patroness of seafarers. Here, in bygone days, could be seen hundreds of these *ex-voto* " church-ships " offered by mariners, either from superstitious or pious motives, to their favourite place of worship. Over the years, unfortunately, both wooden votive plaques and ship models, once suspended from the chapel vaults, have almost all disappeared. Their value was quickly recognized and these models became keenly sought after by dealers.

Such was the case with the model of a Catalan vessel which was originally housed in the sanctuary of St. Simon de Mataro. After many vicissitudes, the model finally found a permanent refuge in the Prins Hendrik Maritime

Museum at Rotterdam, where it was designated by the experts under the generic term of *Catalan Ship*. As a matter of fact, it is the only existing specimen and absolutely unique. Some craftsman must have fashioned the ship not long before the Genoese seafarer, Columbus, chose his vessels at Palos. As can be seen, he worked freehand and certainly without conforming to established scientific principles. Nevertheless it would appear that the model was made to a scale of approximately 1 : 24, whence it can be inferred that the original ship would have been approximately 80 ft. long, 33 ft. in beam and 20 ft. high. In point of fact, these dimensions do not altogether tally with the standard measurements observed by Catalan shipwrights of the time.

The complexity of the details with which the work is embellished leads one to believe that the model represented one of the " round " boats in off-shore service, more or less the usual type of vessel plying between Mediterranean ports. It shows unquestionable similarities with the ships portrayed by Carpaccio as well as with other Venetian merchant units that can be identified in certain canvases by Mansueti in Venice.

Analyzing the principal features of this valuable relic, it can be seen that the vessel is carvel-built in the typically latin caravel style and reinforced by stronger strakes fixed to the upright of the stern and the stem-post. Five vertical frames protect and reinforce the hull where it rises up to form the quarter-deck, which is continued practically half-way along the main deck. There are also the remains of sheathing under the hawse-hole, to protect the bow planking from damage by the anchor when it is raised.

To the side of the prow, another series of stepped planks on each side of the forecastle were almost certainly used to close in the forepeak and pro-

tect it from heavy seas. This area was surmounted by a triangular poop, clearly separated from the rest of the ship. At the extremity of the stern rose yet another smaller raised deck, exposed to all winds and weathers. No painted shields are portrayed but there is an unpretentious gallery, probably serving as a hand-rail for sailors during a voyage. The prow ends in a carving representing an animal, the very stylized lines recalling those employed in the decoration of some Hanseatic ships.

The rudder is fixed to the stern-post while the tiller penetrates the hull and is then lost to sight under the poop. It is not known whether the tiller was managed with tackles or ropes, but presumably something of this nature existed on the original vessel in view of the considerable effort required to work it. A single hatchway opened amidships but there is no sign of any other openings to ventilate the holds.

Our Catalan ship, still blackened by the dust of centuries and the smoke from candles and incense, has none of the glamour and splendour legend normally associates with the ships of Columbus. Popular illustrations and official geographical publications like to picture these ships in vivid colours with banners, standards and colours streaming in the breeze and all sails full as the ships sail out of Palos harbour to the salute of cannon and the applause of the watching crowd.

Be that as it may, we have no hesitation in affirming that this model from St. Simon de Mataro is, so far, that which bears the closest resemblance to the original ships used by Columbus. There can be no doubt as to the genuine and responsible intentions and the thoroughness of past research which has resulted in numerous reconstitutions of the *Santa Maria*. In the light of the model from the Prins Hendrik Museum they can only be considered as picturesque representations.

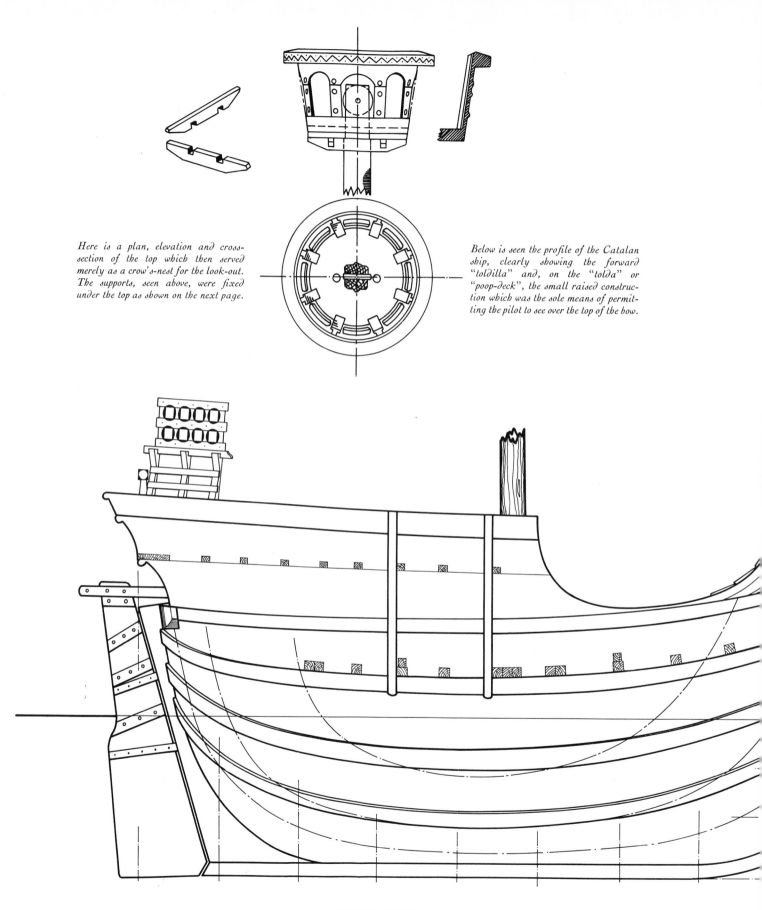

Here is a plan, elevation and cross-section of the top which then served merely as a crow's-nest for the look-out. The supports, seen above, were fixed under the top as shown on the next page.

Below is seen the profile of the Catalan ship, clearly showing the forward "toldilla" and, on the "tolda" or "poop-deck", the small raised construction which was the sole means of permitting the pilot to see over the top of the bow.

PROFILE SECTION

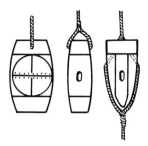

Left: *The first two small sketches show details of a pulley on the model while that on the right represents a block, used for hoisting and tightening the shrouds according to the wind direction and force.*

Below: *This sketch shows a detail from half the forward part of the "poop-rail" on the "tolda"; one of its stanchions is also depicted.*

Below, right: *This detail illustrates how two of these stanchions supported the hand-rail, showing its sturdy construction. Possibly to avoid weakening the structure, no gangways seem to have been provided.*

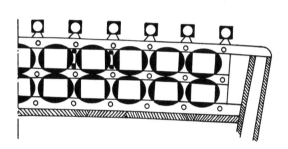

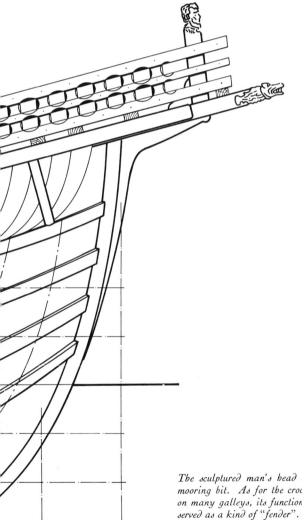

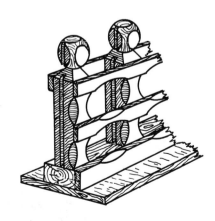

The sculptured man's head seen right forward in this profile is actually a mooring bit. As for the crocodile, reminiscent of the ancient ram, still used on many galleys, its function here is purely decorative, although it might have served as a kind of "fender". The tiller penetrates the hull beneath the "tolda", making it impossible for the helmsmen to see either the sea or the vessel's course; as a result of this, he is obliged to depend on orders from above.

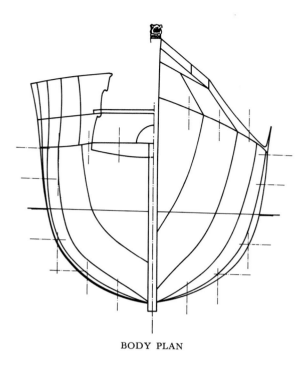

The body plan is an end elevation, looking at the bow for the fore body and at the stern for the after body, represented respectively in the right and left parts of the plan opposite. Anyone with a knowledge of naval architecture will see immediately that the lines of the Catalan ship pay no attention to drag resulting from water eddies, thus cutting down her speed. They may also be surprised at the height of the ship's sides above the water-line. With such a high centre of gravity, considerable ballast must have been necessitated.

BODY PLAN

The upper part of this drawing is the plan or shape seen from vertically above; the other half is symmetrical but the hull seen from below. On the aft part of the plan can be seen the cross-section of the frames between the inner planking and skin planking. At the stern is the "tolda", the platform that later evolved into the poop-deck and, at the bow, the half-triangle represents the "toldilla", an embryo forecastle. The lower part of the drawing is a horizontal section of the ship's lines, known today as the half-breadth plan. In order for the vessel to advance through the water at a fair speed, the lines of the stern should be tapered off, hardly the case here. However, this shape of hull was built much more easily and sturdily, a consideration that outweighed the disadvantage of resulting water-eddies. Naturally, the shipwrights of those times did not draw up construction plans, which resulted in a loss of accuracy, oversight and general consistency. These drawings were made much later.

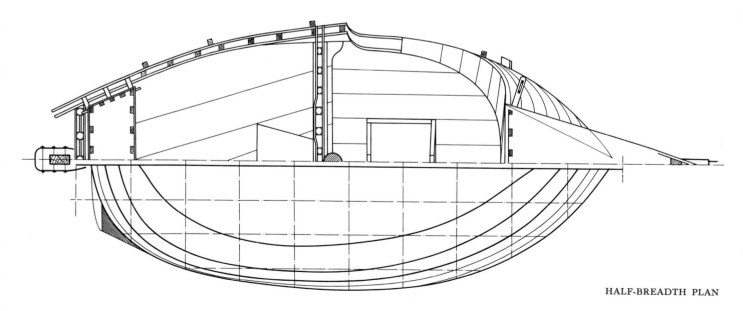

HALF-BREADTH PLAN

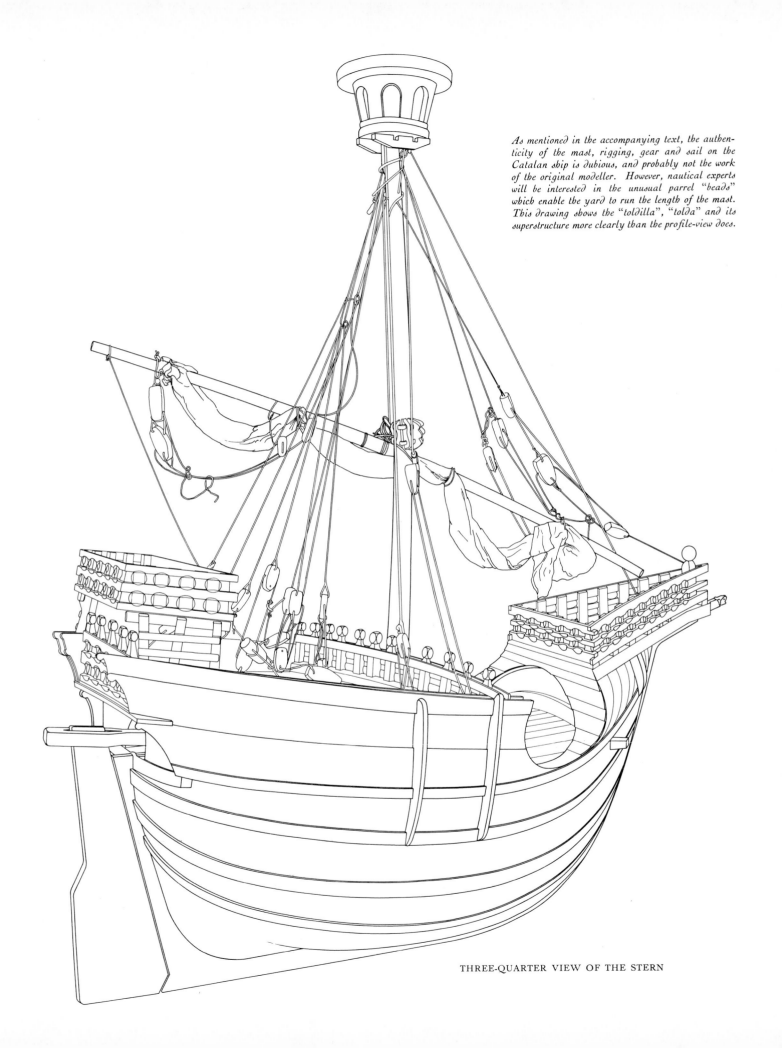

As mentioned in the accompanying text, the authenticity of the mast, rigging, gear and sail on the Catalan ship is dubious, and probably not the work of the original modeller. However, nautical experts will be interested in the unusual parrel "beads" which enable the yard to run the length of the mast. This drawing shows the "toldilla", "tolda" and its superstructure more clearly than the profile-view does.

THREE-QUARTER VIEW OF THE STERN

The "toldilla".

The Catalan ship seen from the bow.

These photographs of the famous ex-voto Catalan ship, now in the Prins Hendrik Museum, reveal the care lavished on its construction by some unknown sailor or ship's carpenter, during his off-duty hours.

A full, and very clear view of the model.

The simple open deck-house to which the Spaniards gave the name "tolda", is not unlike many such "dodgers" on small fishing-boats which are seen today.

A broadside view of the model, showing the reinforcing frames three vertical.

expeditions. He then intended to encircle Islam and form an alliance with Priest Gianni, the mysterious and allegedly Christian sovereign whose realms nobody had yet succeeded in locating, even to the extent of discovering whether they were in Africa or Asia. Finally, the undertaking also had commercial and political undertones for it was clear that if the East could be reached entirely by sea, the spice trade, a monopoly of the Venetians, could be diverted to Lisbon, bringing Portugal incalculable riches as well as greatly enhancing her prestige.

This ambitious scheme was made possible chiefly by the number of stoutly armed caravels the Prince could place at his disposal. " With these ships, I see no reason why it would not be possible to sail to any part of the world ", wrote Alvise da Mosto when he, a Venetian, entered the service of the Portuguese in 1454. His words proved prophetic.

Strictly speaking, it seems that the first expeditions in 1434 were made in small tonnage units called *barchas*, large barques rigged only with lateen sails, when the Portuguese pilot Gil Eanes rounded Cape Bojador on the Mauritanian coasts. Later, the Portuguese used *barineis* or barges, larger ships than usual, in which Alfonso Gonçalves Baldaya reached Rio de Oro and Cape Pedra de Galé two years later. Subsequent expeditions were undoubtedly made in caravels rigged with three masts. Such was the

In 1500, Pedro Alvares Cabral accidentally discovered the coasts of Brazil. In the absence of precise geographical details, the maps drawn in these times, such as the one by Lopo Homem, dated 1519 and shown below, illustrate how rich and colourful were the explorers' tales. Brazil was pictured as having luxuriant vegetation, an unknown species of man, weird animals, and strange, multi-coloured birds which talked.

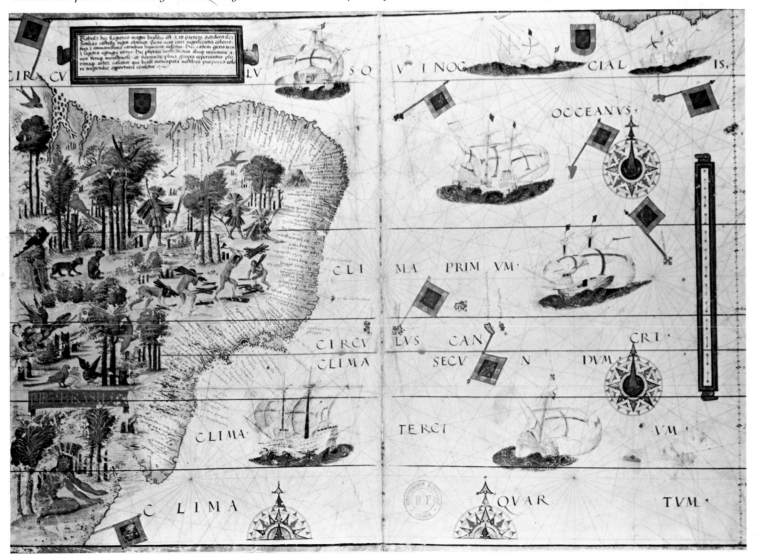

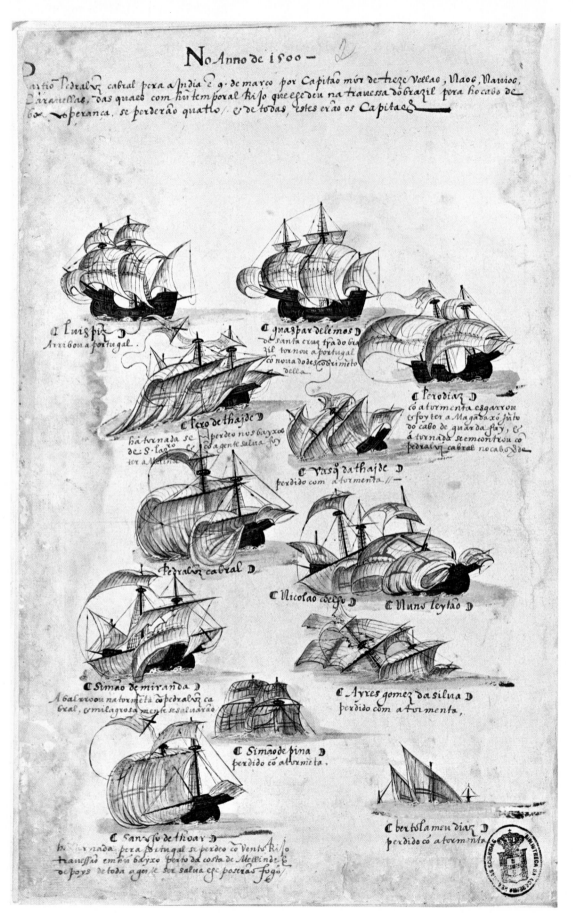

No Anno de 1500

Partio Pedralvz cabral pera a India a 9 de março por Capitão mór de treze Vellas, Naos, Navios, e Caravellas, das quaes com hũ temporal Riso que ehe deu na travessa do Brazil pera ho cabo de boa esperança, se perderão quatro, e de todas, estes erão os Capitães

a Luis Piz Arribou a portugal.

a Gaspar de Lemos de santa cruz tra do brazil tornou a portugal co nova do descobrimto della

a Pero diaz co a tormenta esgarrou e foy ter a Magadaxó junto do cabo de guarda fuy, e á tornada se encontrou co pedralvz cabral no cabo dde

a Sancho de thoar ha tornada se perdeos nos bayxos de S. lazo e a gente salua foy ter a Melinde

a Vasco da thaide perdido com a tormenta

a Pedralvz cabral

a Nicolao coelho

a Nuno leytão

a Simão de miranda abalroou na tormenta co pedralvz cabral, e milagrosamente se saluarão

a Ayres gomez da silua perdido com a tormenta

a Simão de pina perdido co a tormenta

a Sancho de thoar ha tornada pera Portugal se perdeo co vento Riso travessão em hũ bayxo perto da costa de Melinde e depoys de toda a gente ser salua e ge poseras fogo

a bertolameu diaz perdido co a tormenta

After Vasco da Gama opened up the route to the East Indies via the Cape of Good Hope, a squadron of twelve ships under Cabral sailed on March 9th, 1500, to exploit the discovery. Landing in Brazil on April 22nd, Cabral dispatched a messenger to announce the news to the King of Portugal and then sailed on. This admirable record is drawn up as a picture story, destined to immortalize the expedition. It shows the six ships which reached the Indies and, half submerged, all sails aloft, the five which were shipwrecked. In dramatizing their adventures, the artist has shown some of the surviving ships in obvious difficulties. This illustration is taken from the original in the famous "Livro das Armadas" preserved in Lisbon's Academy of Science.

26

This portrait of Vasco da Gama (right) is attributed to Gregorio Lopez. The map (below) comes from a manuscript in which one of Magellan's crew, Pigafetta, described the first of the great round-the-world voyages. The left-hand page depicts the island where "men are as black as in Ethiopia" and where Magellan was killed by the natives. "Having received an arrow in the leg, our Captain, fighting courageously, received a poisoned cane spear in his face, thrown by one of the Indians, and which killed him outright."

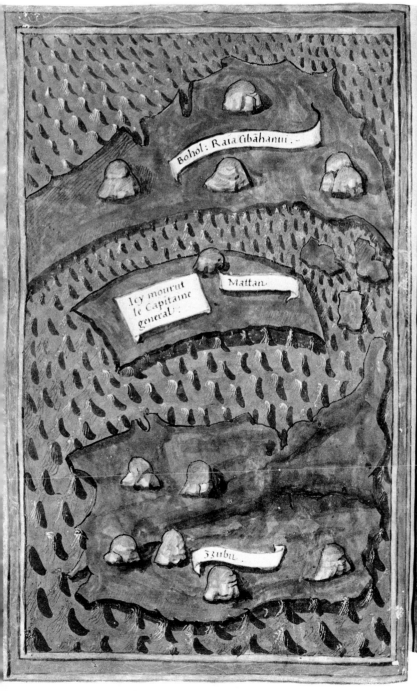

Dixhuyt lieues loing de ceſte iſle de ʒʒubu au cap de laultre iſle, qui ſe nõme Bohol bruſlaſmes ou milſieu de ceſt Archipelague la nauire de la conception. pource quil y auoit tro peu de gens, et fourniſmes les aultres deux nauires des meilleures choſes qui eſtoyent dedans. Puys priſmes la voye de garbin. Et ſur le mydi coſtoyant liſle de Panilõghon (en la quelle ſont hommes noirs comme en Ethiope)

F. Delfinum.

Prom. Gallicum.

In Europe, the voyages and discoveries fired men's imaginations and inspired books, often illustrated with magnificent engravings, such as "The Great Voyages" by J. Th. De Bry, published about 1590, which enjoyed a huge success. But fantasy often prevailed over fact and the various inaccuracies and ingenuous mistakes sometimes appear ludicrous to the modern eye. Two examples are shown here. De Bry depicts the port of Lisbon, purported to be in 1490 (below, left), but crowded with sailing ships of sixteenth century design and not from the preceding century. Wishing to immortalize Christopher Columbus' meeting with the natives (left), he shows Columbus dressed in late sixteenth century fashion. Some natives are proffering elaborate gifts of an impossibly European character. Others, perhaps sensing their ultimate fate, flee to safety.

From De Bry's book, this very lively scene is also based more on fancy than fact. The ships of a Dutch expedition have been driven ashore with all sails spread, wrecked probably as a result of night sailing in unknown waters, and the Dutch sailors have begun to build themselves huts with any materials to hand. Salvaging wood from the wreckage, they have started to build another caravel while others, using trunks of trees as roof supports, construct more comfortable houses, preparing for an indefinite stay. The one on the left even has a hay loft. Other sailors, having prepared the ground, are carefully sowing seeds, providentially included in the ships' stores. Relying on the traditional method of the ancient Phoenicians, after a full season, they could thus grow food and endeavour to build up the necessary supplies to resume their voyage.

29

Sir Francis Drake (1540-1596), Queen Elizabeth's loyal, adventurous retainer, illustrious sailor and author of the Invincible Armada's defeat in 1588.

confidence in this type of vessel that, for fear of possible competition, a royal warrant actually forbade the sale of these ships to any foreign powers. This precaution proved to be of no avail. In the meantime, squadrons of caravels were fitted out by the sovereigns of Castile and put to sea, often in the wake of the Portuguese vessels. The ships of the Prince, however, were easily distinguished by the noble proportions of the large white cross edged in red, the arms of the Order of Christ which were emblazoned on their sails.

Prince Henry, who so well merited his appellation of "The Navigator", died in 1460. He was succeeded by John II, well worthy of the task he had inherited, admirably suited to carry on the great undertaking. His qualities as a statesman and sailor

Drake's fleet has just dropped anchor in Santiago or St. Jacques harbour near the Cape Verde Islands. Two ships anchored in the bay fire a welcoming salvo to a third in the approaches. This base is so well patronized that little space remains, each ship needing enough room to swing.

earned for him the illustrious epithet of *o principe perfeito*, "Perfect Prince", from historians. Under his rule, expeditions were resumed with renewed vigour in the Atlantic Ocean. New ports of registry were systematically founded along the west coast of Africa. In 1470, Fernando Po landed on the Gold Coast where he built the castle St. Giorgio de Mina, commanding a harbour where ships could put in for repairs and revictual before resuming their voyages.

All caravels were already armed with cannon. The orders of King John II of Portugal were unequivocal : to sink with gun-fire any ship sailing under any flag encountered in the locality. The treaty of Alcaçaves signed by Portugal and Spain in September 1479 actually stipulated that the Castile kings, in return for various concessions, acknowledged the absolute sovereignty of Portugal over all territories discovered or to be discovered to the south of Cape No and over the entire route leading to the Indies.

In 1482, Diogo Cao discovered the mouth of a large river, and named it the Poderoso; actually this was the Congo. He believed he had reached the most southern point of Africa but not until 1488 was the Cape of Good Hope rounded by Bartholomew Diaz in command of the caravel *Sao Pantaleao*. Going ashore, on the highest point of the headland, he erected a *pradao*, a stone column bearing the arms of Portugal surmounted by a cross, affirming the sovereignty of Portugal and faith in Christ.

There was no longer any doubt that the Indies could be reached by sea and to this end Lisbon fitted out a squadron with the greatest care, composed of the 50-ton flotilla leader *Saint Raphaël*, the 100-ton *Saint Gabriel*, the 50-ton *Berio* and an auxiliary ship. It was no longer a question of old merchant-vessels converted for better or worse, as had been the case with the caravels of Columbus. These were newly completed ships, especially conceived for such an expedition, and the man chosen to command, of outstanding courage and ability, was called Vasco da Gama. After a voyage full of hazards and every kind of set-back, the effort was rewarded. On May 18th, 1498, the squadron sailed into Calicut, oriflammes and colours proudly flying. At last, the first cargo of spices could be loaded into the holds, an event that had been eagerly awaited. This was the fateful news recorded by Girolamo Priuli in 1499.

The following autumn, the squadron returned to Lisbon. Although only two ships remained, Vasco da Gama was given a triumphal welcome, the King bestowing on him the title of "Admiral of the Indies, Arabia and Persia".

At the *Casa de Mina*, the centre of operations, the first balance-sheet was drawn up. The expedition had made a net profit of six hundred per cent.

This event marks an important turning point in the history of the discoveries. With only three caravels and a handful of men, Vasco da Gama had opened up a new era in Europe, in Asia, and the foundations of a vast colonial empire were laid.

Another squadron, this time composed of twelve vessels, weighed anchor in Lisbon on March 9th, 1500. Under the command of Pedro Alvares Cabral, the mission was clearly defined : to sail to the Indies and there to establish the sovereignty of Portugal. The flotilla followed the usual route down the west coast of Africa. As far as the Cape Verde Islands the trade winds are met head on, obliging the sailors to tack to the south-west with the wind, at least, on the beam, bringing the ships into the vicinity of the Brazilian coasts. During a break in the bad weather, Cabral sighted the country and took possession in the name of the King, calling it Santa Cruz. "It is a land whose northern regions extend to the Antilles, a Castilian possession." And here is part of its description on the chart drawn up by Jorge Reinel in 1519. "The natives are dark-skinned, very cruel and feed on human flesh. One can see parrots of a thousand hues, all kinds of monkeys and a tree grows there named *brazil* which serves to dye cloths purple." Putting out to sea again, the squadron headed on a south-easterly course. Past the Cape of Good Hope, a violent storm caught them unawares and four ships were lost, one of them carrying Bartholomew Diaz. During the same voyage, by a happier accident, another ship discovered the Island of Madagascar. This was part of the price men of these days had to pay in their search for new lands. Their dramatic epic is narrated in the book *Esmeraldo de situ Orbitis* which, as in a movie film, unfolds the sequence of events. The chart drawn up by Reinel, dated several years later, portrays a whole series of ships vastly different from the original small caravels mighty galleons dominating the waves (see page 26).

Times were changing and ships were no longer called upon only to explore the uncharted seas and unknown lands but to conquer empires as well as to transport men and goods. Come what may, the great commercial enterprise, answerable directly to the Crown, must prosper. Obviously, this trade development necessitated ships with more spacious holds to carry all those products the new lands had begun to yield. The tonnage of the vessels thus increased proportionately, as did the crews required to handle them. The internal structure of the hulls, which now had to be strong enough to support the weight of added arms, posed new problems. Hulls now had two decks as well as the forecastle and quarter-deck.

On the sea routes to the Indies, there was no peace between Portugal and Spain. In those areas assigned by treaty to each nation, clashes were frequent and quarrels invariably resolved with exchanges of cannon fire. Moreover, the arrival of the Portuguese ships in Calicut threw the existing economic system into chaos. Shipping lines and trading posts were completely disorganized and the arrangements that had existed for centuries with local traders and transporters who handled the merchandise across sea and land as it progressed through the Middle East, were completely upset. This event provoked a chain reaction from the Arabian Sea to the Persian Gulf, from the Red Sea to the Mediterranean, striking a mortal blow to the Venetian market.

Fierce battles were inevitable, particularly after the Portuguese took to opening fire without warning on any ships in their vicinity. Vasco da Gama and all the admirals and viceroys who succeeded him considered themselves perfectly justified in acting in the same aggressive manner. Had not the king himself conferred on them the title of "Lords of the Seas"? In the skirmishes between the Portuguese and Arabo-Indian fleets, the Portuguese almost always came off best, due as much to the superiority of their sailors as to the weight of their ordnance. These were the determining factors which would ultimately allow the Portuguese and, later, the Dutch and British to consolidate their domination over their newly conquered territories in Asia.

Already the galleon *Flor de la Mar* (see page 14), which flew the flag of Alphonse d'Albuquerque in 1511 and her sister ship, the *Trindade* (see page 15),

were imposing battleships. The *Roteiro de Malaca* portrays them with 32 cannon jutting menacingly from the gunports along their three decks. The naval might they represented could well assert Portugal's rights to the Malay Peninsula and the Moluccas. A convenient interpretation of the treaty of Tordesillas permitted their claim. This agreement, reviving previous arrangements sanctioned by papal bulls, traced a demarcation line from one pole to the other. The line passed 370 nautical leagues to the west of the Cape Verde Islands, delineating the respective areas of Portuguese and Spanish conquests but leaving indeterminate vast expanses in course of exploration, as in the case of the Moluccas which were said to produce all kinds of spices and, later, even known as the "Spice Islands".

Keen rivalry for possession of the coveted Spice Islands was actually responsible for the momentous discovery of a South-West Passage to the Indies', the first round-the-world voyage ever made. Magellan, Portuguese by birth but then in the service of Spain, sought command of a fully equipped fleet to sail to these islands and, once there, establish the absolute rights of Spain under the terms of the Tordesillas treaty signed by Spain and Portugal in 1494. Magellan, convinced that a passage existed beyond the southernmost tip of the recently discovered American territories, wanted to set a westerly course instead of heading to the east and submitted his plan to Charles V, asking for his patronage.

The expedition, comprising five ships, is known to have sailed from Spain on September 20th, 1519, discovering a South-West Passage and finding its way into the Pacific. His own dreams, however, were never realized as Magellan died in a fight with Philippine natives before he ever reached the Moluccas. After countless set-backs, fleeing before the Portuguese ships in pursuit, the leader of the flotilla, *Vittoria*, was the sole ship to survive when, three whole years later, she regained her home port. Among the survivors from the crew, severely depleted by sickness, a Patrician from Vicenza in Italy, Antonio Pigafetta, engaged as a *sobresaliente* or supernumerary man-at-arms. He left a detailed personal account of these dramatic events and his book, *First Voyages Round the Terraqueous Globe* was undoubtedly the best-seller of its time (see page 27).

The long and arduous voyage undertaken by the *Vittoria* across the unknown waters of the Pacific had an immeasurable effect on the seafaring world. Apart from the discovery of a South-West Passage and the Philippines, it proved that the large Asiatic peninsula, thought to lie in the south-west, did not exist and was merely a legend based on a Ptolemaic conception of the world. Furthermore, as a result of this voyage, cartographers could, at last, gain a more accurate idea of the distribution of lands and seas and verify that the earth was, indeed, a sphere.

Christopher Columbus had set his heart on reaching the great eastern empire of Cathay and the land of spices. His grandiose scheme was well known to the English court long before its fruition and had been disclosed to Henry VII, in person, by the navigator's own brother, Bartholomew Columbus, about 1488. At that time, the sovereigns of Castile appeared undecided and were reluctant to give their consent to such an expedition. It seems unlikely, therefore, that the scheme would have been of interest to the English. The voyages and explorations undertaken by the Portuguese caravels along the African coasts were well enough known and Bristol merchants traded with Madeira, the Canary Islands and, possibly, with the Azores. But beyond these islands stood the great, grey wastes of the uncharted Atlantic. Few men could find courage enough to confront the unknown sea space that lay between the coasts of Europe and Cathay, five hundred or more nautical miles, as calculated by the Florentine cosmographer, Antonio Toscanelli. As to what actually lay to the west of Iceland, little was known although certain English ships had been as far as Greenland, fishing and trading.

The Port of Bristol archives leave no doubt as to the departure of an 80-ton vessel in 1480, in quest of the islands expected to be found lying to the west. In 1481, two other boats, the *George* and the *Trinity*, set course in the same direction but nothing is known of them nor the results of their voyages.

It was at about this time another Italian navigator, John Cabot, and his son, Sebastian, arrived in England, hoping to interest the English in his plan and to enlist their much-needed support. This plan had the same basic idea as Columbus', namely to find a west passage to Asia. Cabot's scheme succeeded in whetting commercial appetites in Bristol. Whereas Columbus had established the possibility of making a crossing at the latitude of the Azores, Cabot believed that by following a more northerly parallel from England, the voyage would be shorter and so much the safer. For the first time, England showed some signs of interest in naval expeditions and King Henry VII gave assent, the letters patent bearing the date, March 5th, 1496.

A first expedition seems to have set sail that same year but without results. Another, organized more thoroughly in Bristol, was to have comprised five ships but in the end was reduced to only one ship, the 50-ton *Matthew*. It is said to have been so called in respect to Cabot's wishes to name her after his Venetian wife, Mattea.

With a crew of eighteen, John Cabot sailed from Bristol early in May 1497, setting a course to the north-west and sighting land on June 24th. The exact location of his arrival is unknown but is thought to have been Cape Breton. Cabot went ashore and took possession in the King's name, erecting a cross, the Royal Standard of England and that of Venice. It has never been ascertained whether Cabot believed he had reached the northernmost point of Asia or another continent, as did Columbus.

The *Geographical Atlas* by Martin Waldseemüller, published in 1507, clearly reveals the extent of men's knowledge of the world in those days. Europe and Asia are shown as separate from the American Continent and, while the southern hemisphere is fairly clearly defined, the north is only vaguely sketched in and stops short at latitude 50°N.

The search for a passage to the north-west, a quicker route to the land of spices, was the primary objective of all the expeditions and, after his father's death, Sebastian Cabot carried on the quest with an expedition in 1509, financed by the Crown of England and a group of Bristol merchants sharing in the enterprise. He explored the coast of Labrador and went beyond latitude 60°N., the northernmost point hitherto reached, in following the huge gulf which was later to take the name of Hudson Bay. Sebastian Cabot's explorations rank among the most important in the history of the discoveries and it is, in fact, due to them that the foundations of the vast English colonial empire were laid in North America.

G. B. RUBIN DE CERVIN

Curator of the MUSEO STORICO NAVALE, Venice

THE BIRTH OF THE NATIONAL FLEET

Not a century had passed since the discovery of the New World before the might of an all-powerful Spain was being challenged. Over the oceans and the lands that lay beyond, Holland was attaining her own glory. England was embarking on maritime exploration and colonial development. France was establishing herself in Canada. The navy was already an instrument of military and economic power in the hands of western nations.

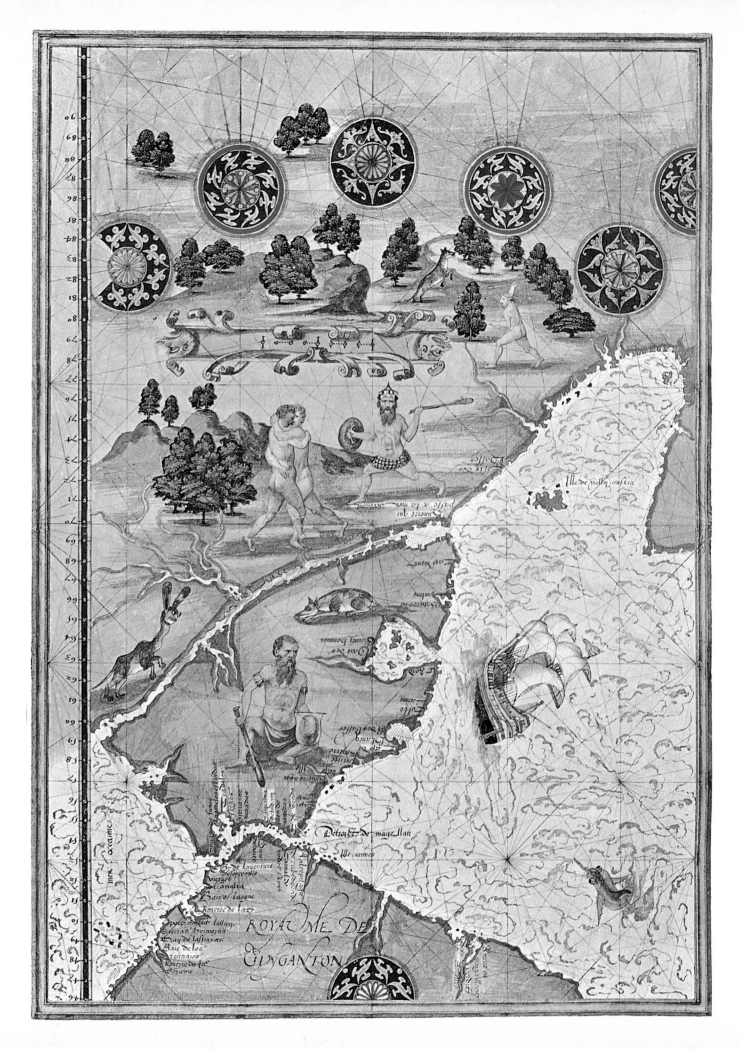

THE SPREAD OF SAIL

The far-flung discoveries of the fifteenth century gave rise in the sixteenth century to colonial empires, whose rivalries and disputes were henceforth to be settled on the high seas. To meet the new demands of armament and endurance that such voyages imposed upon their vessels, shipbuilders of the sixteenth century found themselves forced to emerge from their traditional ways; far from being the skilled handicraft of former times, shipbuilding by the seventeenth century was on its way to becoming an exact science.

Europe's rulers, at the same time, were beginning to understand the vital part that maritime power would inevitably play in determining a nation's rank in the world. Already, the possession of the largest and most luxurious ships ensured the prestige of princes and sovereigns. Furthermore, these ships frequently constituted an important source of revenue, as in the case of the small fleet fitted out by Cosimo I of the Medicis which he hired out to both Spain and the Pope when not employing it to chase after Barbary galleons and Turkish barges. Other sovereigns with more ambitious political plans dispatched stoutly armed galleons to the Atlantic or Pacific Oceans with the intention of plundering merchant convoys or destroying colonial bases which had been established by Spain on the shores of the New World.

Comfortably installed on deck, this navigator makes a great show of measuring the magnetic needle's deviation in relation to the pole-star, by means of an alidad over the compass. His steel sword is hardly conducive to accuracy but, as yet, its deflection would not have been known.

From "Cosmographie universelle" published in 1555 by Guillaume le Testu (circa 1509-1572), this map of the extreme south of the American continent is drawn with the north to the bottom of the page, showing Patagonia below Tierra del Fuego and Cape Horn. Above lies "terra australis", inhabited by nude men and strange looking animals.

That great painter, Peter Breughel the Elder (circa 1525-1569) was not averse to portraying ships and these engravings are superb. However, one must realize that many Flemish painters, as well as old masters and miniaturists of the Middle Ages, often used outdated documents for reference, frequently resulting in chronological inaccuracies. This explains why the ship in the picture on the right, although obviously a carrack, is rigged like a galleon. The small sailing-boat to its right is even more interesting, featuring a spritsail, similar to the three-cornered sail used at that time by Breton mariners. Both of these were derived from the lateen, although less cumbersome, and heralded the gaff-sail. Although more than a century was to pass before capital ships finally adopted the jib, this small avant-garde craft actually has one rigged forward of its mast.

An amusing and lively detail from an engraving by Breughel shows sailors clambering up the rubbing strakes to board their vessel. Those in the ship's boat are left to hang on as best they can. It was actually this row of protective "shields" that gave meaning to the term "bulwarks" and the idea of their use.

Spain, towards the end of the fifteenth century, had become a vast colonial empire the like of which had never been known. By virtue of rights granted by Papal bulls and the Tordesillas Treaty, signed in 1494 by Spain and Portugal, dividing the New World into two regions of influence and outlining the future areas of colonization for both countries, Spain's foreign territories extended from the west coast of Africa to the Philippines, and from the southern coasts of North America to the archipelagos and central shores of that continent. And, with the exception of the Portuguese possession of Brazil, all the vast expanses of South America discovered by her explorers and conquered by her soldiers were a source of fabulous wealth and power.

To Europeans, when ships from the New World brought tidings of the seizure of age-old Incan treasures and the systematic looting of the Temples of Cuzco, it must have seemed that El Dorado had at last been found. When deposits of gold and silver were reported in Chiriqui, Veraguas, Potosi and Veracruz, the available means of transport no longer sufficed to meet the demands of all those who, lured by the mirage of these riches, were willing to brave the discomfort and danger of the long trip.

Today, it is difficult to imagine the rigours of these voyages. The few cabins on the ships of those days, located under the quarter-deck in the free space on either side of the steering gear, were reserved for the ships' officers or distinguished passengers. The remainder, passengers and crew alike, managed as best they could under the forecastle or on the deck, exposed to both wind and sea. Below decks, the available space was even more restricted. The between-decks area was cluttered with guns, ropes and gear, water-barrels, large earthenware jars of oil, wooden chests of biscuits and supplies of salted provisions. The ceiling was so low that a man could not stand upright and, to add to the misery, all the portholes had to be made water tight while the ship was under sail. As a result, there was practically no light or air, the only openings being the central gratings and the hatchway. Living conditions and standards of hygiene naturally deteriorated still further when the ships entered the equatorial zones. The air became almost unbreathable because of the fetid stench of rotting victuals. Fresh water, stored in wooden containers, spoiled in no time. The shipboard diet of salted, smoke-cured meats, biscuit and cheeses, totally lacking in fresh vegetables and vitamins, inevitably led to outbreaks of scurvy, a disease which neither the ship's surgeon nor barber knew how to treat. In practice, a seaman falling sick could not count on treatment, and any chance of recovery depended on his physical stamina. If, after a few days "in bed", the patient died, his remains were simply sewn up in sail-cloth, weighted by a cannon-ball at his feet and, as the captain recited a funeral oration, dropped into the sea.

At first, Spain's territories in the New World were acquired haphazardly by soldiers, merchants, noblemen and adventurers, operating under the guise of a personal warrant from their sovereign. But soon the organization of the entire colonial system came under the authority of the Spanish crown. A vast state monopoly was created, the *Casa de Contratacion*, with its headquarters in Madrid, for the sole purpose of controlling trade and commerce with the East Indies and with the Americas.

The policy adopted in relation to these overseas possessions tended to cut them off completely from the rest of the world. Only the port of Seville was allowed to admit ships carrying gold or other valuable cargoes from America. Trade between the colonies was forbidden, and they were not allowed to import goods from Spain, apart from the barest necessities. The result of these restrictions was the highly lucrative smuggling trade which was conducted on a vast scale by pirates and privateers, mostly of French, Dutch and British nationality.

This, in turn, led to a state of war on the high seas between the European nations, a war which, though undeclared, was legalized by genuine letters of marque issued by the various governments indiscriminately to notorious adventurers and respected mariners, habitual criminals and gentlemen of high rank. A ruthless war, it gave rise to heroic epics as well as to the most sordid episodes, to noble exploits undertaken in the name of honour, and to base assaults having no motive other than lucre and plunder. Although a state of hostility did not officially exist between England and Spain, Queen Elizabeth, standing imperiously behind her "sea-dogs", did not hesitate to allow privateers to fit out in her naval

This unusual and intriguing drawing by Breughel the Elder shows tenders, plying between the quays and the tall galleons, rigged with lateen sails. As can be seen by the long diagonally placed poles, the craft on the left of the picture carry spritsails — the shape of sails to come.

yards and sail the Atlantic routes to the New World, plundering Spanish ships and colonial bases. Since England, converted to Protestantism, no longer attached any value to the Papal bulls which had granted all the American territories to Spain and Portugal, such operations were conducted with a clear conscience. "Westward Ho" became the favourite war cry of British sailors bound on high adventure.

The sailors manning these ships, slave-traders or pirates, came from nearly everywhere. There was Jean Angot from Dieppe who, in 1522, with a flotilla of eight ships, succeeded in capturing three galleons bearing treasures sent by Cortez to Madrid.

Then there was Le Clerc, known as "Peg-Leg", who after pillaging a Spanish convoy en route for the Canary Islands proceeded to sack the ports of Santo Domingo, Puerto Rico and Havana. Other famous privateers were Vincent Basquet of Dieppe and Jacques Sores from La Rochelle. After years of campaigning, adventures and fabulous profits, the luckiest of these seafarers could settle down to a peaceful existence but others, caught at last by the enemy, often ended up swinging at the end of a rope.

The great majority of privateers were English. The exploits of John Hawkins, dubbed "Juan Aquines" by the Spanish, are famous. In 1566, he

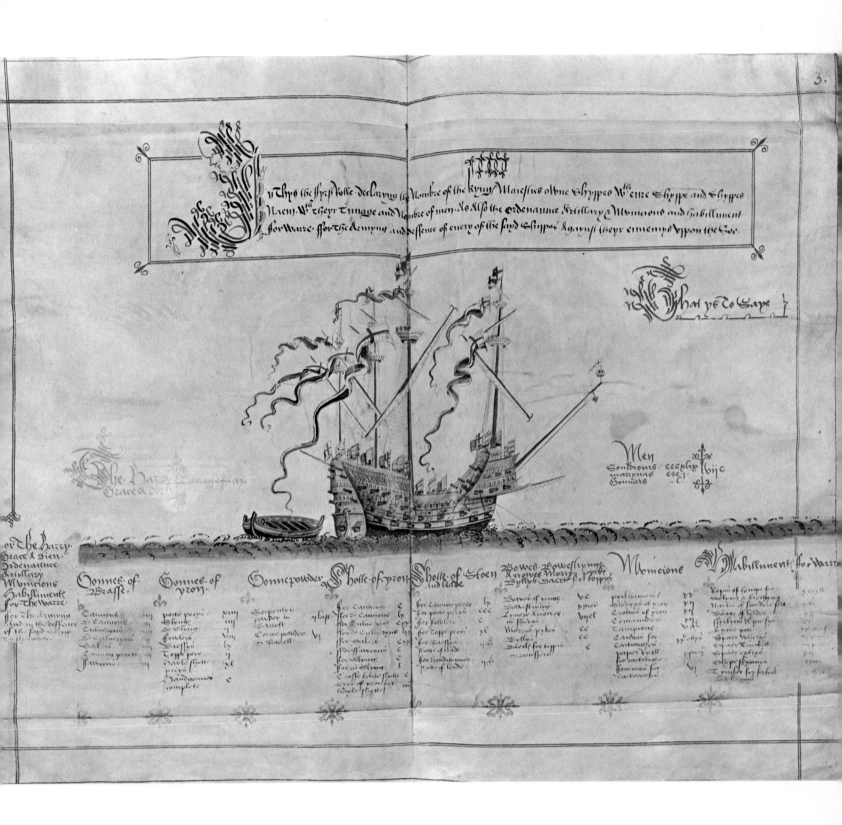

Better known as the "Great Harry", the Henri Grâce à Dieu, as rebuilt in 1545, was the finest ship of the fleet in the reign of Henry VIII. Her ship's complement totalled 700 sailors and artillerymen, and she was armed with 21 heavy bronze cannon, 130 of iron, and 100 lighter guns. The towering stern castle, four decks high, projected far out over the rudder while the forecastle ended in a kind of ram featuring, for the first time in Europe, a carved emblem, the forerunner of the figurehead. The vessel was rigged with no less than twelve sails and carried a colourful profusion of flags, including 28 silk banners embroidered in gold and silver. The pennants at the mast-head were over 130 ft. long.

commanded a naval division of six vessels to which the Queen herself had contributed the 64-cannon *Jesus of Lübeck*. Various successes enabled Hawkins to seize possession of the Portuguese galleon *Gracias De Dios*, whose holds were filled with slaves. After selling them to settlements in the central regions of America, he returned to England where he was enthusiastically fêted, heaped with honours and appointed to a high ranking office in the Royal Navy. Another, Sir M. Frobisher, took part in forays on the Guinea coasts and sailed as far as Iceland in the hope of finding a North-West Passage to the Indies.

NAVAL ENTERPRISE

The most daring and famous of all privateers, of course, was Sir Francis Drake. In 1572, Drake commanded two ships, the 70-ton *Swan* and the 50-ton *Pacha* with which he roved the Caribbean almost unchallenged, even going so far as to sack the town of Nombre de Dios in central Mexico. In 1577, with the financial backing of the Crown, he assembled a flotilla of five ships, the 240-ton *Pelican*, the *Elizabeth*, the *Mary Gold*, the *Swan* and the *Christopher*, for the express purpose of stabbing Spain's merchant trade in the back by attacking her shipping in the Pacific Ocean.

By the time he reached Cape Horn, Drake had lost all his ships except for the *Pelican*, which he renamed the *Golden Hind*. He rounded the dreaded Cape in this ship and then sailed north, hugging the coastline of Chile and Peru. The largest Spanish galleon in Pacific waters, the *Nuestra Senora de la Concepcion* also happened to be heading to Panama along the same route, loaded with a year's worth of all the gold and silver mined in these regions. Drake caught her unawares, captured her intact and took possession of her entire cargo. Pursuing her northerly course, the *Golden Hind* reached the latitude of 43° in quest of a north-east passage leading back to the Atlantic. Not daring to press on still further north, Drake entered San Francisco Bay, which he named "New Albion". He then decided to return to Europe via the Indian Ocean and the Cape of Good Hope.

The *Golden Hind* arrived in Plymouth on September 26th, 1580. Queen Elizabeth herself came to welcome Drake, and went aboard to confer a knighthood and the rank of Vice-Admiral on her captain. The arms chosen by Drake bore the globe and the Latin inscription "Tu primus circumdidisti me — divino auxilio", meaning "Thou first sailed around me — with God's help". Had he perhaps forgotten that F. de Magellan had preceded him by several years?

THE PATTERN OF CHANGE

In order to counter the incessant and systematic attacks by privateers on the strategic points of its maritime routes, the Spanish government, acting through the *Casa de Contratacion*, adopted a series of defensive measures. Each ship bound for the Indies was henceforth to be adequately armed and carry a contingent of soldiers. However, as even these precautions proved ineffectual, convoys were organized to bring regular shipments of gold back to the mother country. This famous "Gold Fleet" set sail from Cadiz each year during the first two weeks of June. Composed of as many as thirty galleons, the flag-officer commanded an impressive staff of admirals, gunnery and infantry commanders, as well as a large number of civilians. The fleet dropped anchor first in the Canary Islands, to take on supplies of fresh water and food. Then, taking advantage of the trade-winds, it headed for the Lesser Antilles, stopping off at Martinique or Guadaloupe, where it split up into two flotillas. One, called the "Convoy of

Towards the end of the sixteenth century, the old unscientific methods of shipbuilding gave way to rigorously calculated plans. Around 1586, Matthew Baker, possibly the man shown wearing a hat above, drew up the plans included in "Fragment of Ancient English Shipwrighty". The seats folded up against the wall suggest that this "drawing-office" was also used for architects' conferences with their associates.

This "goblet" cross-section on the right, brimming with a man on a ladder to illustrate scale, was intended to display the powerful athwart beams. The floor-timbers with their knees are shown here intersected by a series of odd-looking slanting stanchions.

The galleons designed by Matthew Baker are low and shapely. The lofty forecastle, which has virtually disappeared, is replaced by a type of defensive keep with one deck.

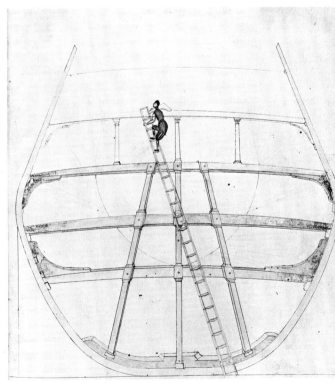

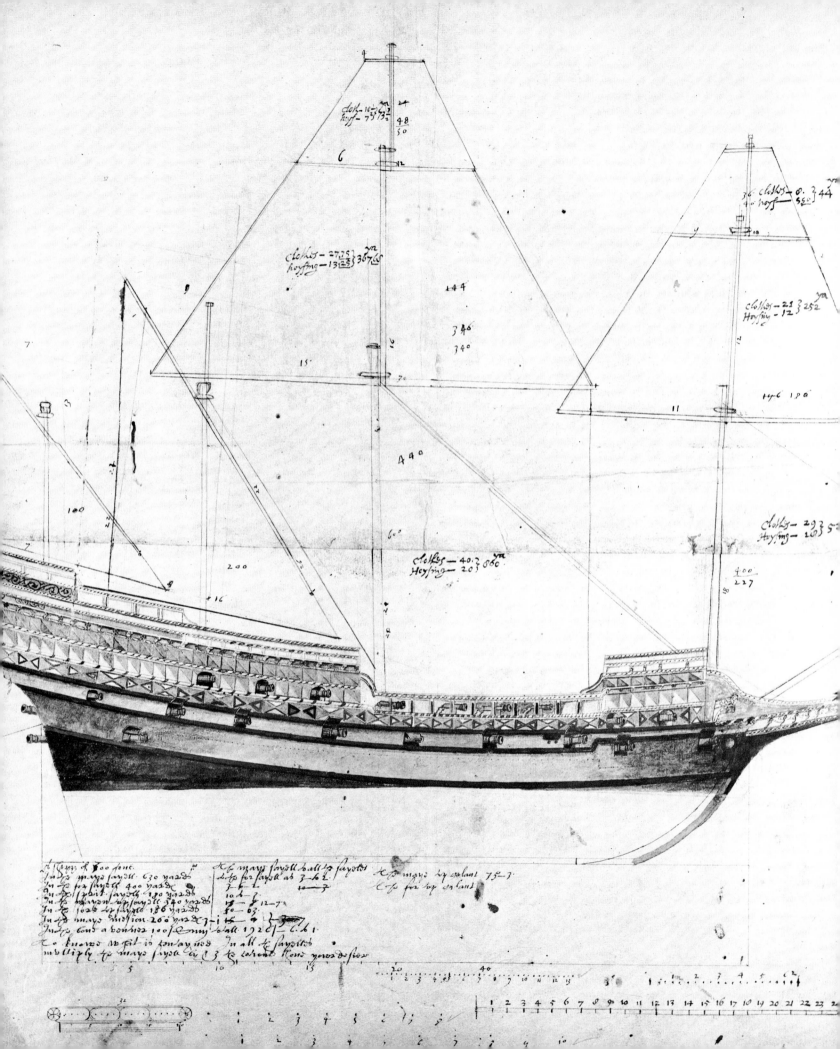

The Santa Catarina do Monte Sinai, *a Portuguese warship, was armed with over 140 cannon, although many were light weapons. Cornelis Anthonis (circa 1499-1556) has shown her mainsail as it was probably rigged when he painted this picture in 1553.*

Here is a sail plan, drawn in very much the same way as it is today. The hull was included merely to provide a base, and the sails only approximately indicated, the prime purpose being to show their angle and elevation. Apparently, Matthew Baker had envisaged equipping the mizzen-sails with lateen sails.

New Spain" sailed along the coasts of the Greater Antilles, calling at the port of Havana, and after entering the Gulf of Mexico reached Veracruz where her cargo was discharged. The other, known as the "Convoy of the Mainland", set sail for Maracaibo and Cartagena and anchored at Portobello in Panama to wait for the goods brought there by the Pacific fleet. Once the vessels were fully loaded, the two convoys reassembled at Havana, and made the return voyage together, first passing by the Bermudas in order to pick up the regular westerly winds which would then carry them back over the familiar sea route to Spain.

The last stage of the trip, which was undertaken in autumn, was the most dangerous. Privateers lay in wait for the "Gold Fleet" hoping to seize a share of the precious cargo. They were so frequently successful that Alonzo de Chavez, one of Emperor Charles V's cosmographers, remarked that Providence had chosen Spain to discover and conquer the Indies so that she might distribute its treasures to the other nations of the world.

To meet the challenges of distance and strength that such voyages imposed upon ships, the cargo-vessel evolved into the "galleon", a refined and specialized man-of-war. The origin of this name is uncertain. It is generally thought to be Spanish, but it is also possible that it comes from "galley" or "galleass", such terms having been used for vessels with certain similarities to the new galleon. For instance, its forecastle, no longer bulging out over the water but set back from the bow, was somewhat like that of the trireme galleys, and the prow now ended in a beak. (This beak, incidentally, should not be confused with the Roman *rostrum*, protruding forward from the fore-foot and designed to rip open the bottoms of enemy ships. In the Middle Ages, when fire-arms were introduced, these beaks or rams were discarded. In their place, tradition demanded that the bows be embellished with symbolic figures, heraldic devices or merely iron decorations.)

The art of naval construction was, at this period, confined to a narrow circle of shipyard foremen who reigned supreme over their shipyards. For the most part, they were simple shipwrights, using ancient unscientific methods handed down from father to son over the ages. Ships were not built according to rigorously calculated plans drawn up in advance, and the vital correlation between the vessel and her rigging was not yet appreciated. Long centuries of experience counselled against deviating from the square body. This formed the basis on which ship-wrights established the other co-ordinating elements. On the keel, the rudder-post at the stern and the stem-post at the bow delimited the skeleton on which the ribs were placed. This method is used to this day in Venetian shipyards when laying down gondolas and other craft serving the lagoons.

Each master shipwright had his "technique", his own trade secrets, with his formula written in a notebook, sometimes in obscure terms. Some of these manuscripts have been preserved, such as *Construction of Galleys* dated 1410, of which nothing is known except that its author was Venetian. Another notebook of 1550 is signed by a certain Theodoro de Nicolo, *Proto dei marangoni* or Master-shipwright, in the naval dockyard of the Republic of Venice. This document contains instructions for the construction of what de Nicolo calls "large galleys", "bastard galleys" and "galleons".

In England, the Tudor kings were quick to appreciate the importance of the navy to English foreign policy. Henry VIII who founded the naval fighting force, took a personal interest in the organization of the Royal Navy. Records of this period reveal that he kept in close touch with all the latest developments in Continental shipyards, going to great lengths to obtain information from Venice on a certain type of "galleon driven by oars", with which he was experimenting at the time. He also looked for a new use for his "merchant-galleys" as almost all of them were lying idle, a result of the Mediterranean's decline in economic importance now the new trade routes led round the Cape of Good Hope.

The fleet commissioned by Henry was not only influenced by Venice, but had also borrowed some of the characteristics of Hanseatic, French and Spanish naval architecture. The illustrated list of the British battle fleet in 1546 shows the 450-ton *Grand Mistress* (see page 47) described as a "large galleon" but classed as a galleass. The sketch might have come straight from the notebook of a naval dockyard foreman in Venice. In fact, she was a hybrid vessel, her stern reminiscent of a galleon, while her bow was

Most painters of this time had little if any seafaring experience and found it hard to portray a sailing-vessel with accuracy, as can be seen here. The Grand Mistress served the English fleet at the time of the Armada.

Quite the opposite is true of this painting by Cornelis Claesz van Wieringen in 1588. This pinnace, used by the Spanish fleet under Philip II, is illustrated with the greatest accuracy.

47

Knave ♣

Don Alphonso Duke of Medina, Cheife Comander of ÿ Spanish Fleete.& John Martin Recalde, a great Seaman.

A sixteenth century English playing-card bears the likeness of the Duke of Medina Sidonia, Admiral of the "Invincible Armada", and John Martin Recalde. Describing the Englishman as "a great seaman" rather infers the other was not. It so happens that Medina Sidonia, also known as the "Handsome and the Good", suffered from sea-sickness at the slightest movement of his ship. In 1588, the Spanish Armada, seen in the anonymous painting below, was made up of 128 vessels and 29,000 sailors and soldiers. The unknown artist does not neglect the high winds that were to prove more effective adversaries than the units of Queen Elizabeth's fleet, in spite of the famous medal, struck by the Mint and bearing the legend "Dux femina facti". It should be fairly stated, however, that Queen Elizabeth I did admit later, "God breathed on them and they were scattered". King Philip II, wryly acknowledging the weather's influence on his strategy, said: "I sent my ships to fight the English, not the gales".

John Hawkins, sometimes known as "the wind's favourite", Admiral of the English fleet. The drawing below is generally thought to be of the Ark Royal, the famous English galleon built in 1545. This vessel, as well as the Spanish galleys and other ships shown opposite, features the sumptuous, encumbering ornamentation that was to remain so fashionable until the time of the French Revolution. Although the high sterns are less extravagantly embellished than in the Golden Age of Louis XIV, the ships' sides and even the tops are encrusted with intricate carving. Bunting seems to have been common but served no obvious purpose. The flowing pennants are a relic from the Middle Ages and are still as long and wide as they were in those early days of sail, when they were frequently made from skins of animals, especially those made in Normandy and England.

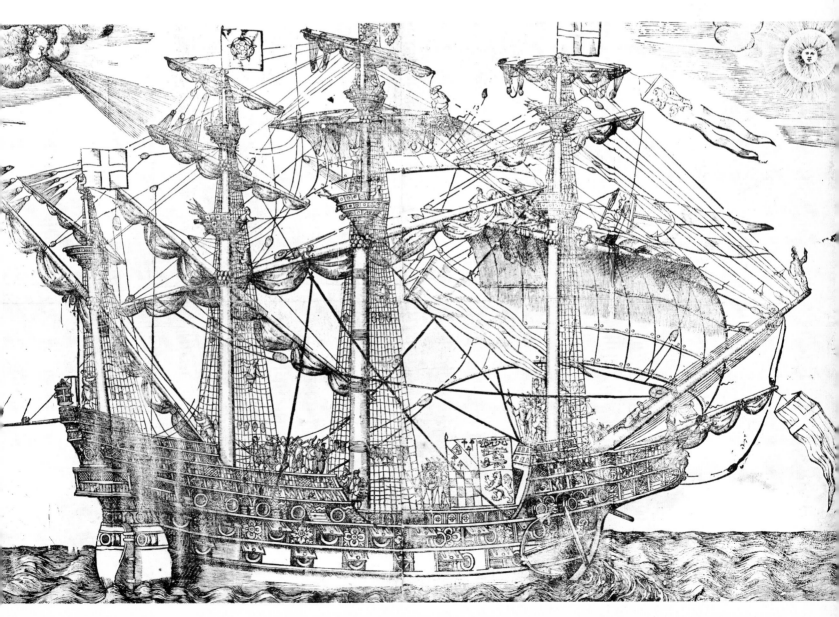

The White Bear *proudly wears the flag of Queen Elizabeth I.*

The Tiger, *swifter and better sailed without a forecastle.*

The Ark Royal *displays very curious "round-houses" forward.*

The Golden Lion *with quarter-galleries more usually placed.*

The Griffin *and, behind her, another craft making scant headway.*

similar to that of a galley. The rigging was mixed with square sails on the first two masts, and triangular lateen sails on the mizzen and bonaventure mizzenmasts. Another earlier vessel, the *Regent*, with its 29 bronze cannon and 151 smaller iron guns, was built in 1489 according to certain specifications established for French ships, such as main topsail on the mainmast and topsails on the three other masts. In 1512 she suffered a strange end: meeting with the French flagship *Marie La Cordelliere* in the Bay of Camaret, she became entangled in the other's ropes. The two ships collided, caught fire, and both exploded.

To replace this prize vessel, the king immediately ordered the construction of another far larger ship, the "Great Carrack". She was to bear several different names — *Imperial Carrack, Henry Imperial*, and finally *Henry Grâce à Dieu* — but she is generally known to history as simply the *Great Harry* (see page 41). The pride of Henry VIII's Royal Navy, her launching was attended by the King, high state and church dignitaries and accredited ambassadors to the Court of England. The vessel, as it descended majestically towards the water, flying green and white flags, the colours of the House of Tudor, her 184 guns firing, seemed to symbolize the supremacy that England was to exert over the high seas.

For all her imposing appearance, however, it was evident right from the time of her launching that the *Great Harry* had serious drawbacks. The excessive height of her topsides caused her to roll dreadfully in high seas, so much so that in 1536 the height of the vessel was reduced and her tonnage accordingly fell from 1,500 to 1,000 tons. No reproduction of the vessel exists prior to this transformation, the only surviving drawing dates from 1545. Even in her reduced form, the ship still carried a crew of more than 800 men, made up of sailors, soldiers and gunners. She was armed with 21 bronze cannon and 130 smaller calibre guns distributed over her four lower decks, while still more pointed from the decks of the castles. According to the iconographic record of a naval officer of those times the rebuilt *Great Harry* was rigged with four towering masts, each divided into three sections. This was a remarkable innovation, permitting a more rational spread of the total sail area. The foremast carried foresail, fore-topsail and fore-topgallant while the mainmast was rigged with mainsail, main-topsail and topgallant. The two other masts, incorrectly termed mizzen and bonaventure mizzen, carried five triangular lateen sails between them. The large hooks at the end of the main-yards were a curious detail, seemingly designed to grip the rigging of an enemy ship in order to hold her firm during boarding. To the same end, a large four-armed grappling iron, hung from the end of the bowsprit, could be dropped onto the deck of the enemy ship, thus firmly anchoring her.

The *Great Harry*, however, never had the opportunity to demonstrate her might. She, too, was accidentally destroyed by a fire in Woolwich in 1553.

This was also an age when painters' imaginations began to be fired by maritime scenes. Flanders was the birthplace of an entirely new school of artists whose meticulous regard for detail and taste for ornamentation have provided us with valuable facts concerning the vessels of their time. Among them was Peter Breughel who, although observing galleons sailing on the grey waters of the River Scheldt, apparently liked to imagine them in the serene seas of the Mediterranean. One of his drawings, executed with a bold and sure touch, depicts three galleons standing out against a landscape of Italianate ruined towers and bridges. The work is especially interesting for the details of ship construction shown therein (see page 38). As can be seen, this was a period of transition with the stern rounded on one vessel, flat on another. During this period, the quickworks of the hull tended to fine down.

Although at first glance Breughel's galleons are still reminiscent of the carracks depicted by Barbari (see page 11), closer examination clearly reveals the changes made to the topsides over the intervening years. The carracks lying at anchor in the port of Venice are shielded from the weather by awnings covering the poop and the deck. These tent-shaped awnings were supported on movable poles so that the entire frame could easily be dismantled when necessary. The galleons drawn by Breughel, on the other hand, have a covering protecting the topsides, which appears to be a fixture, while the deck is entirely free, except for the cannon jutting from gun-ports in the bulwarks. In both illustrations, there is a lack of balance between the underwater parts of the vessel and those above the water-line; the forecastle, the poop and all the masts are very high in proportion to the area amidships. It was, in fact, impossible to raise the ship's centre of gravity without compromising her stability. Another of Breughel's prints (see page 38) shows the stern of a galleon with tapering instead of straight sides, so that the upper deck is narrower than the lower ones. This design was intended to increase the ship's resistance, enabling the guns on the upper decks to be placed as near as possible to the fore and aft line.

As has already been noted, the first Portuguese caravels were already armed with a few light cannon. These were usually muzzle-loaders, placed on the deck and generally pointing out of openings under the poop and the forecastle. Later, when it became possible and necessary to increase fire-power, the larger calibres had to be placed on the lowest decks in order to balance the ship. Thenceforth, the cannon fired through ports in the sides of the hull. This idea of structural modification to the vessel is thought to be due to a certain M. des Charges of Brest, in about 1501. At all events, the range of this line of guns along the lower deck must have been very short and their use limited to battering the hull of enemy ships at the water-line. On most galleons at the end of the sixteenth century, a certain number of guns was also disposed on the various decks which rose in tiers at the stern and bows. In this way, an internal defence system was established which, in accordance with the latest theories on the art of fortification, allowed for cross-fire between the different defence points if a ship fell into enemy hands. As in fortifications ashore during the Middle Ages, the stern castles on these ships formed a stronghold and the last line of defence. From this vantage-point the guns, trained downwards, could sweep the entire deck if enemy boarding-parties managed to reach it after forcing their way through a defence system of nets.

The Portuguese galleon *Santa Catarina Do Monte Sinai* in the picture by C. Anthoniszoon (see page 45) gives a clear illustration of this type of armament. Guns bristle from her ports while others fire from the top of the stern between the shields, standards and oriflammes. She might almost be mistaken for a mediaeval citadel, erected on a headland to defend a port. On this occasion, however, her mission was strictly one of peace and the cannon fire only a

courtesy salvo in honour of the Infanta Beatrice of Portugal. The ship was exchanging a royal salute with the fort at Villefranche, as she entered the roads to conduct the princess to her future husband, the Duke of Savoy. Since the invention of fire-arms, it had become the custom for ships which met on the high seas or entered a foreign port to fire a number of shots into the air to demonstrate, by discharging their guns, that there need be no fear of a surprise attack, a custom that persists to this day.

For her day, the *Santa Catarina Do Monte Sinai* was a marvel, both for her dimensions and her lines. Apparently she was so armed as to be able to fire from 140 mortars spread over her four decks. One is particularly struck by the fullness of her sails, especially those on the main and foremast. They were cut like "wind cones", with a deep pouch designed to catch the maximum amount of air when sailing on "a broad reach" with the wind over the stern quarter. This trim was adopted by ships in the Atlantic as soon as they encountered the Trades, winds which blew regularly at certain latitudes. However, when the winds reached gale force, the area of these vast sails had to be reduced, a laborious and awkward manoeuvre demanding the efforts of the entire crew. First, the very heavy yards were swung back, then the bonnets of the lower sails were unlaced. Later on, when the sail area was spread more satisfactorily, the preferred method of reefing the sails was to have the sailors sent aloft to roll them up and make them fast to the yards.

Towards the end of the century, the winds of change blew through European dockyards, resulting in important modifications to both hull and rig. Simultaneously, ships' decorations increased in proportion to ever enlarging dimensions. On the galleons of these days, the stern, no longer rounded, formed a flat surface on which it soon became the general custom for ships of most nations to display the picture of a saint and the heraldic arms of the royal family or the shipowner, surrounded by such embellishments as caryatids, dolphins, tritons and various other symbolic flourishes. These decorations were already well in evidence on Elizabethan ships like the *Ark Royal* (see page 49) which was richly encrusted with carved motifs predominating in scrolls, the white rose of York and the green and white heraldic colours of the Tudors. From this time onwards, ships of all nations bore sumptuous decorations whose theme was repeated over the entire vessel, terminating in a large carving at the prow, on the cutwater, almost at a level with the waves. Female figures, winged horses, fierce dragons and rampant lions were favourite subjects with artists who generally remained anonymous. These sculptors displayed a keen sense of beauty, skilfully heightening the majestic grandeur of these instruments of war, dispatched over the high seas by their sovereigns. Unfortunately, their creations were doomed to a brief existence, for even if they escaped the ravages of storms or enemy broadsides, they were inevitably smashed to pieces by the wrecker's hammer when the whole ship ended up in the breaker's yard.

Such decorations, with their ornamental paintings and carvings often copied from the classic architectural themes of "stately homes", were not a luxury but a necessity. In fact, it was considered that the richness and ostentation of a ship enhanced the prestige of her flag. Furthermore, it was also believed it would instil fear and respect in the primitive peoples across the seas. For this reason, even vessels bound for distant regions were as richly ornamented as those used for less arduous tasks.

CRITICAL NAVAL BATTLES

These, then, were the vessels sailing the seas of the world as Philip II of Spain prepared to challenge Great Britain between 1583 and 1586. Son of the Holy Roman Emperor, Charles V, and heir to much of his empire, Philip II was determined to crush all opposition to Roman Catholicism. Great Britain, on the other hand, had not only left the Catholic fold but was actively aiding the Dutch Protestants in their revolt against Spanish domination. These two facts, plus the encouragement and support England was giving privateers in colonial waters, were the main causes for the state of war which had existed *de facto* if not *de jure* between the two countries. Now, however, it seemed that there would be open conflict. Both nations were making feverish preparations, mobilizing all their resources on both land and sea. For in this battle, it was Britain's very life that was at stake, while in Spain's case, it was her colonial possessions which lay in the balance.

Philip prided himself, and rightly so, on having organized the coalition of Christians which had halted the Ottoman advance at Lepanto in 1577. His triumph gave him complete confidence in his naval and military forces. Nevertheless there was open speculation throughout Europe about the outcome of this war. Andrea Mocenigo, the Venetian ambassador to the Court of France, hastened to express his concern in dispatches to his government, pointing out that "...Philip II is perfectly aware of the might of the English fleet, both in numbers and ability. The English are men of a very different stamp to the Spanish, and are renowned among the western nations for their skill and enterprise in all naval operations...", a timely prophecy indeed.

To meet this threat, Philip put all his faith in his "Invincible Armada". Tradition has it that the plan for this great fleet was conceived by Admiral Santa Cruz who had submitted it to his sovereign as early as 1583. But Philip hesitated three years before finally giving his assent to the project, and in the meantime Santa Cruz died. The command was entrusted to Duke Medina Sidonia, a brave and gallant soldier but lacking in knowledge of naval matters. As a consequence, Spanish manoeuvres throughout the ensuing war were typical of the pitched battle strategy such as had been employed at Lepanto which, one might say, was the last land battle to be fought on the sea.

The Spanish Armada included 128 vessels capable of embarking 29,000 sailors and soldiers. The son of Isabella of Portugal, Philip II had inherited this kingdom, annexing it to Spain in 1581. He could thus count on the assistance of four Portuguese galleys and twelve large galleons as well as four galleasses furnished him by the Viceroy of Naples. For her part, Queen Elizabeth had entrusted the

This lively view of Flushing in Holland, painted by Cornelis Vroom in 1613 is, from the nautical point of view, extremely accurate. Running into harbour, the Royal Prince is taking in the last of its canvas, retaining just enough sail for berthing. To the right, the small boat with the spritsail is equipped with lee-boards, the one on the weather side raised out of the water. The Dutch used this "beam keel" to minimize the sideways movement when reaching, to the same effect as the modern centre-board. In the foreground, the boat with one sail features a startling innovation, so ahead of its time that it was only at the end of the nineteenth century that it came into general use, and then only for pleasure craft: brailing a triangular sail the length of the mast, the forerunner of the "Marconi", more commonly known as the "Bermuda" rig. Here, the mast is even curved. It is interesting to note as well that all the small craft shown already carry one or, sometimes, two jibs.

This painting by Hendrik Cornelisz Vroom shows "The Happy Return to Amsterdam of Jacob Cornelisz van Nexk's Second Expedition to the East Indies on July 19th, 1599". The awning over the stern gallery is an interesting feature.

command of her naval forces to Charles Howard, First Lord of the Admiralty, who hoisted his pennant on the *Ark Royal*. Her flotillas were commanded by such experienced men as Frobisher, Hawkins and Drake. The composition of the fleet was, however, surprisingly heterogeneous. The Royal Navy itself consisted of only 34 vessels while Drake's squadron was composed of a large number of merchantmen of widely varying types, hastily armed and fitted out. These, plus various vessels offered by the City of London and private shipowners, constituted the total strength of the assembled fleet — 102 ships, some bearing such names as the *Victory*, *Lion*, *Tiger* (see page 50), *Revenge* and *Dreadnought* which were destined to fame in the annals of the British navy.

Philip II's main strategy was centred around the eventual landing, on English soil, of a *corps d'élite* under the leadership of Alexander Farnèse. As for the naval forces of Medina Sidonia, their role was a minor one : they were to cover the operation, disperse the British ships and block their way. As Philip was to learn, his mistake lay in not giving naval operations priority over land action.

By the spring of 1588, Spain's "Invincible Armada" was concentrated at Corunna. Already, its commanding officer was beginning to show symptoms of hesitation and misgivings, aware of the many shortcomings in preparedness and particularly the inadequacy of the victuals allocated to each unit. Nevertheless, on July 12th, the Armada put out to sea and was sighted by the coastguards in Cornwall on July 19th. The alarm was raised and the British fleet immediately sailed out of the ports to challenge the Spanish. Some time later, in describing the Armada, Howard said that never in all his born days had he witnessed such a concentration of ships assembled in one place. Medina Sidonia kept his ships close together, drawn up in crescent formation, intending apparently to repeat the manoeuvre, successfully used at Lepanto, of engaging the enemy at close quarters. This time, however, the Spanish strategy was not successful; the four English divisions simply backed off to a prudent distance and pounded the enemy with their cannon fire.

The first formal engagement took place on July 21st. Drake, sailing out of Plymouth with his squadron, succeeded in manoeuvring around the enemy, attacking from the rear and harrying the Spaniards throughout the night. At dawn, one of the largest Spanish galleons, the 64-cannon *Nuestra Senora del Rosario*, flagship of the Andalusia Flotilla, surrendered to Drake. During the following days, while the Armada slowly sailed up the English Channel, there were numerous skirmishes which, while not decisive, cost the Spanish vast quantities of munitions and supplies as well as men and ships. The English, on the other hand, never far from their bases, were able to take on fresh supplies.

During the night of July 28th, Medina Sidonia, anchored off Calais, was attacked by the fire ships which the English set adrift to float down to the Spanish vessels, where the burning hulks aroused panic and caused untold damage and losses. Unable to establish contact with Farnèse, who had been prevented from putting to sea by rebels, the commander-in-chief of the Spanish fleet decided to withdraw. Setting out to the north, he sailed around Scotland on the return voyage. When the once-proud Invincible Armada regained its home ports, 64 vessels were missing and over 10,000 men, soldiers and sailors, failed to answer the roll call.

Although no real naval battle had been fought, the two fleets never closing in force, the Spanish failure had far-reaching consequences on the further development of European history. England had been saved by the pluck and skill of her sailors and by her "bulwarks of wood", as her naval ships would henceforth be called. The triumph of Queen Elizabeth's fleet marked the beginning of Britain's colonial ambitions and expansion, since possession of colonies in faraway lands overseas depended upon the Navy to hold, supply and defend these — in short, for their very existence. At the same time, the balance of power in Europe began to shift, and other nations entered the colonial scene. Thus, while the Thirty Years War was raging and armies in Europe were battling across the land, other battles were being waged at sea for the conquest or defence of colonies. Spain against England, Holland versus Spain, England allied to Holland against Portugal and later against France : like a game of musical chairs, these five powers pitted their might and strength against each other in a continuous, unlimited conflict, which found its setting against the ocean.

ORGANIZED MARITIME COMMERCE

The Dutch, prompted by severe restrictions to the movements of their ships in the port of Lisbon where they had previously taken on cargoes of spices, decided to ensure their own supplies. In 1592, a group of leading Dutch merchants assembled in Amsterdam to found a company, owning its own fleet and militia, to trade with India. A few years later, the first expedition of four ships set sail under the command of Cornelius de Houtman. This undertaking, military as well as commercial in nature, had dual results. On one hand, it opened up a regular traffic with the East Indies, while on the other it was the cause of a maritime conflict between Holland and Portugal which, in varying degrees of intensity, was to continue for many years to come. In 1602, the States General of the Netherlands recognized the right of the United East India Company to carry on maritime and colonial trade over "all the seas and all the lands beyond the Cape of Good Hope as far as the Magellan Strait, as well as sovereign power over the territories and waters granted to the said company". The downfall of the Portuguese Empire was swift. The Dutch captured the Society Islands in 1621 and founded Batavia. By 1660, Dutch maritime supremacy had drastically reduced the acquisitions in the East of the famed Portuguese seafarer, Alphonse d'Albuquerque (1453-1515), leaving only Goa and a few minor possessions on the African coasts to the Portuguese crown.

In England, demand was growing for spices, sauces and highly spiced beverages. Consequently, when the Dutch, now in control of European trade in colonial produce, announced a rise in the price of pepper from three to eight shillings a pound in 1599, the English merchants demanded the intervention of the Crown to sanction the creation of an English East India Company. This company's first ship weighed anchor for the east on January 24th, 1601. It was followed by others, mostly bound for the Spice Islands. The need to establish a company headquarters and trading station soon became obvious. Initially located at Surat, this post was subsequently transferred to Bombay, a town easily defended with the ships' cannon. Naturally, the English East India Company also possessed its own military defence system on sea and on land.

In August 1639, a new and powerful Latin Armada of 70 units, commanded by Don Antonio Oquedo of Spain, sailed up the English Channel. Composed of Spanish and Portuguese ships, it was supported by an Italian contingent furnished by the Kingdom of Naples. In this case Holland was the enemy. Her ever-growing maritime forces threatened the fate of the far-off Iberian colonies. The Dutch started the battle with only 17 ships under the command of Admiral Tromp, but later they received reinforcements. After a series of inconclusive engagements, Tromp succeeded in routing the Spanish forces at the Battle of the Dunes, off the Kent coast. For Spain, this defeat was a national disaster, heavy with consequence for the future of her colonies.

In 1651, the Cromwellian Parliament passed the Navigation Act which reserved the monopoly of trade between the British Isles and the colonies for British ships, and barred Dutch vessels. This measure provoked a heated reaction from the States General and ultimately led to the outbreak of war between Holland and England. Squadrons of both nations came to grips on several occasions and with varying fortunes. On the Dutch side was Admiral Tromp and, on the other, Admiral Blake. The outcome of the war was decided in 1653 at Scheveningen where Admiral Tromp himself was killed and the Dutch lost 14 vessels to the British forces.

Although peace was concluded in 1654, war between England and Holland broke out afresh in 1665 when the troops of the English Africa Company captured Goree Island, a Dutch possession off the coast of Senegal, followed by the New Netherlands and New Amsterdam in America and finally the Island of Tobago. Once again, the ultimate fate of these territories was decided in European waters. During one of the bloodiest naval battles of its time, fought for four days in June 1665, off the North Foreland, Holland's Admiral Ruyter defeated Britain's Admiral Monk. Ruyter then advanced up the

Thames river and captured or destroyed a considerable amount of English shipping. However, the Breda Peace Agreement signed in 1667 was based on *uti possidetis* or, in other words, the right of the present possessor. England thus retained ownership of New Netherlands and New Amsterdam, later known as New York, while the Dutch received Surinam, a colony considered at the time as being of the highest importance, in compensation. The Navigation Act itself was partly repealed. Britain and Holland clashed in a last indecisive but hard-fought battle in 1674 before the Treaty of Westminster brought an end to hostilities between the two countries. The Dutch then became involved in a series of continental wars with the French which overtaxed the resources of the state, and their naval strength declined. The golden age of Ducth shipping was over. The British, however, doubled their merchant fleet by the end of the century, and continued to expand without interruption throughout the eighteenth century.

THE BREAK-THROUGH IN SHIPBUILDING

At this time, the art of shipbuilding was closely associated with the name of Pett, predominantly in the shipyards in the United Kingdom. Of this family of naval architects, the names of Phineas and Peter Pett stand out as designers and builders of the finest vessels then owned by the Royal Navy. One, the *Royal Prince*, can be seen in a painting by the Dutch artist, Hendrik Cornelisz Vroom (1591-1661), showing the arrival of the Palatine Elector at Flushing in 1613 (see page 54). Its architect, the eminent Phineas Pett, had designed and built her according to Trinity House standards. In this body was invested the authority of the Royal Navy over all shipbuilding. It published standards such as overall dimensions for certain classes of ship, like this one; length 126 feet, beam 47 feet and draught 21 feet. She carried 55 cannon which were distributed over her three decks.

According to legend, King Charles I, upon seeing the *Royal Prince* in the process of construction, commanded Phineas Pett then and there to build another, far larger ship which would be worthy of the name of *Sovereign of the Seas*. Despite opposition from the Admiralty, the King's will prevailed, and the keel of the mighty "Sovereign" was laid down. It measured 172 feet, the vessel's beam was 46 feet and she carried 100 guns on her three decks. The topsides were overlaid from stem to stern with carvings, paintings and gilded ornamentation. The stern broadened out on either side to form those characteristic quarter-galleries which resemble organ-lofts. Projecting out on either side of the large navigation light atop the stern castle were two huge carvings representing the Lion and Unicorn with various other mythological symbols. The taffrail in the centre was embossed with the Royal Arms. Her rigging was equally ambitious. A complex suit of sails was supplemented by royal-sails on the foremast and mainmast. There were three decks, but according to chroniclers of the times, the ports on the lowest deck, being too close to the water-line, always had to be kept closed. Furthermore, the weight of her top-hamper made her so unsteady in heavy weather that the Admiralty decided to scrap the poop in 1652. In 1696, by an unfortunate mischance, a lighted candle fell into a hold, fire broke out and the masterpiece of Phineas Pett was entirely destroyed.

In France, Jean-Baptiste Colbert, Minister of Finance and the Colonies, created a naval force for his sovereign, Louis XIV. He also equipped the harbours of Brest, Dunkirk, Rochefort and Lorient — so called because it was the port for ships belonging to the recently created French East India Company. Colbert's son, the Marquis de Seignelay, was sent on a mission to study new developments in British and Dutch shipyards. The young man reported back to his father with news of a type of merchant vessel which the Ducth called *fluyt* or "flute". Three-masted, with a bulging stern, the ship had a deck that was particularly narrow in relation to the width of the bottom of the hull, a design possibly prompted by a desire to minimize taxation then levied in Holland in proportion to the size of the

main beam. The observant young Marquis noted, as well, vessels called "pinasses", with a three-masted rig, which served as cargo boats or men-of-war, carrying on occasion up to 24 pieces of ordnance.

With the seventeenth century, naval art developed into a science. In the larger shipyards, naval archi-tects now worked alongside shipwrights and master carpenters, drawing up plans, studying the behaviour of hulls in water, and calculating the coefficients of hull shape and stability at different degrees of list. Just as in architecture ashore, where it was customary to establish a wooden miniature of any large building to

be constructed, so the naval dockyards, before laying a ship on the stocks, produced a scale model, accurate to the smallest details. This was submitted for the admirals' inspection and called the "Admiralty" or "Shipyard" mock-up. These models sometimes outlived the ships themselves, serving as the basis for future designs and providing valuable research data. Some became important foundation-stones of later maritime or naval museums, forming exhibits which show us the gradual transformation of the ancient galleon. Out of this vessel, with her very high, exuberantly embellished poop, has evolved the vastly more rational man-of-war. As the bulk of the topsides diminished, the hull below the water-line attained better proportions and it was fined down.

Already at the beginning of the century, small men-of-war with three masts and a single deck were being described as "frigates", a term not to be confused with the Mediterranean frigates of bygone days which, in common with "brigantines" and "galliots" belonged to the family of polyremes long since outdated. As for the galley, its popularity waned considerably in European fleets during the seventeenth century. However, contrary to what is sometimes believed, this type did not disappear altogether, but remained in service for still another century in Venetian waters and in the Turkish and Barbary pirate fleets. The oarsmen were no longer made up of "volunteers" or regular navy men, but prisoners of war, generally Berbers or common-law criminals,

For voyages to the West Indies and Canada, La Rochelle ship owners also commissioned pinnaces, carrying 10 to 12 cannon and a crew of some 20 hands. These vessels are seen to be rigged with a "bowsprit topgallant", even at a time when jibs had already been introduced. The sail on the small boat to the right is still square, rather than triangular, ill-suited to such a small craft. The ships' boats appear sturdily built.

A la Rochelle,

Il y a des Pinasses, basties en arcasses, autrement qui ont le derriere caré, de 150. 200. et 250. Tonneaux que les Marchands font servir pour les Isles de l'Amerique et Canada comme aussi pour la pesche du poisson sec. Celles de 200. Sont montées de 45 boes armées de 10 a 12. pieces de canon, et si on les envoye a l'Amerique elles n'ont que 20 hommes d'équipage

Echelle de 60 p.

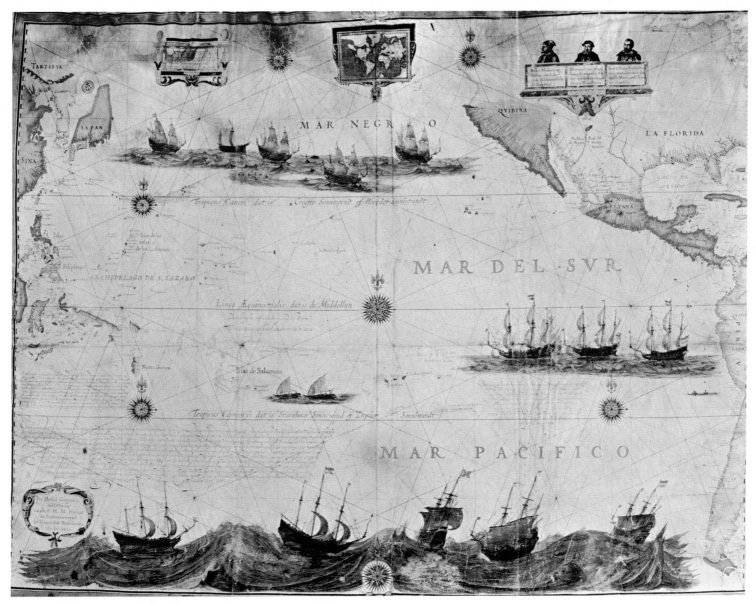

This map of the Pacific is attributed to Hessel de Gerritsz (1581-1652). Although far from complete, it does broadly indicate the extent of men's knowledge of this area in the years around 1630. First surveyed mid-seventeenth century, Australia and New Zealand are not yet shown.

condemned to serve their sentence in chains under the galley-master's lash. In Europe however, the military needs of the major maritime powers made such boats virtually worthless. Naval strength increasingly depended on the fire-power of the ships of the line, as illustrated in the case of the recently rediscovered *Vasa* (see pages 65-70), the great 1,400-ton Swedish man-of-war which was armed with 64 big bronze cannon, including forty-eight 24-pounders, and was designed to carry some 300 soldiers, mostly artillerymen, apart from the crew. Sunk on her maiden voyage in 1628, she remained preserved in the mud of Stockholm harbour to give posterity an authentic example of the great ships of her days.

On the opposite page is a detail from the famous engraving by Jacques Callot (1592-1635), depicting the siege of La Rochelle by the English fleet. Above, all the vessels' sails have been furled but still catch the wind, as they lie to fore and aft anchors, serving as floating gun batteries.

The white elephant, which gave the
ship its unusual name, can be clearly made out on the stern of the
Dutch seventeenth century vessel

B. Velthuysen Excudit

THE VASA · 1628

BY ANDERS FRANZÉN

During the spring of 1628, King Gustave Adolf of Sweden, who reigned from 1611 to 1632, proudly commissioned a new ship for his navy, the three-master *Nya Wassan*, since known as the *Vasa*. By the standards of those days, she was a fine, large sailing-ship with a displacement of 1,400 tons and a sail area of 3,800 square feet. In comparison, the *Mayflower*, built in 1620, displaced a mere 400 tons. The Swedish ship's mainmast rose 160 feet above her keel, as high as a 12-storey house. She was designed to carry a complement of 133 crew and some 300 soldiers, mostly artillerymen. Although no list of the crew has been found, the names of some of the officers who served on her are known to this day. These were Captain Severin Hansson, his second-in-command Petter Gierdsson; Chief Gunner Joen Larsson, Sailing-Master Jöran Mattson, Boatswain Per Bertilsson, Gunnery-Officer Erik Jönsson and Hans Jonsson, Captain of the Royal Naval Dockyard. The *Vasa* was armed with 64 pieces of ordnance, 48 cannons of 24, 8 pieces of 2, 2 guns of 1 and 6 mortars, a formidable total of 80 tons of bronze, ready to spit cannon-balls or grape-shot. Vividly painted and sumptuously decorated, here was a ship to inflame national pride and instil fear into the hearts of all enemies of Sweden.

And this was, indeed, the King's plan. Already he saw political storm clouds blowing up on the coasts of the Baltic. Indeed, Emperor Ferdinand II of Hapsburg (1619-1637) and Gustave Adolf were at war, wrangling over the Baltic which, in King Gustave Adolf's opinion, should be under Swedish jurisdiction. For this reason, the King of Sweden took a personal and very energetic interest in building up, by all possible means, the strength of his navy. He is even reputed to have said : "...After God, it is the Navy which will determine the future prosperity of our kingdom..." In the spring of 1628, the *Vasa* was towed from the shipyard in Blasieholmen Island where she had been built and launched the previous year, to the naval dockyard near the Royal Palace of the Three Crowns, where she was to take on ballast, have her armament stowed in place and embark her crew and complement of soldiers.

Between three and four o'clock on the afternoon of August 10th, 1628, the *Vasa* got under way to proceed to Älvsnabben in the islands off Stockholm where, under the King's orders, she would join other ships and hold herself in readiness "... to set sail, on such day and hour as it may please Us for whichever destination We ordain ..." In the big church nearby, Vespers had just finished and a crowd assembled on the quay to wish Godspeed to this proud man-of-war as the sails filled with a light breeze from the south-south-west. The *Vasa* was towed into a head-wind to Södermalm where the fore-topsail, main topsail, foresail and lateen mizzen sail were hoisted. Less than a mile away, a squall lashed down from the heights of Södermalm and heeled the ship over so savagely that water poured through her lower gun-ports. Despite all efforts, the *Vasa* capsized and sank in several minutes "...under sail and dressed over all..."

Apart from the crew and the gunners, the *Vasa* had various dignitaries on board, as well as the wives and children of a number of servicemen on their way to Vaxholm. Although no absolutely reliable records exist, fifty people are estimated to have been drowned in this shipwreck. The finest ship of the realm had been lost at a particularly crucial time, worth 100,000 Riksdaler, the equivalent of about US $50,000,000 in our days. It was no less than a national catastrophe.

The very next day, a court of enquiry was convened to hear the evidence of the ship's surviving officers and those who had been responsible for her construction. Why had the *Vasa* foundered? Was she badly built, badly loaded, badly commanded?

The Gunnery-Officer, Erik Jönsson was the first to be questioned. He stated he had inspected the guns and made sure they were properly secured. All had appeared normal to him. In his opinion it would have been impossible for the ship's centre of gravity to have been affected by more ballasting, as the lower gun-ports were only three to four feet above the water-line, highly vulnerable in any storm.

The second-in-command, Gierdsson, who had been in charge of the *Vasa*'s rigging, informed the court of enquiry that he would never have believed that any ship could be capsized under the pressure of such a light wind. The interrogation of Sailing-Master Jöran Matsson was dramatic. He was blamed for having "... neglected his functions and his duty by failing to ensure that the ballast was correctly stowed and other details were in order, in accordance with his duties and orders received ..." and to have incurred the loss of one of His Majesty's ships. Jöran Matsson defended himself courageously. He had seen to it that the ballast was correctly loaded and distributed and had, personally, inspected the work. But he pointed out the ship had too much top hamper, that Captain Hansson had known this, and Admiral Fleming had witnessed clear evidence of this during the roll trials that Matsson himself had carried out in his presence. He concluded his evidence with a very apposite thrust. "If the ship had been incapable of standing up to a light wind when carrying only four sails, how would she have fared in a strong wind with every stitch of canvas spread?..." This statement exploded like a bomb-shell and its full blast fell on the Boatswain, Per

The plan showing masts, sails and rigging was recon-
stituted from records of the period. It is quite conventional,
scarcely differing from those of contemporary French ships,
built early in the seventeenth century. The hull itself is
unusual, already showing a marked break-away from the
galleon, not yet overburdened with the superstructures so
fashionable throughout the closing years of that century.

Length :   217 ft. $^1/_3$ in.
Breadth :   42 ft. $^2/_3$ in.
Depth :   about 17-18 ft.
Armament :   64 cannon : 48 24-pounders
                              8 3-pounders
                              2 1-pounders
                              6 mortars
Crew :   133 men and 300 soldiers

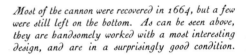

Most of the cannon were recovered in 1664, but a few were still left on the bottom. As can be seen above, they are handsomely worked with a most interesting design, and are in a surprisingly good condition.

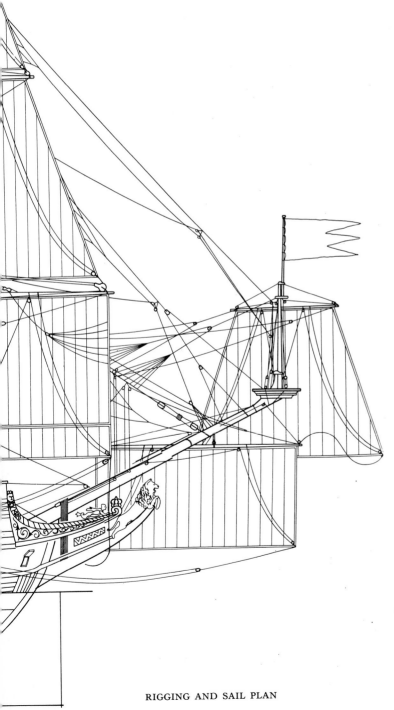

Bertilsson. He was asked why "... he had not concerned himself, as he should, with his duties and checked the sails and gear and whether he had not, perhaps, had too much to drink and was intoxicated ..." He vehemently defended himself and, in reply to the last question, affirmed that on that very morning, before the vessel sailed, he had received Holy Communion.

The court went on to question Hein Jacobsson, who had been responsible for the completion and delivery of the *Vasa*. He was asked why he had constructed such a narrow hull with so little bluff. He replied he had carried out the instructions as to the ship's dimensions, and had indeed followed the specifications to the letter. In actual fact, the dimensions of the *Vasa* had been determined by none other than the King himself.

In short, this long enquiry proved inconclusive and was closed with no grounds for prosecution. Meanwhile, attempts were made to salvage the wreck, for the mainmast of the *Vasa* still projected above the surface of the

RIGGING AND SAIL PLAN

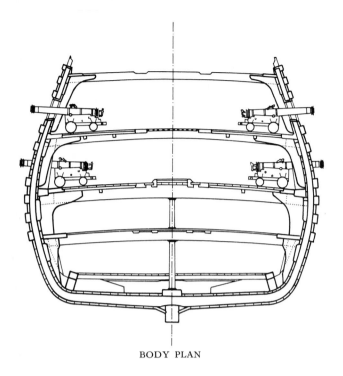

BODY PLAN

water. This undertaking was found to be impossible with the equipment available at that time and in December the same year, Admiral Fleming wrote despondently to the Council of the Realm: "... The weight is far greater than I would ever have supposed ..."

Hans Albrecht von Treileben attempted a new salvage operation in 1664. He recovered fifty or so cannons (and gutted the hull of everything of value). At the time it was considered an amazing achievement to raise one to two tons, the weight of a cannon, from a depth of one hundred feet. In 1956, after being forgotten for many long years, the wreck of the *Vasa* was rediscovered, buried in mud in over 100 feet of water. Between 1957 and 1961, various possibilities were investigated to raise it to the surface and this was accomplished during the summer of 1961, after immense efforts and infinite precautions. Since 1962, the hull of the *Vasa* has been on display in a provisional museum at Djurgarden, in Stockholm.

Although the fate of the *Vasa* was by no means a glorious one, she has another claim to fame. Today, she stands as the world's oldest ship to be fully identified and perfectly preserved. The *Vasa* thus provides an inexhaustible mine of information for naval historians who can derive a wealth of evidence on the art of naval architecture, and life aboard in the seventeenth century, thanks to some 20,000 objects discovered on or near the ship.

The *Vasa* has earned her letters patent of nobility in becoming a historic monument to naval archeology. Nevertheless, nobody knows to this day why this great sailing-ship, Sweden's pride, so inexplicably foundered.

As is well known, the mud of the sea bed is an excellent wood preservative, providing the water is too cold to be inhabited by the destructive teredo ship-worm. So it was that "drakkars", the boats Vikings used as tombs, have been unearthed from peat-bogs, virtually intact after a thousand years. However, to find a large ship so well preserved after more than three centuries was a new and unique achievement. The illustrations on page 69 show how perfectly the Vasa has been preserved, both inside and out. Only those parts that were not submerged in the mud have rotted and been destroyed, as can be seen in the last photograph. Unfortunately, earlier salvage operations resulted in most objects of any value being removed from the vessel, but a certain number of utensils remained, giving us interesting glimpses of life aboard in the seventeenth century. The hull itself provides a mine of fascinating and almost endless information for naval archaeologists and architects. It is only now, restored to the open air, that the Vasa may begin to deteriorate and age in the normal way, although the authorities in Sweden are naturally taking all possible precautions. Exceptionally enough, it was possible to design and draw up the plans on the facing page by referring directly to the original model.

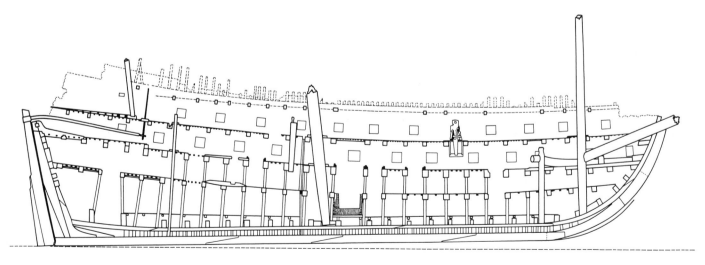

LONGITUDINAL SECTION

These four carvings, miraculously untouched by time, are typical examples of seventeenth-century Swedish art, especially the figure in armour with his plumed helmet. The lion's head adorned a dead-light, covering the gun port from which projected the cannon. The photograph above clearly shows the interior of the battery-deck, which was remarkably high for a ship of that period.

To the left, the arms of the King of Sweden. Below, cannon are unshipped from *Vasa* as she lies in the empty dock where she was towed, and is actually afloat.

ÉTIENNE TAILLEMITE

Curator of the ARCHIVES NATIONALES
FOR THE MINISTÈRE DE LA MARINE, Paris

ROYAL GLORIES

Nothing is more impressive nor so befits the
majesty of the King than that his ships bear the
finest ornamentation yet seen on the high seas.

JEAN-BAPTISTE COLBERT (1619-1683)

ROYAL GLORIES

During the first thirty years of the seventeenth century, the modern concept of the battle fleet emerged for the first time in the navies of the leading nations. Powerful men-of-war, heavily armed with cannon, were needed in quantity, and the task of supplying this demand changed the face of shipbuilding forever. The empiric methods of the small shipyards, their limited equipment and knowledge were outpaced by the special problems which now arose. Shipyards and foundries were obliged to expand, to develop new skills and refined systems of production, and naval construction, in the process, became one of the first large flourishing modern industries the world had ever known up to that time.

The first consideration was the supplying of shipbuilding materials — and of these the most important was, naturally, wood. Oak was needed for hulls, pine for masts, poplar for ornamental carvings and elm for gun mounts. To secure these, each maritime nation had its own jealously guarded sources of supply; and these had to be continually expanded to meet the needs of shipbuilders.

The Dutch were principally supplied by the Baltic countries, by Norway (with pine) and by

The drawing below, and those on the next six pages, are reproduced from the " Album de Colbert " preserved by the Service Hydrographique de la Marine in Paris. Here the stern-post, suspended from sheer legs, is about to be joined to the supported keel with its stem-post to the right.

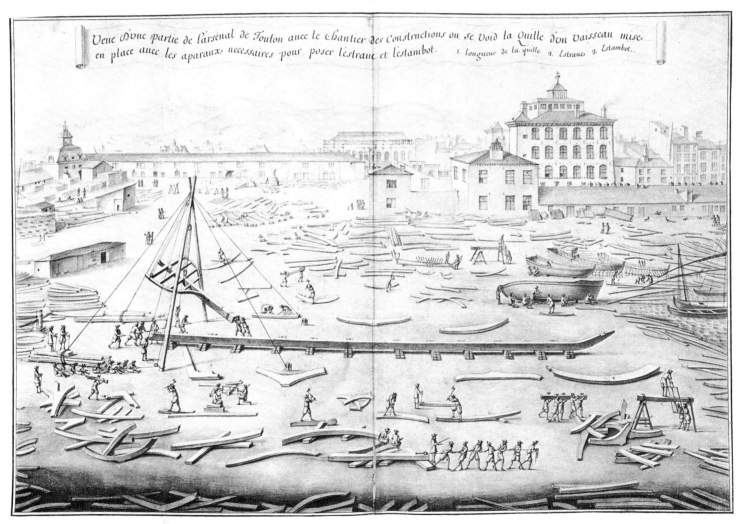

This drawing of the Royal Charles *by* Willem van de Velde the Elder (1611-1693) *exemplifies the elaborate work undertaken to achieve the prestige attached to the royal fleets.*

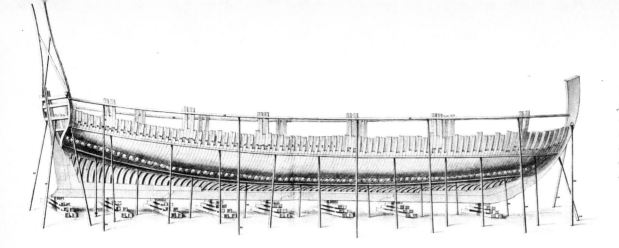

On the stocks, this hull already has floors and futtocks, the lower sections of the frames being joined to the keel. The timbers rising aft are actually the sterncastle and poop-deck frames which at this stage oddly resemble the shape of a lyre.

Outside planking has now given shape to the quick works, the hull below the water-line. The second futtocks are built up to form the sides, held in position by rib-bands, the longitudinal spars that ensure the frames will remain regularly spaced throughout construction work.

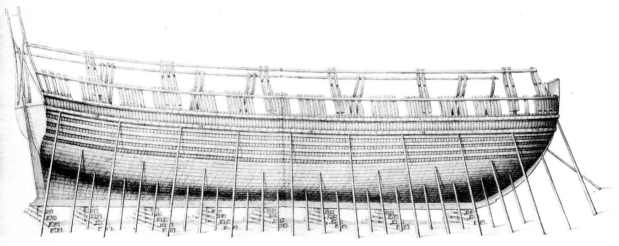

A third series of futtocks adds to the height of the frames and are in position. Spaces left between some of them will be used as ports. Thicker and wider timbers, the wales, strengthen the ship's sides but, as can be seen, neither bulwarks nor final strakes are yet in place.

74

Germany. In England, all oak trees were reserved for the Royal Navy. The counties of Essex, Sussex and Hampshire yielded the best quality but these local resources had to be augmented by wood from northern countries as well as from the American colonies in New England and the West Indies. In France, Jean-Baptiste Colbert, that indefatigable minister of Louis XIV who controlled the navy from 1669 to 1683, laid down strict regulations to protect the resources in construction woods. In densely forested provinces such as Burgundy, Franche-Comté, Lorraine, Alsace, Auvergne, Dauphiné, Provence, the Pyrénées and Brittany, officials marked those trees suited for naval use and only the navy could fell them. But France, too, soon found her domestic supply insufficient and turned first to

Once completed, the hull is hauled slowly down to the water by an elaborate system of blocks and tackle that ensure against mishaps during the ever critical launching. While the ropes on either side are pulled by men on the shore, other crews operate the capstans on two beached pontoons.

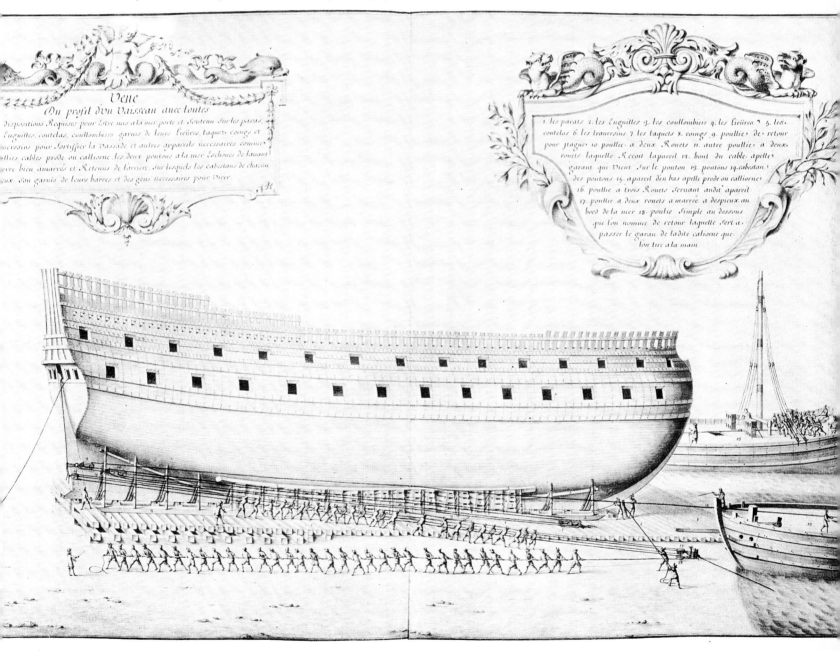

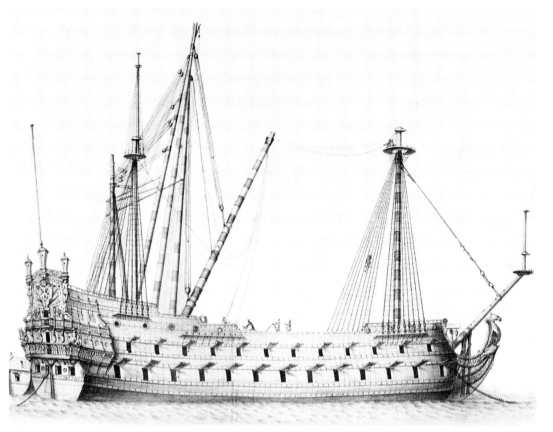

Finished, the ship receives her head, the poop with its galleries and deadlights, chain-plates and navigation lights. Bowsprit, foremast and mizzen-masts have already been stepped. Between the fore- and mizzen-masts the sheer-hulk sways up the lower section of the mainmast into position.

Barges, pulling on the ship's masts, have heeled her over, while still afloat, to be careened. Gun-ports and other openings are battened down to keep as much water as possible out of the hull while the work is being carried out. In tideless waters it was a nearly impossible task to beach a ship of any size for careening.

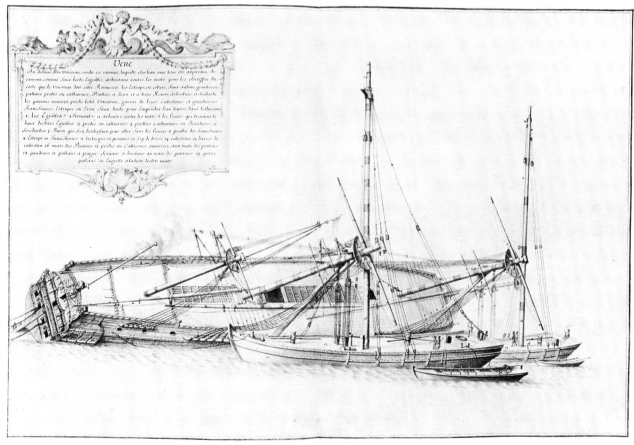

Scandinavia and the Baltic countries, Riga long being the centre of this trade; then to Spain, Italy, Bohemia and Germany. Timber was sought as far afield as the Black Sea, southern Russia, Canada and the West Indies, particularly for the very hard guaiacum mostly used for pulley-blocks. All this wood was floated, towed behind ships, or transported in specially fitted-out vessels to the naval dockyards.

One can well imagine the amount of wood used up by the navies of those days when it is realized that a ship of 110 guns represented approximately 100,000 cubic feet, or 4,000 oak trees. Felling techniques varied from one country to another, the English cutting the trunk just above the roots and below the first branches, maintaining that this method prevented the trunk from splitting. These trunks were not squared up but simply stripped of bark, the logs piled up and left to dry in the open air, except in the case of elm or the pine intended for masts. Huge timber-yards, where the felled trees were stocked and allowed to dry in the free-flowing breezes, were established near shipyards. Some shipbuilders advocated preserving the new wood in sea water, a method which had certain advantages and which was frequently adopted for the wood used in making masts. Consequently, nearly every shipyard had its own mast-timber pond in use. Iron, too, was needed in quantity for naval

With shrouds and masts straining, the ship is heeled over for cleaning and repainting. Installed on a raft alongside, the caulkers have lit a fire to soften the old pitch before scraping the bottom planking. Afterwards, the seams between the planking will be stopped up with oakum, filled with thick pitch and tarred over. By this method, all the caulking work could be accomplished while the careened hull was more or less dried off.

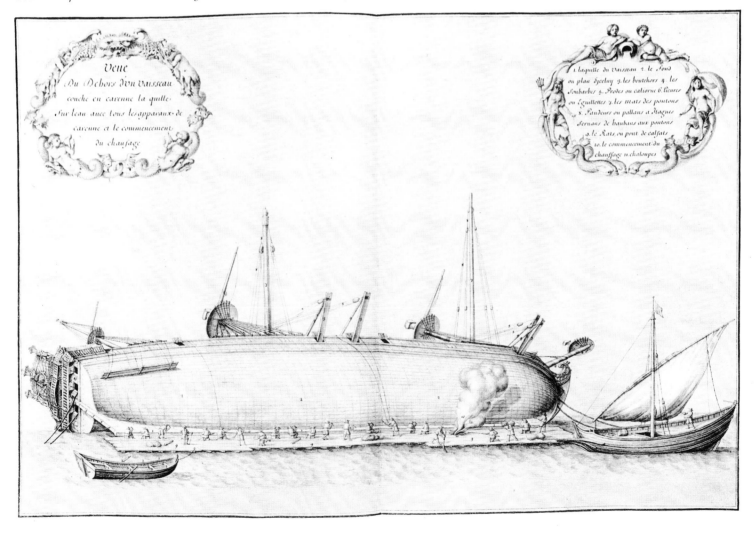

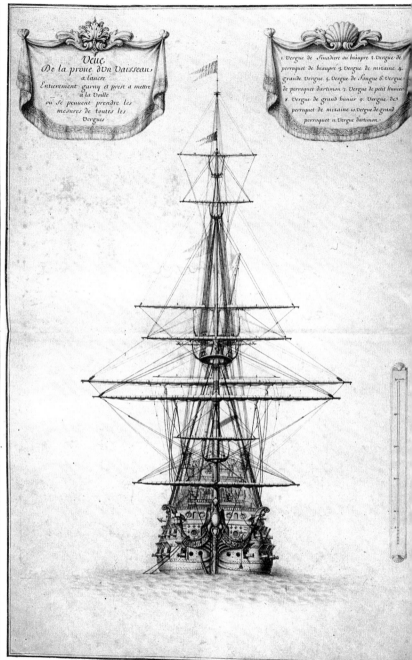

Seen from the stern, this fully rigged, fitted out and armed French ship is ready for sea. Magnificent decorations grace her poop and galleries ; her cannon are in review order, barrels level below the ports.

Seen from the bows, the same ship with sails furled on her yards rides at anchor on one hawser ; chains were not yet adopted. The illustration on the left shows her held across wind by an anchor aft.

construction and its production steadily increased. More iron nails were used for joints, and various fittings in metal, such as hand-rails, became increasingly common. Local ores were used for all iron fittings ; in France, the forges of Nivernais specialized in the making of anchors while those of

Dauphiné, Périgord and the ancient province of Angoumois mostly produced cannon. To supplement local production, iron was brought in from Sweden, lead from Britain and zinc from Holland, while copper was shipped from Sweden, Hungary and the Levant, especially during the seventeenth century,

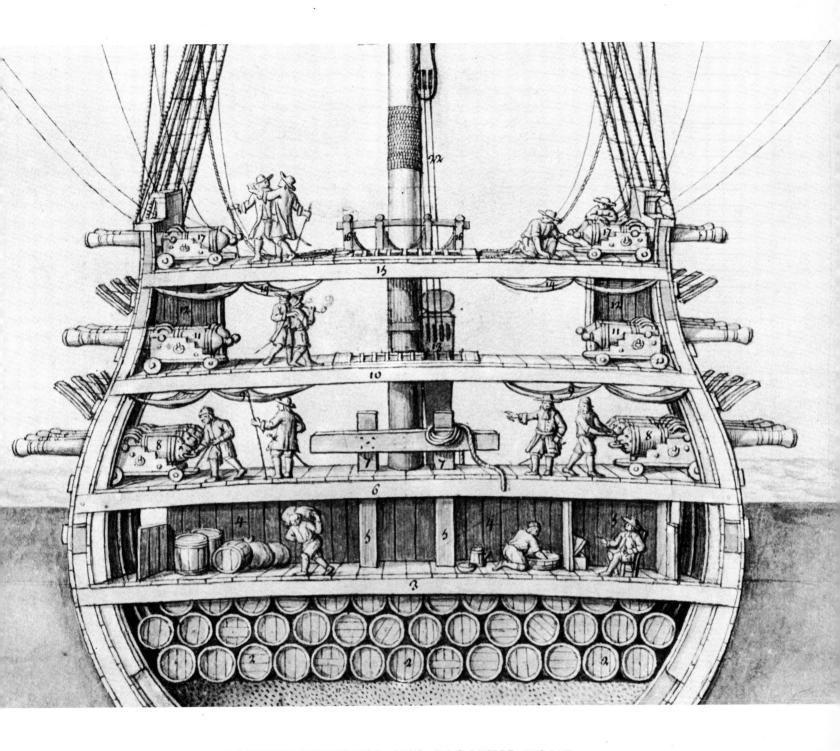

MOBILE FORTRESS AND FLOATING HOME

A sectional drawing reveals the internal structure of a man-of-war. In the centre are the mizzen-mast, its giant pulley-blocks and the mooring bitts where the mizzen is stepped deep in the hull. Excluding the castle, this ship has four decks, making three between-decks, an upper deck and a hold where casks of fresh water and other provisions were stored on top of the sand or gravel ballast. Above are the ship's stores. Below the water-line, this deck is usually protected from enemy fire but if the ship heeled over it became exposed. To block up cannon-ball holes, access passages are provided the length of the hull. The battery decks above also provide crew accommodation. Cannon, decreasing in weight from the lower to the upper decks, are level in review order below the opened ports. They would not normally be visible through the ports on both sides of the ship. The men's hammocks were slung above the guns and, in fact, hung much lower than shown here, and it was difficult to move about beneath them without bumping into the occupants. Albeit a man-of-war, this was also a sailing-ship and the huge pulley-blocks, one for swaying up the foremast yard and the other for hoisting the mainsail, as well as the heavy bitts for mooring cables about the mast foot, are interesting.

Every detail of this ship is meticulously accurate in this work by the famous sculptor Pierre Puget (1620-1694), painted one year before his death. Puget was well acquainted with his subject, having decorated many of the King's ships. Sailors are hauling on the mainsail and fore-topsail sheets and, in the lower battery, a cannon has just fired. Three stern lanterns denote a flagship but Puget leaves her nameless.

THE DUTCH FLUTE · 17TH CENTURY

BY E. W. PETREJUS

There is no doubt that the flute was ingeniously designed to meet the exigencies of commerce and the times. Towards the end of the sixteenth century, Dutch merchants were industriously capturing a large portion of the cargo trade, not only within a few days' sailing of their own shores but pushing their commercial frontiers east and west across the world. This increasing foreign trade called for larger, faster vessels than the *boyers* and *flyboats*, and these needs were satisfied by the flute, a new and very successful type of cargo-ship.

In general shape and proportions the flute was not unlike the musical instrument with her narrow deck, rounded hull and conspicuous length. Four times as long as she was broad, her unusual proportions are well illustrated by the fact that up to the introduction of the flute, ships were built to the standard of 80 lasts (about 160 metric tons) on a keel of 30 ells. Thirty years later, a keel of this length was considered unreasonable for a ship of more than 40 to 50 lasts.

It is rare in the annals of naval history that a new ship design finds mention in the chronicles of the time. However, in the first edition of his chronicles published in 1604, D. Velius, who kept the official records of the city of Hoorn, mentions that the new type of ship called "flute" was first built there in 1595.

One of the leading sponsors of this new cargo-vessel was Pieter Jansz Lioorne, a merchant trading with the Italian port of Livorno, hence his name. It is questionable whether the flute was an entirely new type of ship or merely a radical development of an existing design. However, of light construction with a large cargo capacity, shallow draft, good sailing qualities with a small crew, she was inexpensive to build and run, proving an economic success. Demand rapidly increased and within eight years over

eighty of these ships were flying the flags of Hoorn owners and bringing in handsome profits. Fear of competition quickly led more merchants to replace older ships with the new vessels.

A flute was easily recognized by the rounded stern and planking sharply curved into the stern-post, a peculiar athwartships helm port which admitted the tiller under a narrow taffrail and the unusual tumble home of her sides and quarters. In some ways, the flute bore a resemblance to the herring-buss, similarly built but much lower aft and with less tumble home. Flutes trading to the north and east were also characterized by their blunt bows, narrow decks and pear-shaped quarters.

According to the existing regulations in these waters, flutes could be classified as much smaller than other vessels with the same carrying capacity. This classification reduced the export duty and passage tolls levied by the Danes on vessels carrying timber from Norway and when passing through the Sound. This tax advantage lasted until 1669 when new legislation governing ship classification and measurements amended the regulations. With no further advantage to be gained by the extreme design, the exaggerated tumble home disappeared.

Smaller flutes were simply built with only one cargo hold and a cabin on the after deck. The head was seldom built up and the only decoration on the ship was some painting or carving on the taffrail surrounded by gingerbread-work. As simple as the hull construction, rigging consisted of two square sails on the main and foremast, a triangular sail on the mizzen and a spritsail under the bowsprit. Basically the same as the old *razeils* with its six sails, the flute's masts were proportionately higher, with shorter yards and less rake to the foremast. This rig was an improvement on the short three-masters of earlier times and, with her narrow beam, the

flute was a better sailer under most wind conditions. She sailed well on the wind and, unencumbered by fore and after castles, made less leeway.

Throughout the seventeenth century, this cargo-vessel was the foremost Dutch merchant ship in European waters, making an impressive contribution to the development of Dutch maritime trade and, indeed, constituting one of the most powerful arms in Holland's long struggle to gain control of the cargo trade in European waters and between Portugal and Brazil.

As time passed, various classes of flutes developed. These included those trading with France, Spain and the Mediterranean countries. Others shipped timber from Norway and grain from the Baltic ports. The Dutch whaling fleet was composed mostly of flutes. They were owned by large companies trading with Brazil and the West Indies. And, from their outset, flutes were in service with the Dutch East India Company in the Far East, where they collected cargo, subsequently shipped home in costly "return ships". According to records in 1653, flutes had lengths of 100, 120 and 140 Amsterdam feet. In the second half of the century, the Spaniards and Portuguese were no longer so much feared and flutes made the long ocean voyages to and from India. However, in this region the flute was less successful than the *pinas*, as the sharply curved planking tended to spring in the heat of the tropical sun. Although often used as transports by navies of the major sea powers, flutes were never considered suitable for adaptation to men-of-war.

Over all these classes of flutes, there were many differences in size, rigging and armament. Obviously, ocean-going vessels of this type were more strongly and solidly built than those used for local European trade to the north and east. Of necessity they had to have better sea-going qualities,

To an uninitiated eye, the flute's rigging appears bewilderingly complicated although it is, of course, elementary compared to that of the large sailing-ships to come. Instead of the blocks of the Middle Ages, the shrouds are now hauled taut with the more convenient dead-eyes and lanyards. The sails had a very simple, uncluttered line.

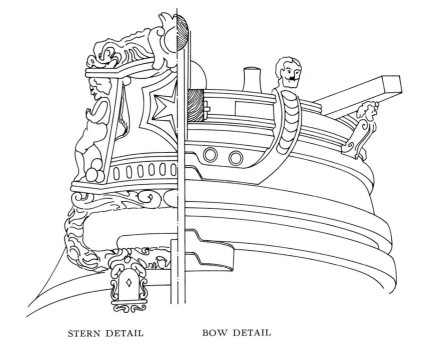

STERN DETAIL   BOW DETAIL

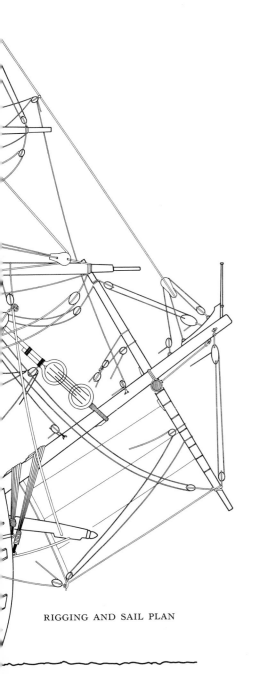

RIGGING AND SAIL PLAN

sides built higher and the cabin larger to shelter a larger ship's complement for defence against possible aggression. Such flutes carried the same rig as other ships of their size. Those which sailed routes passing through the Strait of Gibraltar were also broad and solid, more heavily armed, and carrying a larger crew than those sailing the safe waters to Norway and the Baltic. All these larger classes of flute were built with heads and, in some cases, side galleries.

Flutes serving as timber ships were plain vessels without a head, only lightly armed and carrying a small crew. They had timber ports cut in the stern through which the lengths of wood were loaded or discharged, and ballast ports in the sides. When serving as whaling ships, they had bows doubled as a protection against the ice, were broader and more sturdily built than those used for cargo. They were easily recognized by the boats they carried aboard and, particularly, the heavy boat davit athwartships borne near the stern.

Not only used in their country of origin, flutes were also built in Britain, France, the Scandinavian countries and Germany, where the first was

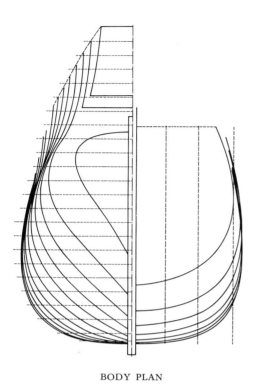

BODY PLAN

built at Hamburg as early as 1618. However, the success achieved by the Dutch could not be attained merely by copying the lines of these vessels. A deal of knowledge and experience had been built into the flute, not always apparent to the observer. British and French shipbuilders seem to have been satisfied with copying its general characteristics while Danish, German and Swedish shipyards followed the Dutch methods more closely.

In the second half of the seventeenth century, other varieties of the flute appeared, one of these being the *hek-boot* or *hagboat*. The main difference was seen in the shape of the stern surmounted by a wing transom which, in effect, widened the hull aft, increased her loading capacity and accommodation space, while allowing enough room for contemporary decoration. The taffrail was small and there were no side galleries. The hull of the *bootschip*, on the other hand, resembled that of the eighteenth century galliot built up in much the same way as that of the flute, but with the upper part of the stern much wider because of reduced tumble home. These vessels were ship-rigged but had the mizzen-sail carried on a gaff instead of a yard. During the eighteenth century, the *bootschip* mostly served in the whaling fleets. Another related type of ship was the "cat" whose hull was a mixture of *boyer* and flute. With only one deck, the cat was a simple vessel designed to carry as much cargo as possible, flat-floored with very little rake to stem and stern-posts. Mostly used as timber ships, those in Britain carried coal from the north to London and the Continent. The rig was unusual, fore and mainmasts being single poles or, if in two sections, with the topmast lashed to the lower and no tops were used. Courses and topsails were lowered on to the deck to be furled. The mizzen, a tall narrow sail, was bent to a small gaff and spread by a boom. However, this odd rig was replaced eventually by the normal ship rig throughout the eighteenth century.

The flute was still very much a " round " ship and these plans tempt one to compare it with a clog. The Dutch required ships with large cargo capacity, yet capable of manoeuvring in the shallow coastal waters as well as in the open sea. These lines have survived to the present day, in all kinds of small fishing craft, now equipped with lee-boards — a feature which was sadly lacking on these large flutes of the seventeenth century.

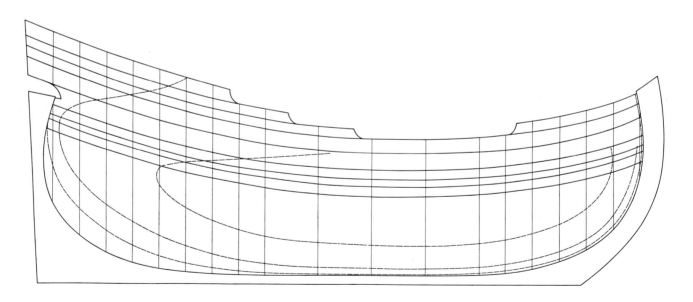

PROFILE

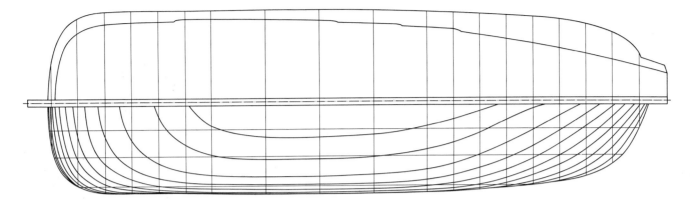

HALF-BREADTH PLAN

Above : The lower part of this drawing traces the waterlines. One realizes that the vessel made considerably better headway by sailing backwards, the egg shape being more hydrodynamic with the rounded end forward and the tapering end aft. The flute's side is seen to be straight.

Below. The construction plan, clearly demonstrating the main features of the flute and showing the dimensions. The vessel is undeniably on the heavy side, rather a " tub " as sailors would say. This excellent plan, doubtless drawn up after the ship had been completed, reveals every detail of her construction. As in the Middle Ages, the rudder still penetrates the hull beneath the stern castle but what cannot be seen here is that it is worked by a tiller passing through the planking of the poop, enabling the helmsman to see at last where he is steering. The ship's hold is still all in one, without an intermediate deck, similar in this respect to the hold of coastal sailing-vessels and barges of today. The ornamentation is restrained. At the bows, the inclined bowsprit is secured by ropes to counteract its tendency to lift. Just below is the cat-head for the anchor.

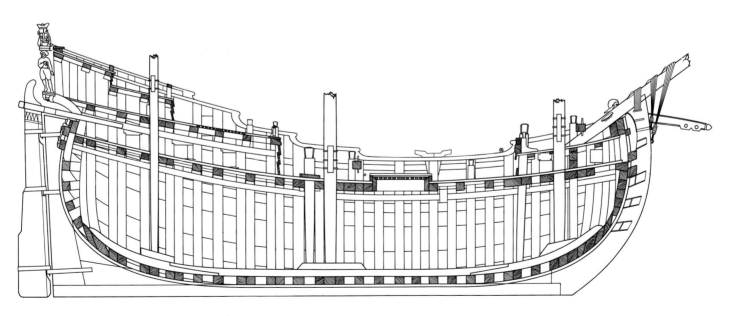

CONSTRUCTION PLAN

On the left, this model of the Houtpoort, dating from 1700, served as a basis for the plans on the preceding pages. The hull is built with meticulous accuracy and the few cannon are interesting, although the sculptor has clearly lavished his most loving care on the rigging. Apart from the pulleys, which are rather too heavy according to the scale, the rest is modelled with a lifelike and rare accuracy. Below, the flute seen from the stern and the other, shown broadside on, are simply models posed on the water or wedged, at low tide, in the sand which is ridged with extraordinary regularity. The flute in the picture above, approaching the vessel hove-to is, on the contrary, full of life, the fresh breeze filling her sails and ruffling the water. This anonymous engraving from the late seventeenth century, representing a third-rate Dutch "Oorlogschip", as well as the two illustrations below, are now preserved in the famous Prins Hendrik Museum at Rotterdam.

and, sometimes, even during periods of hostilities. Other essentials were sails and ropes. The Dutch, French and English, with their mills at Bristol and Ipswich, were the major producers of sail canvas. In France, Colbert developed this industry in Brittany and also tried his best to establish it elsewhere. Hemp rope was needed by the mile to fit out the ships; here again, the major producers were in the Baltic States, centred on Königsberg and Riga. They supplied all the large fleets and, frequently, complemented the inadequate production facilities of the various nations.

Ship completion and, particularly, maintenance also used up considerable quantities of tar and thick pitch. These wood extracts were manufactured on a large scale in the north European countries. France, too, had its full share of this trade, producing these materials in the area of the Landes and shipping large quantities to England and Holland during the seventeenth century from the ports of Bayonne and Bordeaux. Except for Scotland, Britain produced very little, relying on supplies from the Baltic countries, France and New England. Coal-tar was used by the British in the eighteenth century with much better results as a wood preservative, as it was found to be highly resistant to rain and heat and hence adaptable to many climates.

Thus, by the very diversity of its needs and by the size of its labour force, naval construction in the seventeenth and eighteenth centuries emerged as a dominant industry. Naval dockyards changed the aspect of certain towns: at Chatham, one of Britain's most important shipbuilding centres, 1,500 to 2,000 workmen were employed in twenty graving docks with an output capacity of about ten vessels a year. Plymouth, Portsmouth, Deptford and Woolwich boasted the largest British ordnance works, with foundries for making cannon and other armaments. Woolwich employed about 500 men and concentrated on the building of frigates and other small craft. In Holland the main shipyard was at Amsterdam, so well laid out and well equipped that it drew the admiration of all visitors. The Danes also had a fine shipyard at Copenhagen, the Swedes at Stockholm and, in Russia, Peter the Great established naval yards at St. Petersburg. Spanish shipbuilding was mostly carried out at Cadiz,

Ferrol and Carthagena. In France, the major yards were located at Toulon. The oldest of the French shipyards, however, was at the Channel port of Brest and was originally founded by Richelieu and Rochefort, on Colbert's instigation. Another important shipbuilding centre was at Lorient, but until 1769, when it became a Royal Dockyard, it had been exclusively used by the India Company for building and for fitting out. In every country, an infinite number of small shipbuilders still supplied the needs of the merchant navies. Sometimes, during the eighteenth century, they were contracted to build light units such as frigates or corvettes. According to the course of national or international affairs the amount of work carried out in these yards varied considerably; in periods of hostility or of prosperous maritime trade, they were kept extremely busy. In the thirty years between 1763 and 1792, no fewer than 422 ships left the Honfleur yards in France alone; but there were also times when work came to a virtual standstill.

During the seventeenth century, naval construction was still essentially empiric in applied techniques. Shipwrights were artisans without professional training who worked out their designs by rule of thumb, following traditional methods handed down from father to son, inheriting secrets closely guarded by each family. Their methods fell into a strict pattern, each shipwright having his own individual habits which he would not easily relinquish. This jealousy and obstinately conservative attitude delayed progress in construction techniques. Most vessels were built on a slip inclined towards the sea or in a horizontal position in a dock sealed off by watertight gates. Methods of construction varied from country to country and even from one region to another. Ships built on the Atlantic coast of France were reputed to be less graceful than those which left the Toulon yards.

How was a ship built during this century? Once the keel was laid, the curved wood frames were mounted perpendicularly upon it, forming the skeleton on to which were fixed the planks that formed the hull. These were of two kinds, "skin planking" on the outside of the frames and "inner planking" on the inside. Decks were constructed on a series of athwart timbers, or deck beams, which

Wenzel Hollar (1607-1677), although born in Prague, spent long periods both in Britain and Holland. He made numerous engravings of sailing-ships, which display great accuracy and a good understanding of ship construction. In the engraving opposite, he depicts the stern of a Dutch merchant-vessel which has been fitted out for a voyage to the West Indies. Although the decoration is generally restrained, the embellishments on the stern seem quite superfluous and extremely fragile, being bereft of any kind of support.

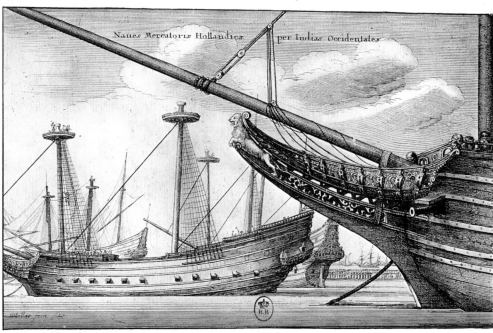

Other details of ships taking part in the same voyage are shown in the second engraving. The carved cutwater on the vessel to the right is no longer a support for the bowsprit but merely allows access to it. It is also used as the heads. The tops observed in the background appear enormous and do not seem to have been provided with the necessary stays. Although fitted out as merchant-vessels, these ships were always armed with cannon against the ever-present risk of attack at sea when the captain had to rely solely on his own resources.

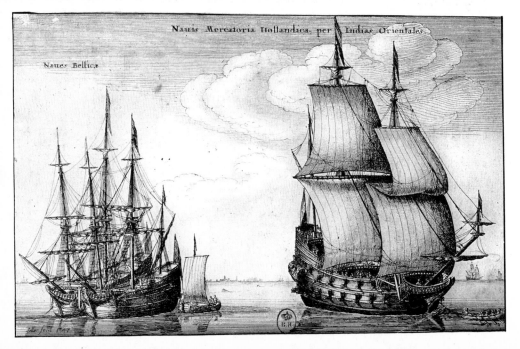

In this engraving, Wenzel Hollar seems to invite comparison between merchantmen and men-of-war. In actual fact, the difference between them was extremely slight and depended more on the ship's armament and mission than on her actual lines. Ships under the same company or national flag often sailed together for reasons of safety, although occasionally naval units from the battle fleet escorted the merchant-vessels. However, the system of organized convoys, as we have come to know them today, had not yet been developed.

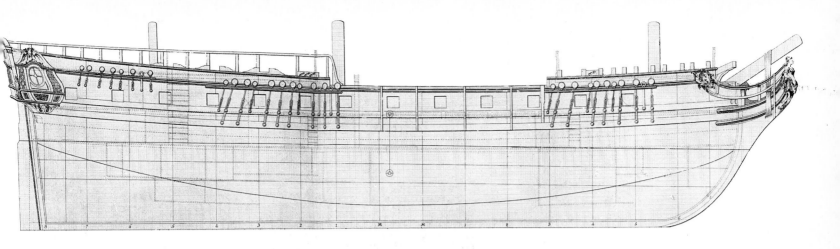

CHAPMAN
GENIUS OF THE DRAWING BOARD

When King Gustave III of Sweden (1746-1792) took upon himself to restore his navy to its proper place after its deterioration since the death of Charles XII, he chose Frederic-Henry Chapman (1721-1808) for this task. Chapman earned his fame mainly by publishing, at the age of 47, his " Architectura Navalis Mercatoria ", acknowledged ever since as one of the best collections of eighteenth-century maritime drawings. His work was the result of considerable study, foreign travel and correspondence with scholars and shipbuilders. Chapman was familiar with the work of Newton and Alembert and, particularly, such treatises as " Scientia Navalis " in 1749 by the mathematician Euler, " Elements of Naval Architecture " in 1752 by Duhamel du Monceau and also Murray's " Treatise on Shipbuilding " published in 1754. Chapman was especially noted for his mathematical calculation of a ship's centre of gravity, laden or unladen, carefully marked with two small concentric rings, joined by a line, in the central part of his profile. The diagram above is that of the Sirène, *a frigate commissioned by the King of France, and the one below the English King's* Unicorn. *Each ship was armed with batteries of 24 to 26 eight-pound and 8 to 10 four-pound guns on the forecastle and quarter-decks. Apart from the occasional figure-head and other small details, there were hardly any features that distinguished ships of one nationality from another, making their identification extremely difficult.*

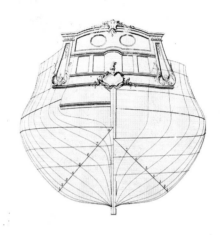

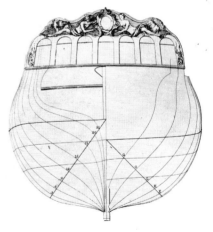

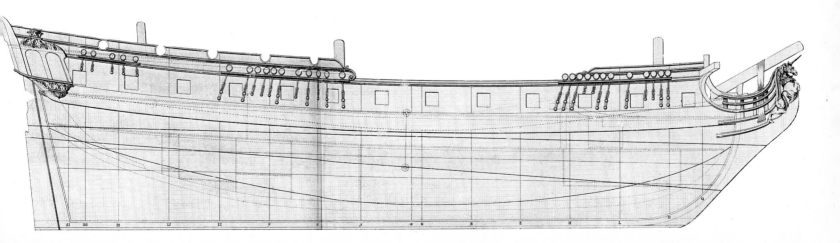

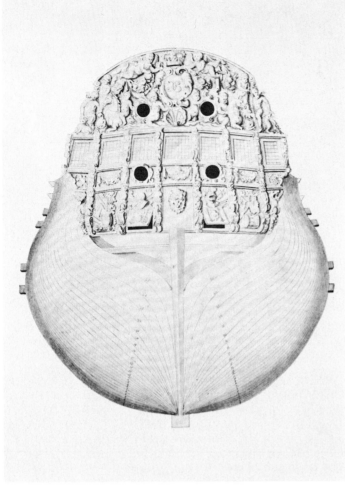

were overlaid with planks, binding-strakes and water ways. The deck beams were fastened to the sides of the hull by triangular braces known as "knees", which in later periods were often reinforced with metal pieces.

The construction of ships called for a considerable amount of curved wood. In England, this was bent or shaped in troughs of boiling water, a method which produced a sweeping curve; the Dutch favoured a type of steam bath. Copper and iron nails or bolts served to fasten many of the joints, though the British and Dutch endeavoured to minimize the use of iron, as when it rusted it rotted the surrounding wood. Consequently, they favoured wooden pegs or trennels for those parts of the hull below the water-line. These wooden fixings, swelling with the ever-present damp, gave a much more waterproof joint.

After planking, it was necessary to caulk the seams. Cracks were plugged with strands of oakum and then filled with melted pitch; this in turn was overlaid with thick tar. However, caulking was not very hard wearing and had to be frequently refurbished, a task which constantly occupied the crew.

Once the building of the hull had reached a stage when floating was possible, it was launched. As a rule, the ship was put into the water when the

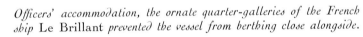

The stern of the British vessel shown on page 90, seen from the side. Surmounted with navigation lights, the castle is comparatively modest.

The cutwater, although decorated, is also quite restrained and foreshadows the straight stem that was to reduce the effect of heavy seas.

Officers' accommodation, the ornate quarter-galleries of the French ship Le Brillant prevented the vessel from berthing close alongside.

Reminiscent of the ram of ancient galleys, although not so used, the cutwater of Le Brillant unfortunately allowed her to ship heavy seas.

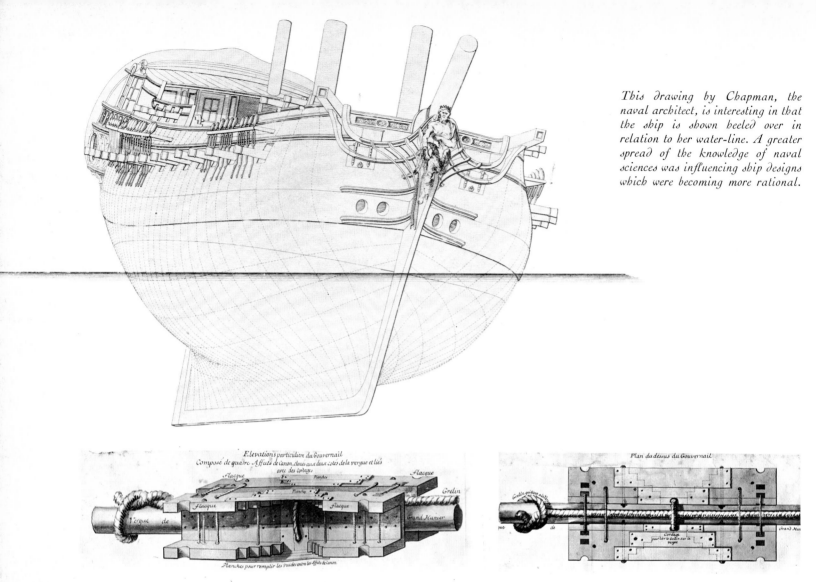

This drawing by Chapman, the naval architect, is interesting in that the ship is shown heeled over in relation to her water-line. A greater spread of the knowledge of naval sciences was influencing ship designs which were becoming more rational.

Elevation particulière du Gouvernail
Composé de quatre Affuts de Canon, cloués aux deux cotes de la vergue et liés avec des Cordages

Plan du dessus du Gouvernail

During the eighteenth century the use of plans became widespread, even in preparation for emergency repairs, as can be seen from these drawings made on the orders of the Chevalier de Luynes after his ship had lost her rudder during a sudden gale in the Kattegat in September, 1733.

In another clearly detailed drawing by Chapman, a ship is depicted as though beached to display some interesting features of the equipment as it was disposed on deck. Thus, for example, stout reinforcements of the bowsprit have a double function : its cheeks, while serving as a check, simultaneously provide two sturdy bitts to which anchor cables and other gear could be belayed. Judging by the sheave-holes, probably leading into pulleys, the two spars jutting from either side of the prow would seem to serve more as cat-tackle for the anchors than bumkin tack for the foresail. The capstans are used for swaying up the heavy yards on the three masts, explaining the placing of one forward of the sterncastle.

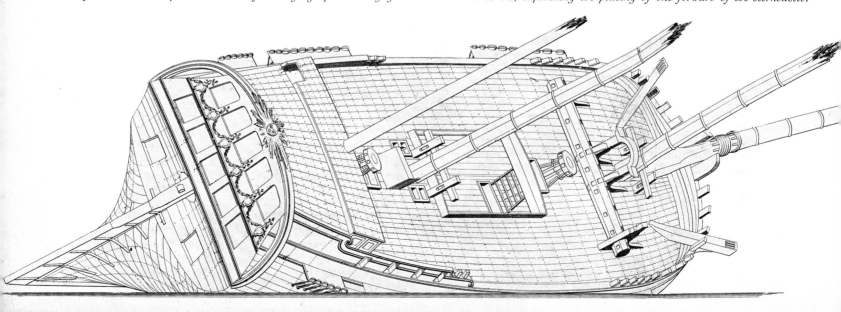

Wenzel Hollar's engraving is of a Dutch merchant-ship which was built for very long voyages and used for trading with the East Indies, including the route round the "Cape of Storms", now known as the Cape of Good Hope. The topsides are being painted with long-handled brushes called tar-mops.

The same ship presents its imposing stern-castle joined to tiers of poop-decks. This castle is not just a luxury but a real necessity to accommodate officers, pilots, petty officers and passengers. The height of the upper poop-deck provides a good post for a look-out and a clear view of the top deck.

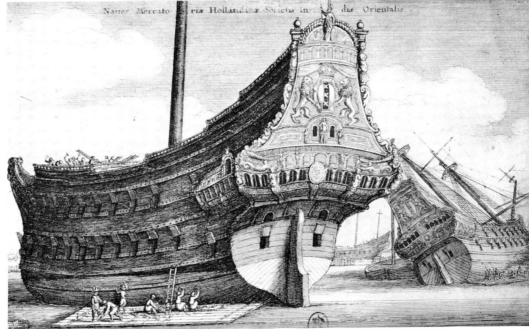

Lying up at the head of a harbour, a ship is in the hands of shipwrights and caulkers. To the right of this engraving by Reinier Nooms are boats with lateen yards, the word "lateen" coming from "a la trina" meaning triangular. These small boats, although not renowned for their sturdy build, were fine sailers and excellent on a beat to windward.

Above can be seen the numerous shrouds that held the mast erect and, between them, the ratlines on which the sailors mounted to work on the yards.

This section shows clearly how important the top was as an anchorage for the bracing of the upper mast. Reef-points were in a double row at the top of the canvas ; sail area was reduced by the process of gathering the sail in folds almost up to the yard.

These pictures and those on the opposite page are details from a large engraving by Sbonski de Passebon, featuring a 112-cannon flagship, flying the French King's colours. Of Polish origin, de Passebon was both an engraver and a naval officer. He first saw service in a galley at Marseilles, March 1670, and attained the rank of captain. He died on January 20th, 1705.

A sail set under the bowsprit enabled the ship to pay off : the dreaded spritsail, so difficult to handle that it was responsible for the death of many a sailor. Just above the flag can be seen a fore-and-aft staysail, carried on a small mast at the very end of the bowsprit. Slanting from sprit to yard, the furled canvas without a yard is the first form of the jib, as we now know it.

Tops are illustrated even more clearly in this detail. It can be seen that shrouds were hauled taut with lanyards reeved into wooden blocks pierced with holes, called dead-eyes as the position of the three holes resembled the eye-sockets and nostrils of a sheep's skull. The man sitting astride the yard, which is not yet fitted with foot-ropes, is laboriously passing a gasket round the furled sail.

In order to balance the lateen yard, the almost triangular mizzen-sail or spanker had to be set so far in front of the mast that it became a serious encumbrance. Only much later came the idea of dispensing with the forward part, which did little useful work, and of attaching the sail to the mast by hoops, thus forming the first quadrilateral fore-and-aft sail, now known as leg of mutton.

second deck was laid and the deadworks had risen as far as the second gun deck. This was the method used in France and Holland. Some Dutch builders submerged the partly finished hull after launching and kept it under water for a whole year. It was believed that this greatly strengthened the wood, prevented residual sap from fermenting and gave the ship a longer working life.

The British, by contrast, only launched their ships when the hull was completed, the interior fitted out and the deadworks in place. A ship of 110 cannon took three to four years to build as extreme care was taken to ensure the wood was absolutely free of sap, thereby minimizing its tendency to work or warp. Sometimes, in the initial stages of constructions, as much as six to eight months were allowed for the sap to drain from the frames before the planks were fastened on to them.

Launching methods also differed. British ships were always launched stern first while, as can be seen from the drawings in Colbert's Atlas (see page 75), French vessels were launched bow first, with jacks to push the hull if the weight proved insufficient to move the vessel down to the water.

Fitting out was continued after the hull was afloat. Superstructures were added to the hull and the masts stepped deep into the bottom of the hold, a tricky operation requiring powerful hoisting gear. The masts were then stayed by a veritable welter of shrouds. The interior fittings completed, the boat received her suit of sails and was ready for service. Since no vessel could be perfect in every particular, it was then up to the officers in command to trim their vessel themselves, by trial and error, until they got the best sailing qualities out of her.

Different countries built their various ships in different ways, but during the seventeenth century the British were recognized as the master builders. An account written in 1672 describes them: "...the British vessels stand out from those of other nations for the sturdiness, artistry and grace of their construction..." British hulls were sleeker, the topsides lighter and the general shape more hydrodynamic, with rounded sterns resulting in a more sensitive helm and greater manoeuvrability. They were more seaworthy, rolled and pitched less, were better rigged with ropes which were light, supple and easier to handle. The arrangements of the ports allowed more cannon to be carried on board. Certain refinements of detail were also characteristic: the more spacious galleys, the ovens for baking bread installed at the aft of the hold to relieve weight on the bows. The pulleys, capstans and anchors were all of excellent quality. And from the beginning of the eighteenth century, a very practical wheel helm, with all the advantages pertaining to this new development, was generally adopted. The supremacy of British construction was such that in 1785, returning from a visit to England, Captain de Kersaint, a Frenchman, was inspired to record: "A British ship built today is in every respect a model of perfection; the finish and strength of her construction, the care and work lavished on all that goes into her have endowed her with such advantages that no comparison can be made with anything put to the same use in ships of other nations." Visitors admired the organization and method that prevailed in British shipyards. Each unit under construction had its own individual stores holding all the gear that could possibly be needed. This excellence of construction contributed greatly to the success of the British fleet during the eighteenth century as well as the Empire period.

Dutch ships, too, were of high quality. Their design was appropriate to the coasts of the Low Countries: flat and very wide-bottomed, nearly horizontal in profile, they were of sufficiently shallow draught to allow them to ground on the low sandy coasts with little damage. Wide at the keel, the round-bellied hull sloped in towards the bulwarks, making them very seaworthy and capable of carrying large cargoes for trade or war. Towards the end of the seventeenth century, however, Dutch shipbuilding design had become stereotyped and was outstripped by the British and French developments in naval architecture.

Curiously enough, certain methods of construction, considered ultra-modern today, were widely used as far back as the seventeenth century. Prefabrication was common practice in French dockyards even during Colbert's lifetime, while "jumbo-isation", the practice of cutting a ship in half in order to insert a midsection and thus increase its capacity, was quite common in the Dutch yards from

Drawn by Jean Berain (1640-1711), these two prows date from the seventeenth century. The prow of the Saint Louis, on the left, bears a warlike motive while that in the right illustration is inspired from mythology. There are only slight differences between them. An interesting feature is that these projections are built into the stem-post and only tenuously joined, sometimes being purposely severed by the crew. By the eighteenth century, however, as can be seen in the drawings below, the cutwater was solidly attached to the ship's hull and no longer had open lower levels which shipped seas so easily. Carved ornamentation still remained martial or mythological; the shields on the bows in the left pictures are not unlike those that formed Viking ship " bulwarks ", while the other prow has the characteristic all-seeing eye of old Asian vessels.

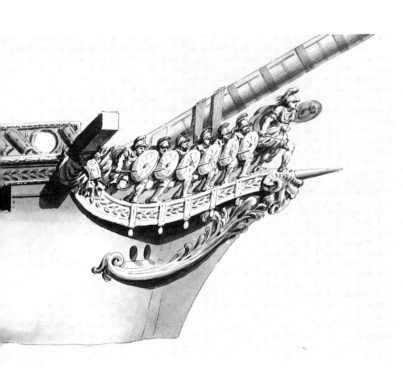
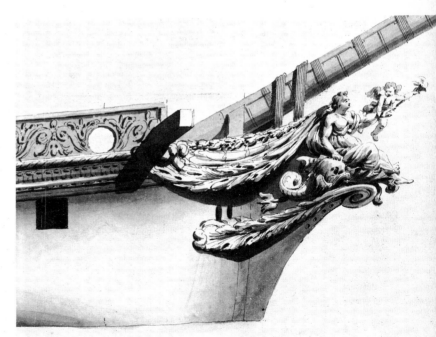

about 1670. According to a contemporary account : "... They lengthen their ships, when they are found to be too short, by cutting them across the middle and giving them four or five frames more than they had previously had. They then replace the outer and inner planking over them, so well curved and so blending with the rest of the construction as to be hardly noticeable and the ships give as good service as though, from the beginning, they had been built in such fashion..." These methods were seldom adopted by the French but were also used in England during the eighteenth century. French ships, around 1680, had the reputation of being heavy, bulky and not very manoeuvrable; they were built of wood that was cut too thick, and were overburdened with iron fittings. Admittedly strong,

This quarter-gallery was designed by Pierre Puget (1620-1694) a famous French sculptor who was long attached to the dockyard at Toulon. Even the greatest artists willingly contributed to ship decoration, despite the difficulty of accommodating to the awkward and elaborate shapes to which their designs often had to be affixed.

This cartoon for a ship's decoration by Charles Lebrun (1619-1690), demonstrates structure and composition worthy of great Renaissance draughtsmen-sculptors. It is also an example of over-elaborate and unnecessary work on what was, after all, a very vulnerable vessel. All this splendour was, no doubt, admired and further adorned by the seagulls. These carvings were often "gilded" in a yellow colour hardly pleasing to modern eyes and simply achieved by white paint over tar — superficial grandeur concealing the wretchedness of life aboard.

their sailing qualities left much to be desired; the hull designs of most French warships followed, too closely, the characteristics of merchant-ships.

This state of affairs, however, took a general turn for the better in the early part of the eighteenth century. As navigation methods became more and more scientific, naval architecture improved in its turn. Mathematicians, among them Bernoulli, Euler, Duhamel du Monceau and Borda, tackled the theoretical problems. The first technical schools for naval architecture were founded around 1750; theoretical treatises were published and, thereafter, the shipwrights, those preservers of the hand-me-down design, were gradually superseded by engineers.

Chapman in Sweden (see page 89) and Sané in France produced notably successful ship designs.

Sleek and graceful, they were more seaworthy and had the advantage of greater manoeuvrability. By the end of the eighteenth century, French naval construction was so highly esteemed that it was even copied by the British; as Kersaint noted in 1785, the French navy had "... certain recognized advantages such as the theory of ship construction, an advantage admitted by the British themselves, to which they pay the most signal homage by modelling their own ships on those captured in battle from us and, by means of repairs and refitting, prolonging their useful service life..." This was a tribute indeed.

ARTISTS AND SHIP DECORATION

Ornamental carvings on ships first appeared in the seventeenth century. Until then, as in olden days, the decoration on sails and hulls was confined to painted designs whose colours slowly faded. Hanseatic ships, around 1660, wore their armorial bearings on the spritsails and carried the Maltese Cross or various other emblems on other sails. By 1630, the threshold was crossed into the true golden age of decorative sculpture embellishing prow and stern. Figure-heads became the rule rather than the

Pierre Puget made several cartoons for the decoration of ships sailing under the flag of Louis XIV, among them this design for the Argos. *The object looking like a spade and projecting from a false hawse-hole recalls the steering oar which was later replaced by the stern rudder.*

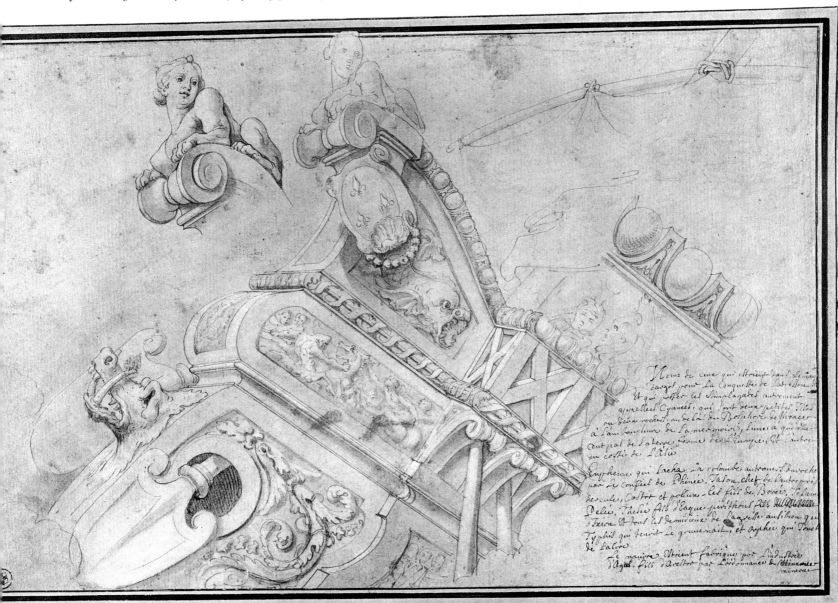

exception in most navies. On British ships they were nearly identical, representing the heraldic British lion. The French figure-heads, on the other hand, covered a wide range, generally portraying the name of the ship, as often as not that of some Olympic deity. Danish ships were adorned with a swan or a lion. The upper part of the stem, the head-rails and the kind of beakhead awning stanchions enclosing the forecastle also bore richly carved ornamentation. The tendency to discard the forward castles led to a reduction in this ornamentation and the decoration on the bows steadily dwindled over the following years.

Most of the ornamental work decorated the stern, the high-rising part of the ship from where the captain and officers commanded a view of the entire vessel, and reached the peak of its extravagance midway through the seventeenth century with the blossoming of fantastic sculptures. Huge escutcheons, in vogue from about 1640, lent themselves particularly well to sculpture and were equally favoured in France, Britain and Holland. Often the stern was graced by two or three galleries, one above the other, according to the height of the ship and the number of decks. First appearing on French ships, this fashion was copied by the British and occasionally by the Dutch, the decoration extending along the sides of the hull. Various emblems, often gilded, were carved on the upper castle : in the centre, a shield bearing the national arms and the name of the ship, surmounted by an ornamental frieze and the navigation lights.

Various countries naturally evolved their own artistic styles and, from time to time, tried to outdo each other in the sumptuousness of their creations. The *Hollandia*, flying the flags of Admiral Tromp and Admiral Ruyter, had a magnificent poop, its gallery supported by caryatids and flanked with statues. Underneath the gallery, between two figures, a coat-of-arms depicting a lion was crowned with a gilded pediment featuring a woman surrounded by cherubs and mythical animals. Other statues embellished the timber joints completing a harmonious design. Dutch ships were generally characterized by statues and huge, over-decorated stern rails. It is interesting to note that " taffrail ", the naval term commonly used for the top of a vessel's stern, comes from the old Dutch word "tafareel" meaning "picture". Although this trend towards ship ornamentation was universal, the British vessels were somewhat more restrained with fewer statues and numerous bas-reliefs.

The French, wishing to reflect on the high seas the glory of the *Roi-Soleil*, Louis XIV, overloaded their ships with galleries and balustrades altogether worthy of Versailles, portraying martial scenes, with bas-reliefs and caryatids. Shipbuilders did not hesitate to recruit the services of the greatest artists of the period — Pierre Puget and Charles Lebrun (see pages 98-99) created many of the works of art gracing these vessels and for quite some time the French navy maintained a team of sculptors. But all this rich luxury was cumbersome and unsuited to a man-of-war. The elaborate projections hampered the ship's handling at sea and in harbour. Under the influence of Duquesne a trend towards simplification emerged around 1670, resulting in a major reduction in stern castles. In consequence, decorations steadily diminished until the nineteenth century when they practically disappeared altogether. Thus the fashion changed to an increasing simplicity of line in fleets of all nations. By the middle of the eighteenth century, with adoption of the " horse shoe " form by the Dutch and then by the French, the stern topsides developed a simple, graceful curve. Later, the general tendency to rounded sterns was responsible for the gradual disappearance of pictures, galleries and taffrails, leaving only one or two small rails, supported at each end by caryatids. These and the figure-head were all that finally remained of the splendours of the past as the trend in design shifted from the fanciful to the functional.

Often as not, extravagance was also evident in the officers' quarters. Painted and carved interior décor, marquetry and figured woodwork were by no means rare. In 1768, Bougainville, admiring the inlaid panelling of the ward-room in a Portuguese ship under construction in Rio de Janeiro, declared it a masterpiece " . . . which would do credit to the most skilful Parisian craftsmen . . . " The bigger merchant-vessels, principally those belonging to the powerful trading companies, such as the Dutch East India Company, also bore rich decoration

W. van de Velde the Elder (1611-1693) is responsible for this excellent drawing, a stern view of the British ship of 46 cannon, the Mordaunt. *Constructed in 1681, she was shipwrecked twelve years later.*

The Soleil Royal, built in 1669, was one of the finest sailing-vessels in the fleet of Louis XIV. Colbert had entrusted the execution of the preliminary designs for the stern to Jean Bérain, artist at the court.

which, either by chance or design, tended to give them very much the same appearance as warships.

During this time ships were not only carved but some parts were also painted. In the seventeenth century carvings on bows and stern were gilded; later they were painted in black on British ships and blue in the French fleet. Towards 1780, British vessels were the colour of natural wood with painted bands of black and red. In the French navy, the hulls were blue, the batteries brown and the port deadlights painted red. Nelson was responsible for the Royal Navy's adoption of a band of yellow ochre running along each row of ports, edged in white against the black background. Much later, in the nineteenth century, the chequered black and white pattern came into general use. By then the splendours of the Louis XIV era were left far behind, and a very big step had been taken along the road to the drab grey camouflage of modern times. Obviously, little thought was given to camouflage as, apart from the short range of the cannon and low speeds, capital ships gave ample warning of their approach. Their poles and skysails appeared over the horizon some time before the hulls came into sight.

This etching by Ozanne, entitled "Plans of a Ship Presented to the King by the Provinces of France" recalls how, under Louis XV, Choiseul brilliantly evoked nation-wide interest in naval affairs. The Provinces dedicated ships bearing their names, such as Artésien and Bourgogne.

The Jaarsveld, *a Dutch ship here shown painted by the same artist, displays highly accurate details in spite of a vague line-and-wash treatment. With their long wooden stocks, the three anchors, including the one catted on the far right, seem identical to those used in ancient times.*

PRESTIGE ON THE HIGH SEAS

It was only in the seventeenth century that the major European nations, pursuing a trend which began with the Great Discoveries, fully grasped the importance of the sea as a strategic and economic area of operations. The increase in the powers assumed by the rulers of France, Britain and Holland had enabled them to build up powerful national fleets requiring heavy expenditure to maintain. Thanks to her naval strength, Spain had opened the way in the preceding century with the founding of her colonies in North and South America, which gave her a temporary lead in the ceaseless struggle for supremacy over the other European maritime powers. The opening of the wide oceans led to a surge in

Shown on the opposite page, the Royal Charles *was built in 1655 and originally named the* Naseby. *In 1667 she was captured by the Dutch. Van de Velde seems to have sacrificed fact to fancy; the pennants are streaming in a different wind direction to that shown by the sails.*

international trade and created new appetites for products from the tropics, such as sugar, coffee and spices. By the seventeenth century, a great political power could, in fact, no longer maintain itself without naval power. This truth did not escape Richelieu, whose political testament sets forth his well known views on this subject; nor Colbert, who set himself the task of competing with the Dutch prosperity in maritime trade and the protection of the sea lanes now slowly linking the continents.

Commercial expansion involved the creation of distant colonies to supply the mother country with tropical products. This course was followed successively by Spain, Portugal, Holland, Britain and France. Each of these nations perforce had to secure its maritime lines of communication with the sources of supply in Africa, America and Asia. Increasingly the prosperity of any nation came to be measured by the extent of its maritime trade. This trade enriched the Italian Republics of the Middle Ages and, later, Holland, Britain and, to a lesser extent, France. Similarly, the diminution of Spanish naval power at the end of the sixteenth century brought about that country's economic and political downfall through the loss of her maritime trade to Dutch, British and French rivals.

But the sea was not only of economic importance. From the seventeenth century it was a vital factor in the military strategy of the competing nations. During the Dutch war of 1672, for example, it was Admiral Ruyter's fleet which, preventing the French from landing on the home coasts, saved the country from almost certain destruction. Some years later it was the power of the British fleet that frustrated the attempts by Louis XIV to put James II back on the British throne. In the War of the Spanish Succession, the naval aspect of the military operations was of major consequence. The supremacy of the British naval forces allowed Archduke Charles to disembark on the Iberian Peninsula and to consolidate his position so strongly that it took eight years of bitter fighting to dislodge him and his armies from their positions.

Perhaps the most important success of the British fleet during this war was the almost unbelievably easy capture of Gibraltar in August 1704. Command of the Straits gave Britain convenient access to the Mediterranean and later enabled her to control the approaches to Egypt and the Red Sea.

But the sea also saved France and Spain. The Royal Navy, powerful as it was, could not stop the convoys of Spanish galleons from crossing the Atlantic under the escort of French ships and thereby replenishing the coffers of Philip V who, but for this aid, would have had to renounce his throne. Similarly, the profitable trade campaigns conducted from the west coast of South America all the way to China by the St. Malo privateers, saved the French Treasury from bankruptcy and enabled Louis XIV to negotiate acceptable peace terms in Utrecht, particularly in ensuring that his grandson remained on the Spanish throne.

All through the eighteenth century until 1815, the rivalry between France and Britain was merely one long struggle for mastery of the seas. In the Seven Years War, the determining factor was the supremacy of the British fleet. British ships prevented the French from landing in England and were largely responsible for the loss by France of her North American colonies, as well as the downfall of her plans for an Indian Empire. French settlements overseas, deprived of all assistance through the inadequacy of the French fleet, were driven to surrender. The Treaty of Paris, signed by Britain, France, Spain and Portugal in 1763, laid down that Canada and the territories to the east of the Mississippi belonged to Britain. Under the same treaty, which ended the Seven Years War, France also lost her Indian possessions, except for five small enclaves, leaving the field clear for expansion by the English East India Company.

The American War of Independence presented another pertinent example of the weight of the naval factor. The re-established French navy played a decisive role in this conflict, both in providing the Americans with invaluable assistance in arms, war materials and troops, and in foiling important attempts by the British to land reinforcements. The independence of the American colonies was achieved on September 5th, 1781, when Lieutenant-General de Grasse, victorious over Graves at the mouth of Chesapeake Bay, compelled the British army to surrender at Yorktown for lack of reinforcements. One is inclined to agree with Washington when he

This painting by the younger van de Velde (1633-1707) shows the Gouden Leeuw, or Golden Lion, the flagship of the famous Dutch admiral, Cornelius Tromp, lying in the crowded harbour of Amsterdam in 1680.   107

wrote: "In all operations and in all circumstances, one must consider a positive naval supremacy as a fundamental principle and the basis on which all hope of final success, and ultimate victory, rests."

The French Revolution and the Empire Wars provided further proof of the perspicacity of this view. All French victories on land were in the end negated by defeats at sea. The British navy was already feeling confident of its strength. When, during the years 1804 and 1805, Napoleon was massing troops and transports at Boulogne for the invasion of England, Admiral Jervis remarked in the House of Lords, "I do not say, my lords, that the French cannot come. I only say they cannot come *by sea*." The almost total destruction of de Brueys' fleet by Admiral Nelson at the Battle of the Nile off Aboukir in 1798 sounded the knell for Bonaparte's ambitions in the East, just as Trafalgar involved, in the long run, the collapse of France's drive towards European domination. The British with their mastery of the seas were able to maintain a virtual monopoly of maritime commerce and to conduct increasingly successful forays on the coasts of the Continent as when, in 1814, British naval support enabled Wellington's army to reach Toulouse.

Naval sea power was a vital factor in the destruction of the Napoleonic Empire, which had relied too much on its land forces while leaving its principal enemy in full command of the sea. Although not sufficiently appreciated at the time, or by historians ever since, Austerlitz was a far less decisive battle, strategically, than Trafalgar.

The results of naval power were readily apparent. Because of naval power the Dutch were able to amass a fortune, the British to reign unchallenged over world trade and the world's economy for more than two centuries, with all the political advantages accruing from such domination. Supremacy at sea assured Britain an unequalled prestige. It made her the arbiter of human destiny by enabling her to found an infinitely farther-flung and more strongly knit empire than that of Charles V. With her network of judiciously located bases, Great Britain could keep watch over the most important sea trading routes of the world and ensure an economy of a prosperity hitherto unknown, a factor essential to this independent policy. And the whole stately edifice of the British Empire rested on the Royal Navy, protecting the foremost merchant fleet the world had ever seen to that day.

ARMAMENTS

Armaments on warships developed little between 1650 and 1850, the main weapon remaining the smooth-bore, muzzle-loading cannon.

The first pieces of ordnance designed specifically for navy use were introduced during the first half of the seventeenth century. Until that time, ships simply used the same types of weapons that were used ashore. The Dutch, Italians, Germans and Scandinavians had long excelled in the difficult skills required to cast these guns. In France, foreign foundry workers, imported by Colbert, established training centres, but until about 1665 French vessels were still equipped with weapons made in other countries. These guns, at first cast in bronze, were gradually superseded by iron guns. Foundry methods then used and the quality of

workmanship were only able to achieve an approximate diameter of bore. No way had yet been found to produce a series of castings of absolutely uniform dimensions and accidents during trials were not uncommon. And since the cannon-balls were often made with a difference of several millimetres between their diameter and the bore of the cannon, the resulting "windage" made for certain inaccuracies.

If these cannon left much to be desired technically, their rich decoration often transformed them into veritable works of art. The chase was decked with various motifs, such as thunderbolts, astragals, the armorial bearings of the king or admiral and other heraldic devices, while the breech handle often bore the head of a man, a satyr or some animal. The iron loops for manipulating the gun were in the form of dolphins which has resulted in them actually being called by that name.

These artistic flourishes were short-lived, however; after 1670, they were increasingly rare. The iron cannon, then being brought into use, were strictly functional in appearance. Between approximately 1670 and 1700, calibres gradually became standardized, the French navy opting for cannon whose sizes were defined by the weight of the ball they threw, i.e. 4, 6, 8, 12, 18, 24 and 36 pounds. Iron being found to cost four times less, guns were no longer cast in bronze, but those that remained continued to serve. The *Soleil Royal*, Conflans'

flagship in 1759, carried a bronze cannon cast in 1670 and certain Russian ships were still armed with such pieces in 1786. Experience gained in naval action during the war of 1688 resulted in a trend towards large calibres and, after 1692, the number of guns of 24 and 36 pounds appreciably increased and, with them, the ships' fire power.

Not for a long time was any progress made and the cannon produced at the end of the reign of Louis XIV were not fundamentally different from those in action during the Napoleonic era and at the time of Trafalgar. At the end of the seventeenth century, Commandant Denoix reported that the

This florid and heavily allegorical seascape by Ludolf Backhuysen (1631-1708) suggests that power and glory belong to whichever nation enjoys supremacy at sea. The magnificence of the ships' decorations inspired as much awe as the thunder of their guns commanded respect.

"cannon has acquired such power that the outcome of a battle depends entirely on its use. The ship has become merely a floating gun-carriage. Naval tactics will henceforth be confined to manoeuvres aimed at placing the cannon in the best possible positions..."

The eighteenth century brought few innovations but towards 1755, a Swiss metal-founder, Maritz, serving in the French navy, perfected the modern method of solid casting, boring out the cannon with a machine of his own invention. This machine worked on the same principle as a screw-cutting turning lathe used internally. Smelting techniques, unfortunately, had not kept pace with other develop-

ments so that Maritz' design did not change the salient features of the cannon, whose range and accuracy were not improved.

The first truly new development came from Britain in 1774 with the carronade, actually cast in Scotland. This was a light, quick-firing gun, initially intended for the defence of merchant-ships against pirates, capable of firing cannon-balls or charges of grapeshot at the rate of one in three minutes and handled by only three men. Adopted by the British navy in 1779, the carronade proved very effective against crews and rigging. It was well suited to the armament of smaller craft, although it obviously

More diagrammatic than artistic, this sketch provides details on hoisting and loading methods. On the left, a cannon is being shipped aboard while, on the right, heavy guns are being handled with the aid of complex lifting tackle mounted on a pontoon which can be towed to the ship.

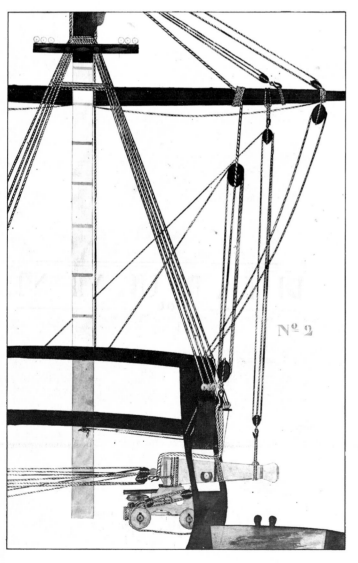

This drawing was intended to teach the novice how to secure a gun with a breech-tackle that checked recoil. Set out, in true text-book fashion, around the cannon, are the barrel cleaners, ramrods and other ancillary equipment used by the gun-crew during duty hours.

CLASSIFICATION OF WARSHIPS

	France	Britain
First-rate	17 to 20 cannon	90 to 120 cannon
Second-rate	60 to 72 cannon	
Third-rate	50 to 60 cannon	64 to 84 cannon
Fourth-rate	30 to 40 cannon	60 to 50 cannon
Fifth-rate	34 to 36 cannon	32 to 44 cannon
Sixth-rate	—	20 to 28 cannon

Mortars are simply lifted on board by an elementary sling. Ropes and pulleys were often used in this way by the mariners.

The guns are secured by warps to prevent them from rolling in heavy seas which could cause terrible damage inboard. These drawings, dating from the beginning of the nineteenth century, provide a typical example of the instruction manuals which began to proliferate in many countries.

could not replace the heavy guns on big ships because of its inadequate range and penetration.

The evolution in naval armament speeded up about 1820 when all calibres under 18 pounds were discarded in favour of carronades. Not long after, a cannon of 30 pounds was adopted by the French navy as standard armament in all ships built after 1835. At about the same time, the work of a French artillery officer, Commandant Paixhans, resulted in another important development, the introduction of the explosive shell. Early attempts at producing contrivances of this kind could be traced as far back as the fifteenth century. Around 1680, bombshells invented by a Basque engineer called Renau were comparatively successful, as were the explosive cannon-balls produced by the French metal-founder Logivière during the same period. In 1770, the Russians bombarded the Turkish fleet with explosive shells but these were considered — notably by the Algerians and Genoese, their first victims — as "... a diabolical invention which it is to be hoped will be forever forgotten..." Alas, this was not to be. In 1824, Paixhans was responsible for the casting of a 220-pound howitzer which fired an explosive shell or a charge of grape-shot. Missiles of the same kind had also been used during the French Revolution and the Empire period. Around 1805, Colonel de Villantroys perfected a large, very powerful hybrid gun, between a cannon and a mortar, but it was never carried aboard ship and used only to equip coastal batteries. A cannon of this weight was somewhat premature and Paixhans had little trouble in proving the superiority of his shells.

Indeed, a gun such as Paixhans' howitzer by its fire power alone tolled the passing of the wooden fleets. Unable to withstand such attacks, they gave way to the accelerated building of metal ships. The period from 1820 to 1850 saw smooth-bore cannon and the wooden ships they armed reach their peak; from then on, they declined.
Men-of-war were not armed with cannon alone. They also carried fire-balls and canister bombs, earthen receptacles packed with grenades and gunpowder which were hurled by hand on to the enemy ship. Mortars, invented by Renau, fired explosive and incendiary bombs which wrought serious damage. Generally, these were carried by a special craft, known as a bomb ketch or *bombarde*; certain other warships, such as those in action at Béveziers in 1690 and in 1704, at Velez-Malaga, also had them on board to the dismay of their enemies.

Ships were also equipped with light arms such as perriers, which were small guns placed in the tops or quarter-decks and mounted on a pivoting fork. Capable of fairly quick fire, they proved effective at close range. In addition, selected squads of men armed with muskets were trained to fire at close range on enemy ships — it was a ball from a musket that killed Nelson at Trafalgar. To complete the ship's weaponry, side-arms were also carried to be used by boarding parties.

Throughout the period under discussion here, the disposition of armament remained virtually the same, as did the handling of the weapons. Cannon were placed between decks along the length of the ship, firing through gun-ports which were closed with deadlights when not in use. The heavy pieces, like the 24- and 36-pound guns, were placed on the lowest batteries for obvious reasons of stability. Although having the heaviest fire-power, these guns, situated so close to the water-line, were often swamped by high seas or when the ship heeled over during manoeuvres. Upper batteries and the quarter decks were armed with the lighter guns, the calibres decreasing progressively towards the top deck. During the seventeenth century, light cannon were often installed in the bows and stern for action in pursuit or retreat, an ineffective arrangement that was soon abandoned. No other major changes were evident in the disposition of the guns until the latter part of the nineteenth century. Also unchanged was the usual plan of having each battery composed of pieces of the same calibre to facilitate the supply of ammunition in the haste and strain of combat.

As has been noted, the cannon were the same type as used ashore, merely installed aboard complete with their wooden carriage on wheels. When fired, they recoiled, running back on their wheels; the shock of the recoil was checked by a stout rope, the gun-breeching, which secured the gun mount. To reload, the muzzle had to be pulled back inside the gun-port. When not in action or engaged in exercises, the guns were lashed to the sides of the hull with a system of bridles, often more elaborate than efficient. In a heavy sea it was not uncommon for a gun to break loose from its moorings and leap into a wild dance inside the battery, to the extreme danger of the crew on duty on the battery deck.

Weighing two to three tons apiece, these cumbersome armaments necessitated a gun crew of large, strapping sailors, whence the classic, humorous description of gun-crews in olden times as " big, strong and stupid ". These sailors worked in the most difficult and unpleasant conditions. The gun decks, less than six feet in height, were very dark, the only light coming from the gun-ports which were partly obscured by the gun chase. The constant gloom was intensified still further when the dead-lights had to be closed against enemy musket fire or to avoid flooding in heavy seas. The thick smoke from cannon fire, often blown back by the wind, quickly fouled the atmosphere so that it was nearly impossible to breathe. In the cramped space, the men were crowded on top of each other and had to spread salt to keep their footing on the slippery decks. Netting strung along the sides of the ship provided but little protection against the lethal wooden splinters which showered from the planking when hit by enemy balls. The gun deck of a ship during combat, with its piles of grape-shot, stacked cannon-balls, cartridges and huge tubs of water to douse the gun-bores when they overheated, was no place for a pleasure cruise. In spite of their numbers, the gunners could not man both sides of the ship at once so that the prospect of being engaged in a pincer movement and fired on from both sides was a constant nightmare to the admirals.

Loading the cannon was a delicate, dangerous operation. Linstocks were used to fire the guns; flint-locks were not introduced for ship armament until 1746, and then only in a very limited way. In the French navy, they did not come into general use until after 1780. The rate of fire was slow, averaging one shot every five minutes even with well trained gunners; the British generally proved faster than the French. The ammunition supply amounted to about sixty to seventy cannon-balls to each gun around 1780. Bores wore out so quickly that after 100 to 150 shots firing became wildly inaccurate and the guns had to be taken out of service and returned to the foundry for overhaul.

Until halfway through the nineteenth century, aiming a cannon was wholly irrational. Various instruments had indeed been invented, such as Tartaglia's square, dating from 1531 and based on the principle that a cannon's maximum range was achieved at an angle of 45°, but for some unknown reason they were never used. Admittedly, sea battles were fought at very close quarters due to the limited effective range of the ordnance — the maximum was about 800 to 900 yards. In practice, however, even heavy cannon had little effect beyond 350 to 450 yards when used at sea. Distances were judged by eye and their accuracy depended entirely on the gun-layers' individual skills, acquired solely through experience and training. Spasmodic attempts were made, notably in Britain, to teach gunners at least the rudiments of mathematics; by the eighteenth century, especially during the Revolution, British gunners invariably obtained better results than their counterparts in French men-of-war.

Gunnery techniques varied from navy to navy. The British favoured firing "into the dead-works": in other words, aiming for the hull of the enemy ship to put her guns out of action, kill her crew and thus force her either to surrender or retreat. Gunners could scarcely hope to sink an enemy ship, for the large vessels had an extraordinary capacity to remain afloat: holes made by cannon-balls filled rapidly as the wood swelled. The French gunners, on the other hand, preferred dismasting, aiming to immobilize the enemy ship by bringing down her rigging; they would then follow up the attack by boarding her. To this end, the French navy sometimes used chain-shot, cannon-balls linked together with a chain or an iron tie. This double missile, spinning as it hurtled towards its objective, could wreak havoc with masts and rigging. The technique was reasonably successful in engagements against pirates but proved less effective in the more important naval engagements, combats involving whole flotillas. Thus, for two centuries, the gunner, making the best use he could of rudimentary implements, remained an "artist", relying chiefly on individual knack and trusting to luck. The new trend towards mathematical precision both in the construction of armaments and their use was very slow in gathering momentum and adoption by major maritime powers.

SIGNALS

Sailing in flotillas composed of increasing numbers of units — convoys of 200 ships were by no means uncommon in the eighteenth century — posed certain problems in communications, such as transmitting orders to subordinates. Signals had to be coded to deal with increasingly complex manoeuvres, and the first signal codes made their appearance about the middle of the seventeenth century. It fell to the Dutch, in particular Admiral Tromp, to put some order into the existing chaos. The systems thus evolved were copied by the British, then by the French in the squadrons commanded by Tourville. Naval tactics as a result were able to follow a predetermined pattern, and battles ceased to be what they had always been since early times: a series of confused free fights, a succession of engagements between single vessels, the men-at arms of each trying to fight their way on to the other.

By Experiens Silleman (1611-1653), this grisaille shows the vessel on the right flying a flag on the mizzen topmast, denoting that the ship belongs to a royal fleet. All other flags, which are extremely varied, are hoisted in accordance with the conventions prevailing at the moment.

Entering the roadsteads to the Bay of Satalieh in southern Turkey, this British flute, observing the traditional custom, signals its arrival by hoisting a flag to the top of the mainmast and another at the stern, as illustrated in this grisaille, dated 1677, by Jan Peeters (1624-1677).

Line ahead formation first made its appearance around this time. The ships moved in as straight and close a line as possible, great care being taken to avoid any gaps which might enable the enemy to break up the formation. Amply justified by the limitations imposed by the artillery, which was only capable of firing broadsides, this battle formation was universally adopted and rigidly adhered to until the middle of the eighteenth century. Certain English admirals, Hawke for one, began to introduce some flexibility into fleet manoeuvres but no radical innovations in the conduct of massed vessels came

about until the time of Suffren and Lord Nelson. By day, signals were made by means of coloured flags hoisted to the mast top or to the end of a yard by ropes called signal halyards. "Signal balls" were also common, these black canvas spheres being handled in much the same way as flags.

At night, lanterns were used, also signal rockets and coloured flares, with the addition of cannon fire. Signal towers on shore were used as well to communicate with coastal shipping. In good weather, the flags could be seen from a distance of about six miles, but during any action, thick smoke from the

The pennants and lights on these two pages were part of the signal code used by the squadron under the command of Abraham Du Quesne in 1657.

Ozanne depicts the launching of the Duc de Bourgogne which was achieved simply by gravity on a greased slipway. Not completed, the ship is not yet flying her colours although the branches of foliage indicate that the shipwrights have "topped out" — i. e. finished their work on the hull.

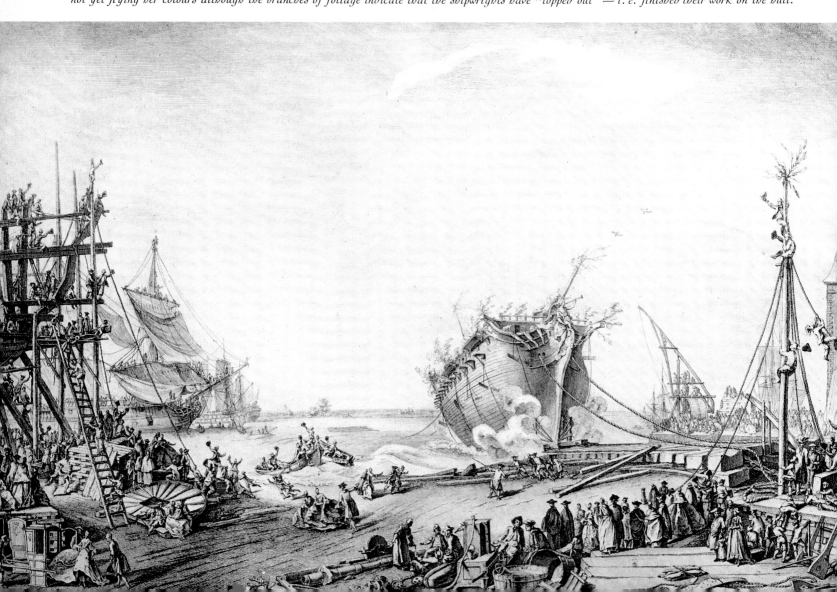

Interpretation of the flags depended on their combinations which were changed according to the day's orders and kept under the strictest secrecy.

This billowing " laundry " creates a mood of carefree jollity, captured extremely well by the artist, Ozanne. Cannon are discharged, standards are flying, flags, pennants and sails are streaming and flapping about in the breeze as the crew, throwing a party, welcomes guests aboard.

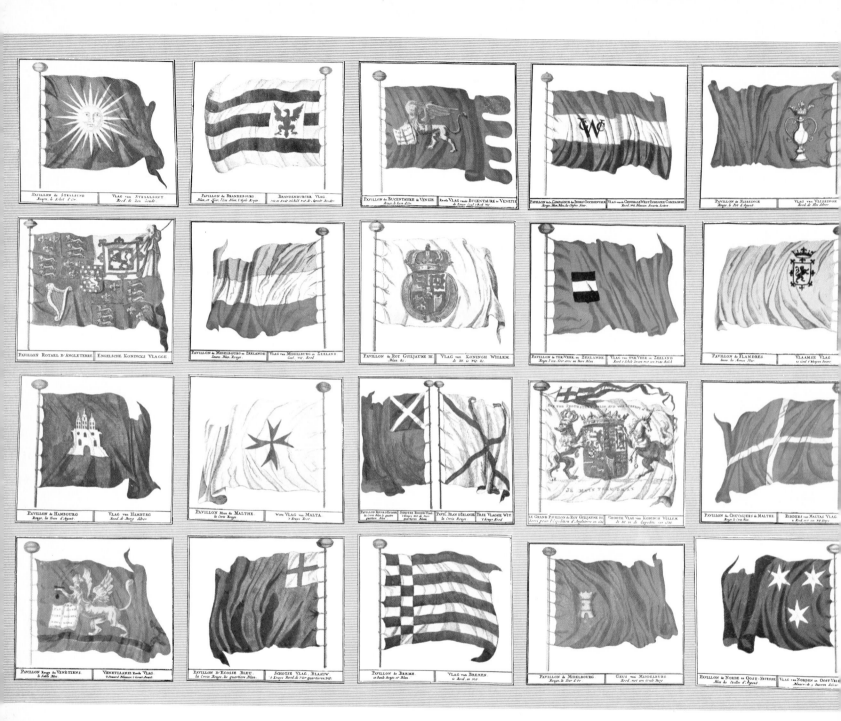

SOME OF THE NATIONAL FLAGS
FLOWN DURING THE EIGHTEENTH CENTURY, AT SEA

Reading from left to right, the following flags are shown on this plate : Stralsund, Brandenburg, Bucentaure of Venice, East India Company, Flissinge. 2nd row: King of England, Midelbourg of Zeeland, King William III of England, Ter-Weer of Zeeland, Flanders. 3rd row: Hamburg, Malta, Scotland (red ground) and Ireland (white ground), the standard of King William III of England, the Knights of Malta. 4th row : Venice, the blue ensign of Scotland, Bremen, Midelbourg, the Norde flag of East Friesland. Only long years of experience or a rigorously up to date flag list enabled the identification of a ship's colours. It was complicated still further by the fact that some captains would deliberately hoist false flags to confuse the ships they encountered, or to allay any inopportune curiosity concerning their mission or cargo.

cannon hampered visibility. Where is the admiral who has not justifiably grumbled about the faulty transmission of his commands?

In the seventeenth century, existing codes were very rudimentary and had constantly to be modified to prevent the enemy from uncovering their secrets too easily. The evolution of signalling made very slow progress; in 1766, d'Estaing was still complaining of the inadequacies which forced him to rely heavily on his captains' intelligence. "It will be a vital need", he said, "to have a code of signals that is capable of expressing all orders, simple or complex." In some small measure, his wishes were about to be fulfilled. Around 1770, Popham in England and Cheyron du Pavillon in France had begun to establish what would eventually become an ever more comprehensive sign language. Fairly elaborate signal books emerged, setting forth the number and kind of signs employed with different combinations and methods of flying them. So it was that a series of signal flags was compiled, each bearing a name and a number. With such a series in which each signal had a different number, the admiral could at any moment modify his code and mislead the enemy. It was also important to ensure that, even in a light breeze, the colour combinations were such that there could be no risk of confusing one flag with another. Each admiral had his own code and

The ship in this drawing by Ozanne is not being towed by its ship's boat; the position of a mooring hawser is simply being changed. The historian owes a great debt to Ozanne and his successors for the accuracy of their records, compared to the misleading caprices of earlier artists.

This fine grisaille by W. van de Velde of a squadron of seven Dutch men-of-war flying the red, white and blue flag is marred by artistic license in the falsely represented sea, porpoises and cannon.

issued it to each of the officers commanding his units before setting sail. When the squadrons included large numbers of vessels, certain ships were assigned to repeat the signals so that all ships could read them and follow the admiral's orders.

MANOEUVRING UNDER SAIL

With the wind as the sole motive force, a ship under sail is almost bound to be sailed in one of four main ways or, in other words, the sails are trimmed in these ways to suit the desired course. Such changes to the sail trim are necessary. The course of a sailing-vessel through the water depends on the angle between the direction of the wind and the centre line of the ship.

Four main "trims" were recognized in sailing ships (and, as a matter of fact, still are today): close-hauled, running before, on a broad reach and reaching. For each of these, the sailor had further terms for finer shades of meaning; for example, "in irons", when the ship was set aback by the wind; "sailing free" and "by the lee", when the ship is running before but with her fore-and-aft line about 20° to port and starboard of the wind direction.

A boat was said to be close-hauled when she was sailing as closely as possible into the wind. It is readily apparent that this trim was difficult to hold and severely strained the vessels; they shipped heavy seas by the bows and their sideways drift under the pressure of wind and waves was considerable. Running before, when the ship was sailed with the wind directly astern was, in many ways, almost as difficult. Forward sails tended to be blanketed by those aft, causing them to flap wildly and preventing them from doing useful work. On a broad reach, the ship was sailed with the wind over the stern quarter, a slightly more favourable angle, although the foresails still tended to be blanketed by the mainsails. Reaching, a ship was sailed with the wind on the beam, at right angles to the wind direction. This made best use of the sails.

Whatever the course sailed, the qualities and faults of each vessel had to be taken into account.

122

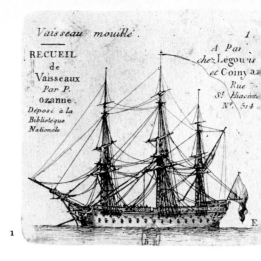

Vaisseau mouillé.

V^{au} au plus près.

V^{au} au plus Près

V.^{au} Arrivant.

A FLEET OF SHIPS DRAWN BY PIERRE OZANNE

Here is an example of documentary perfection from the stylish pen of Pierre Ozanne, who served in the French navy for 59 years.

Some of these ships are riding at anchor, clearly showing masts and rigging. Only the third ship (No. 18, page 124) retains an after-sail, catching the wind abeam, so as not to swing at its mooring.   N°s 1, 5. 18

Many of these ships are shown as close-hauled, sailing as closely as possible into the wind, difficult with a square sail rig although greatly facilitated by the introduction of jibs. These triangular foresails, although not yet replacing the spritsail and less extensively used as can be seen, nevertheless ousted the frightening topgallant. They also performed the same functions of casting and balancing the sail plan far better.   N°s 3, 4, 6, 7, 9, 12, 13

Several of the ships are shown paying off to leeward, turning the head away from the direction of the wind, changing the sail trim from close-hauled to a more effective disposition of the sails to take advantage of a fair wind.   N°s 2, 8, 10, 11

After this manœuvre, the ships will be "running free". The two related drawings on page 124 actually show them on a broad reach, practically running before. Trimmed in this way, neither the lateen spanker nor the jibs serve any useful purpose and have been either gathered in or are idly flapping.   N°s 14, 16

The easiest trim to hold with a square rig is running before the wind, when the cumbersome driver is furled and the square mainsail, set low on the mainmast, is stowed. These sails blanketed the foresail, the square lower sail on the foremast. However, this foremast, seen on No. 13 (page 124), also carries studding-sails, rectangular sails on small booms projecting from the yards to give greater width to the spread of canvas, and the spritsail has been set under the bowsprit. Trimmed in this way, carrying all this canvas forward. The ship answers to the helm better and is much less difficult to hold on a steady course.   N°s 15, 17

V.^{au} au plus près.

V.^{au} Arrivant.

Vau au plus pres 9.

Vau Arrivant. 6.

E. 11

12

Vau au plus pres.

13 E.

Vau Vent largue 7.

14

Vaisseau Vent arrière 3.

15 E.

Vau Vent Arrière 4.

17

Vau Vent largue 8.

16

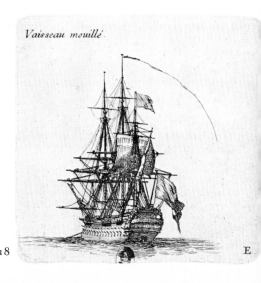

Vaisseau mouillé.

18 E.

A sailing-ship even in those days was a complex structure, sensitive and capricious, with her own idiosyncrasies. Often, only slight alterations to her masts and yards or redistribution of weight on board was enough to improve or impair her drive.

Obviously, the problems involving sailing qualities altered considerably with the passage of time and with increasing knowledge of naval architecture. Ships of the best design were those built in accordance with scientific principles, emerging about the middle of the eighteenth century. Improvements in rigs brought about by reason of changes in sail balance, the adoption of jibs, royals and, later, spankers, helped while the sheathing of hulls with copper and the progressive fining down of the topsides all enabled the ship to make best use of the wind when manoeuvring and to achieve maximum drive. From about 1760, serious attention began to be paid to the stowage of cargo and various other stores, and their best possible distribution on board.

Ozanne has drawn every detail in this picture correctly, even to the sea-spray and the sky. The shrouds are alive with sailors, swarming up the rigging to the yards as fast as their legs will carry them to alter sail as the ship, already beginning to heel over, is struck by a sudden squall.

Engineers and naval officers sought the ideal solution and various theoretical works appeared, one of the most noteworthy being *Treatise on Stowing Ships* published in 1789 by the future Admiral Missiessy. Still more marked progress was achieved in the nineteenth century with the great American, British and French clippers. The handling of these splendid ships, which were capable of attaining sprints of twenty knots, no longer bore any relation to the manoeuvring of the old sailing-vessels of the past.

THE GREAT VOYAGES

At the beginning of the seventeenth century, vast areas of the globe still remained practically unknown, merely skirted in passing by a handful of sailors. The progressive advancement in naval equipment and navigation instruments enabled the resumption of the long distance voyages which were to fill in many of the blanks in world cartography. This vast undertaking was marked by several distinct phases. The first of these extended from the beginning of the seventeenth to the middle of the eighteenth centuries. This was still the Age of Adventure, the heyday of the freebooters in American waters, when seafarers, frequently lacking in any scientific training, were more concerned with material benefits and the search for commercial openings than collecting scientific information. Such was the case in the eleven voyages round the world between 1711 and 1719 by French captains who set out from St. Malo or Port Louis. Reaching the South Seas and the coasts of Chile and Peru, they crossed the Pacific to Canton, making their return via Manila, the Indian Ocean and the Cape of Good Hope. These expeditions were of a strictly commercial nature and no thought was given to the discovery of new lands nor to making astronomical or geographical observations. Their sole objective was to bring back valuable cargoes. Many years were to pass before there was a break-away from these politico-economic expeditions which, in other respects, were not always unproductive in terms of long-range knowledge.

With the publication of certain theoretical treatises which were important aids to navigation in the seventeenth century, a new movement of discovery was given impetus, though it would be a hundred years or so before it produced any positive results. *Hydrography* by Father Fournier in 1642 and *The Science of Geography* by Father François in 1652 were the first of these. At about the same time, the work conducted by the Dutch geographers Vossius and Varenius and the study centres established in Rome by the Popes and Jesuits, as well as the founding of learned societies such as the Royal Society in London and the Academie des Sciences in Paris opened up the minds of scholars to the possibilities of furthering scientific studies by means of maritime exploration. Slowly but surely, this academic influence led to expeditions being better organized. More and more precise instructions were issued to mariners, drawn up in collaboration with scholars of such subjects as astronomy, botany, medicine and zoology. Scientific research was on a flood tide from about the mid-eighteenth century. Ships were transformed into veritable floating laboratories, specially fitted out and carrying mariners as well as authentic research teams equipped with all the latest apparatus that had then been designed for navigational and observation purposes.

This was the threshold of what could be termed the golden age of maritime exploration, extending from about 1740 to 1840 and destined to reveal at last the true face of the globe. Coastlines that had hitherto only been indicated by dotted lines were gradually filled in and the legendary lands and mythical isles of the old geography books slowly faded into the mists of times past. One voyage succeeded another until the mid-nineteenth century when very little else remained to be discovered.

The true conception of discovery actually dates from the years around 1750. Until then, the subject had been surrounded in the strictest possible secrecy, cartography being regarded as a type of secret weapon, vital knowledge to be guarded at all costs.

ISLande

patrixfiord vu Du Mouillage le matin

Marine artists were no longer concentrating all their abilities on representing ships alone. Illustrated nature was an increasingly important record of the voyages of discovery. Among the illustrations on the following pages, trees and plants can be seen, drawn with as great an accuracy as romanticism allowed. In this view of Iceland, Ozanne is at once both geologist and meteorologist, recording the stratification of the hill and the early morning calm. Humourist as well, he depicts the two Scandinavian shallops, on a visit to the French ship, raising their oars in salute.

Painted by N. Dance is this striking portrait of Captain James Cook, one of the most daring seafarers of the eighteenth century. The chin is determined but the expression is wise and thoughtful, although seeming to betray a slight impatience for the sitting to come to an end.

The Portuguese Government punished by death anyone revealing the contents of maps drawn up by navigators. Severest precautions were also taken by the Dutch to prevent the disclosure of their navigation secrets in the Indian Archipelago, which was considered an exclusive preserve. Bougainville still refused in 1769 to disclose the exact position of Tahiti in longitude and latitude, maintaining this

to be a "government secret". But gradually this attitude changed and, as early as 1774, the same navigator wrote: "... Gone are the days when each discovery was shrouded in mystery..." Expeditions became further and further removed from their original purely self-seeking quests for new markets and new colonies. After Bougainville's time, emphasis shifted temporarily, at least, to entirely scientific objectives and a warm climate of international collaboration developed between navigators and scholars, the first important evidence coming to light with the observation of the path of Venus across the sun on June 3rd, 1769. On occasion, collaboration even weathered periods of diplomatic storms, such as the American Revolution during which all French officers are known to have received orders to render all possible assistance to the famous British explorer James Cook (see page 128) should they encounter him. Another example occurred in 1800 when the French explorer, Baudin, setting out for the Australian coasts, was provided with a British passport as protection.

Maritime exploration had relatively static periods, alternating with times of intensive activity. During the seventeenth century, the Spanish, Dutch and English were the most energetic pursuers of discovery; the following century, the French were conspicuous in maritime activity up to 1840. Encouraged by Peter the Great, Russian seafarers also made a noteworthy contribution to the knowledge of certain regions, particularly in the area of the North Pacific, and the islands abounding.

At times, efforts were concentrated on one particular region of the globe. The Indian Ocean

All the voyages of Cook's period were illustrated by charming pictures, water-colour paintings or drawings in line-and-wash. Nature itself and even human movements are treated in a romantic style. Accompanying Captain Cook on his first voyage, the painter James Cleveley (born about 1750) left to posterity several paintings of Resolution and Discovery. On the left, they are shown leaving England. On the facing page, they are depicted in the Owyhee River and, right, at Moorea.

William Hodges (1744-1797) was the painter accredited to Cook's second voyage. His highly romanticized representation of a storm, spectacular but hardly lifelike, follows contemporary conventions with two unruffled figures on the shore.

and the Far East attracted seventeenth century navigators, while during the next century, attention was centred on the Pacific, then practically unknown, and the mystery of *terra australia incognita* whose existence, affirmed by Ptolemy, had long fired imaginations. Discovery was still a matter of national prestige, tinged with economic motives, the British trying to consolidate their rich commercial empire which had been steadily expanding since 1715 while the French sought to offset their losses sustained during the Seven Years War.

The most significant stages in these discoveries can easily be summarized. The first half of the seventeenth century was marked by considerable activity. Queiroz, a Portuguese serving with the Spanish forces, crossed the Pacific between 1605 and 1606 and sighted the New Hebrides, mistaking it for the long sought *terra australia*. Diego de Prado and Torres sailed down the coast of New Guinea in 1606 and 1607, passing through the strait which today bears Torres' name.

The Dutch displayed great energy in the Far East, especially after the founding of Batavia in 1619, which served as a base for several expeditions along the coasts of China and Japan. In 1639, Abel Tasman sailed up as far as Sakhalin; then, between 1642 and 1643, he sailed around Australia and pushed on to New Zealand. Unaware of

Torres' discoveries, Tasman believed Australia to be joined to New Guinea. A few years earlier, in 1616, two Dutchmen, Jacob Lemaire and William de Schouten, had discovered Cape Horn and crossed the Pacific, reconnoitering the Tuamotu, Samoa and the Solomon Islands.

The British, for their part, concentrated all their interest in the northern areas of America and in the Arctic regions which, since the sixteenth century, had been popular whaling grounds. In the course of three expeditions between 1607 and 1611, Henry Hudson visited Greenland, Spitsbergen, Nova Zembla and the American coast from Chesapeake Bay to the river which now bears his name; he then sailed up the Labrador Peninsula and was lost in Hudson's Bay. Navigators still sought the elusive North-West Passage, hoping they would discover and open a direct route from Europe to China without going the long way round Cape Horn.

The second half of the seventeenth century, troubled as it was in Europe by long wars, was not noteworthy for voyages of importance. Nevertheless, William Dampier, an Englishman with fine qualifications as an hydrographer and botanist, made three very important expeditions between 1683 and 1710, rounding Cape Horn, sailing up the coasts of California and voyaging over the Pacific and the Indian Archipelago.

Paradoxically, during the first half of the eighteenth century, the Indian Ocean was widely explored by the Indian trading companies of the British, Dutch and French. In 1745, the French hydrographer d'Après de Mannevillette published *Neptune Oriental*, a series of ocean charts which, despite numerous errors, long remained the authority on navigation in this region. Attention was also turning to the North Pacific where Bering, in the service of Russia but of Danish nationality, discovered the strait named after him between Asia and America, in 1728. An international scientific mission also founded the town of Petropavlovsk in Kamchatka five years later and surveyed the coasts of the Aleutian Islands and Alaska.

Taking into account the round-the-world expeditions accomplished between 1721 and 1724 by Roggeven, a Dutchman who discovered Easter Island, and between 1740 and 1744 by the British explorer Anson, whose published log was an immediate success, the scientific achievements in charting distant seas over this period were considerable.

After 1760, maritime discovery gained fresh impetus and wider horizons. Exploration of the Pacific was initiated, primarily by the French and English, marking the beginning of scientific explorations as we know them today, conducted by teams of scientists and scholars. Improvements in ship-building and relatively more wholesome and hygienic conditions on board made these voyages easier for crews to bear than those that preceded them. Bougainville's loss of only seven men during two years and four months of sailing was considered quite an achievement at the time.

From 1764 to 1790, the British made ten circumnavigations under Byron between 1764 and 1766, Wallis and Carteret between 1766 and 1768 and Cook, who made three voyages between 1768 and 1779. The French flag flew at the masts of the ships led around the world by Bougainville from 1766 to 1769, La Pérouse from 1785 to 1788, and Marchand between 1790 and 1792; and Malaspina, a Spaniard, made one voyage during the years 1789 to 1795. These voyages covered the Pacific in all directions from Alaska to the Antarctic and from Chile to Japan. Slipping on board one of the frigates commanded by Bougainville, Jeanne Baré, disguised as a sailor, became the first woman known by historians to have travelled around the globe. The same period also witnessed voyages with more modest objectives. Kerguelen between 1772 and 1774, and Surville and Marion-Dufresne between 1768 and 1773 attempted, without notable success, to locate the austral lands. Research into navigation instruments led to voyages planned for purely scientific purposes. Between 1767 and 1772, the French navy, itself, fitted out four expeditions to test the functioning at sea of the new chronometers invented by the watch-makers Leroy and Berthoud. The results were conclusive and ushered in the era of modern navigation by chronometer. Other expeditions were concerned with hydrography, such as those by Joseph-Bernard Chabert (1724-1805) and Antoine Chastenet de Puységur (1752-1809) who published his charts remarkably detailed of the inlets and bays of the Santo Domingo littoral in 1787.

H.M.S. VICTORY · 1760

BY R.J. COLLINS

In 1758, England's Senior Surveyor, Mr. Thomas Slade, was instructed to design a three-decker which would be superior to any of her predecessors. The calculations and drawings took little more than six months. The dimensions given were "Length of the lower Deck 186 ft., Length of the Keel for Tonnage 151 ft. 3 in., Breadth Extreme 51 ft. 11 in., Depth in Hold 21 ft. 6 in., Burthen in Tons 2162 22/94." She was to differ from the earlier first rates in having her lower gun ports over five feet from the water-line instead of the more usual two or three. Other differences, probably unintentional, were to make her an exceptionally steady and fast sailer, fast, that is, for a three-decker.

The Admiralty wished her finished in less than three years instead of the five or more it generally took, and preparations were started immediately. Large three-deckers were sometimes built in dry dock and the Old Single Dock at Chatham was prepared for the new ship. The keel was laid on a bright sunny morning of 23rd July, 1759. Made of teak, 21 inches square amidships, it had seven pieces scarfed together to reach an overall length of 151 feet. As usual with keels, its width narrowed at each end, to 18 inches at the stem and to 16 inches at the stern. The curved stem made of several pieces of oak and the stern-post were added, held in place by shores. The stern-post was the largest piece of wood in the ship—30 feet long, 36 by 16 inches at the base and 26 inches square at the head.

The frames of oak, over a foot square at the keel, were then erected and held in place by more shores. A three-decker, carrying 100 guns was no small structure. Detailed measurements are given on page 133. There were over three hundred thousand cubic feet of timber in the completed ship and at least twenty acres of oak woodland had to be cleared to supply it. Her inner planking averaged five inches thick and the outer, seven inches. The men on the lower gun-deck thus had about two feet of solid oak for protection. The lower masts were "built", that is, made up of a number of pieces fitted together and bound around at intervals with bands of rope known as "wooldings". Later these were replaced by iron straps. The mainmast was a few inches short of 117 feet high and at the partners, the level of the middle deck, was 39 inches in diameter. The golden truck on the topgallant mast towered 200 feet above the water. The main yard was 102 feet 4 inches long.

The guns were in three complete tiers, thirty 42-pounders on the lower or gun-deck ; twenty-eight 24-pounders on the middle deck and thirty 12-pounders on the upper or main deck. The quarter-deck carried twelve 6-pounders. During her long life this armament was subject to only slight variation.

On October 28th, 1760, the new ship, the seventh of her line, was christened *Victory*. By the early days of 1765 the hull was completed at a cost of £63,176. On May 7th, water was admitted to the dock and the *Victory* floated out. Now no longer an urgent priority, she was equipped with only her lower masts in place.

England was again at war in 1777, so fitting out of the *Victory* was completed and as the flagship of Admiral Keppel, she put out to sea with the fleet. In July 1778, the *Victory*'s guns were fired for the first time in action. Keppel's battle of Ushant was indecisive. The French fired into the English rigging and the English fired into the French hulls. The enemy casualties were heavy but this did not prevent them from making a quick getaway.

In 1781, with the flag of Richard Kempenfelt flying from her mast, she led the fleet which met the French again off Ushant in December. This time there was no doubt about the result. Fifteen captured transports were escorted to Plymouth.

Lord Howe, ordered to relieve besieged Gibraltar and land supplies, chose the *Victory* as his flagship. On October 20th, 1782, he successfully fought the Battle of Cape Spartel and his fleet with transport vessels entered the Bay and relieved the fort. From then until 1787 she was employed on normal duties as a ship of the line.

On the outbreak of the wars of the French Revolution, she wore the flag of Lord Hood and served with the fleet at Toulon in 1793. The following year, after being present at the capture of Corsica, she returned to England, carrying Lord Hood home to his retirement. Under the command of Admiral Man she returned to the Mediterranean but not as a flagship. In the Battle of Hyères she led the line and was once under fire from three French ships at the same time.

In July 1796, she served once more as flagship, this time under the command of Sir John Jervis. As Admiral of the Fleet, he was a very different man from his predecessor. One of his earliest general orders threatened with "public admonishion" any officer who failed to raise his hat when he came upon the *Victory*'s quarter-deck. On February 14th, 1797, with fourteen other ships she was again in action against twenty-seven Spanish ships, six of which were larger than herself. It was in this famous Battle of St. Vincent that Nelson in the *Captain* so distinguished himself by capturing two of the enemy, the *Victory* herself taking one. She was now due for another rest and, in November, returned to her birthplace at Chatham to be laid up. From her proud position as a flagship, she was reduced to serving as a prison hulk. In 1799, however, it was decided to bring her back once again into service. Placed in dry dock, she was practically rebuilt and when

Length :   151 ft. 3 in.
Breadth :   51 ft. 11 in.
Depth :   21 ft. 6 in.
Armament : 102 cannon : 30 42-pounders
                        28 23-pounders
                        30 12-pounders
                        12 6-pounders
                         2 60-pounder carronades
Crew :   850 men

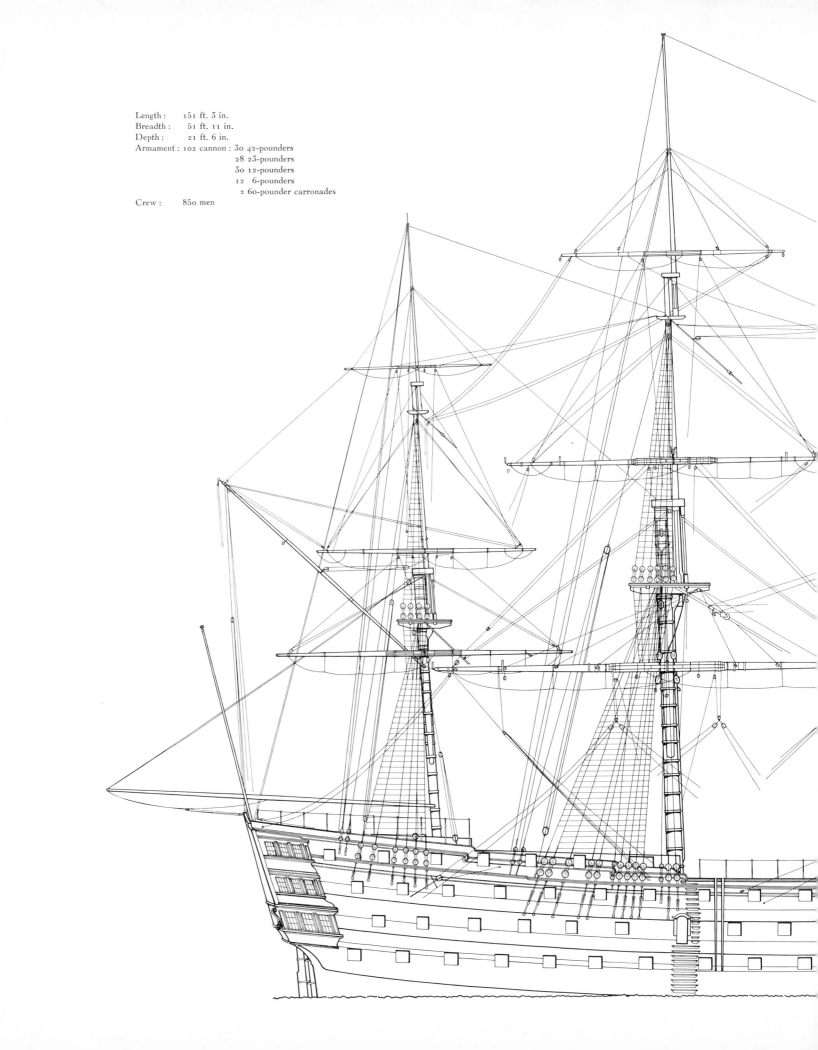

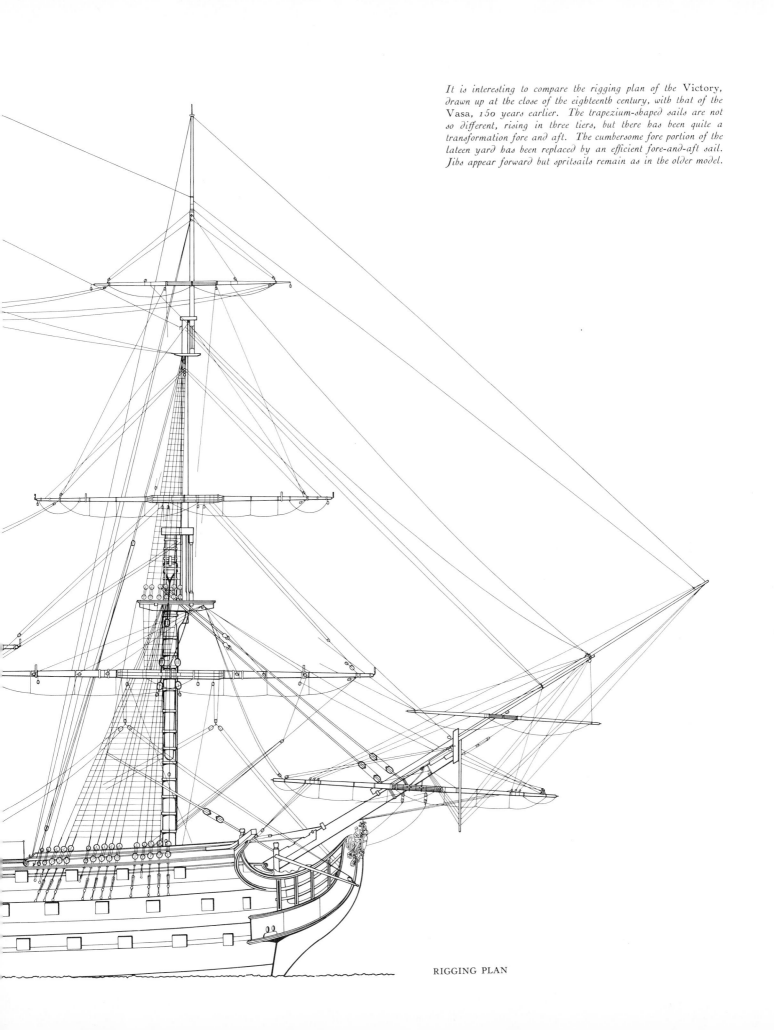

It is interesting to compare the rigging plan of the Victory,
drawn up at the close of the eighteenth century, with that of the
Vasa, 150 years earlier. The trapezium-shaped sails are not
so different, rising in three tiers, but there has been quite a
transformation fore and aft. The cumbersome fore portion of the
lateen yard has been replaced by an efficient fore-and-aft sail.
Jibs appear forward but spritsails remain as in the older model.

RIGGING PLAN

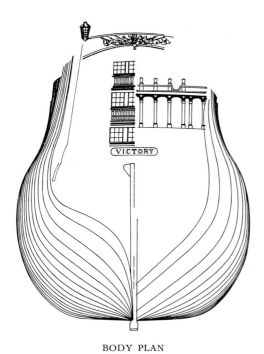

BODY PLAN

recommissioned in April 1803 her appearance had totally altered. Nearly all her ornamental gold work had been removed. Her channels had been raised and, above all, she had lost her open stern galleries. Her mizzen-mast had exchanged the lateen yard for a gaff. It was at this time that her 42-pounders were finally exchanged for those of 32. She looked then as she looks now. On Saturday, July 30th, the *Victory* arrived in the Mediterranean under Captain Hardy and hoisted the flag of Lord Nelson. On January 19th, 1805, while at her anchorage between Sardinia and Corsica, news arrived that the enemy were at sea. Then followed the search which, on October 21st, culminated in the famous Battle of Trafalgar and Nelson's death. The detailed account of the battle and the events which led up to it have been written so many times there is no need to repeat them. Badly damaged during the fighting, the *Victory* was towed to Gibraltar, temporarily repaired, and sailed for home and a complete refit. She was paid off in January 1806.

Recommissioned in 1808, she sailed twice to the Peninsula, helping to bring home Sir John Moore's army from Corunna. As the flagship of Admiral Saumerez, Nelson's second in command at the Battle of the Nile, she served in the Baltic until the end of 1811. After the defeat of Napoleon, she returned with the fleet to England. She dropped anchor at Portsmouth and, once again, was paid off. It was here that the last "active" entry was made in her log by the captain: "Friday, December 18th, 1812, moderate breezes and snowy weather. Employed returning the remaining stores to the Victualling Officer and dockyard".

The Victory was known as a three-decker although, in actual fact, she had five decks, and even six at the poop, as can be seen in this longitudinal section. Its designation was based on the all important number of decks or, more precisely, number of between-decks above the water-line, suitable and strong enough to be used as adequate gun batteries. Here, the 100 cannon are distributed in three main batteries with lighter guns mounted on the poop. Because of less weight, this poop battery does not require the support of such large beams or deck timbers as in the batteries below. It is remarkable how these beam sections diminish in size, progressively towards the stern. The body plan, representing, as is the custom, the aft half of the vessel on the left and its fore half on the right, clearly shows the tumble home, later known as "frigating". It was also called "tuliping", a description as apt as it was elegant, the hull end elevation indeed closely resembling a tulip bulb. The lines of the submerged part of the hull show a marked progress from preceding centuries but although the form is much more hydrodynamic, the lines are still not conducive to high speed, manoeuvring, or good sailing qualities when beating to windward during unfavourable weather conditions.

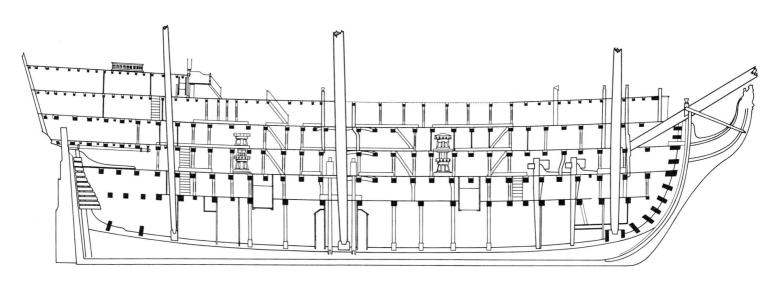

LONGITUDINAL SECTION

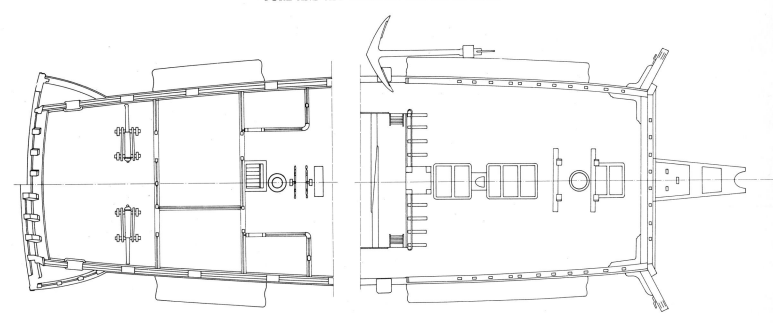

However, she was repaired once more and the shape of her bow was altered to the closed form. Although ready for service she was to see no more action for 130 years.

As there were no more wars for her employment, she was condemned to be broken up and her timbers sold. Such was the public outcry that her fate was averted. Lovers of the ship today should thank John Poole, author of *Paul Pry*, whose article in the *Brighton Gazette* aroused the public's indignation. In 1825, she was commissioned as Flagship to the Admiral-in-Chief, Portsmouth, and she re-

tained this honour until 1869. Thirty-two years later, in 1901, it was restored to her. And there she lay for years at anchor, saluted by all ships of the Royal Navy which passed.

Wooden ships cannot last for ever. By the early years of this century it was feared that she might sink at her moorings. In 1921, the Society for Nautical Research, under the Presidency of Lord Milford Haven started a crusade to save the ship and, on January 12th, 1922, she was berthed in the oldest existing dry-dock in the world, No. 2 Dock at Portsmouth. The Admiralty recognized the Society

Officers as official advisers and, when sufficient money had been raised, the old ship was rebuilt and rigged just as she had been in the day of her greatest triumph, October 21st, 1805.

Even in her retirement, the *Victory* could not steer quite clear of the dangers of battle. During an air raid in the Second World War, a bomb exploded between her hull and the dock wall. A large hole was blown in her side, but the rest of her hull stood up to the concussion extremely well. Fortunately, her upper masts and rigging had been already removed for safety. Today she is fully repaired.

These three drawings show details of the upper decks. Above, on the left, is the poop; the unwieldy tiller has been replaced by two wheels, as two men are required for the helm. The other drawings show two different levels of the forecastle with the booms to which were attached the cat purchase used for weighing the anchors, getting them aboard and vice versa according to need.

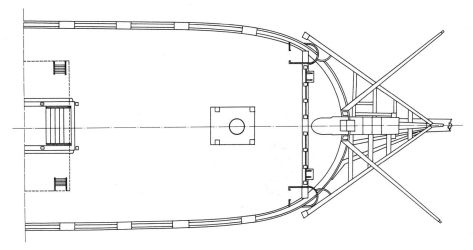

OPEN FORWARD SECTION OF THE FIRST BETWEEN-DECKS

Four portraits of the Victory. The engraving at the top of the page is by C. Bowles, the oil painting below it by T. Butterworth and the water-colour on the right by N. Pocock. Lastly, the oil painting below by R. Dodd shows the Victory leaving Spithead in 1791.

This composition by Nicholas Pocock shows the five vessels that are most closely linked to the career of Horatio Nelson (1758-1805). The large three-master on the right is the famous Victory, *which has been preserved to this day, lying in the naval docks of Portsmouth.*

Some of the missions ended in tragedy. Surville unhappily drowned on reaching Peru, Marion-Dufresne was killed and eaten by the Maoris in New Zealand, and Cook met his fate in the Hawaiian Islands on February 14th, 1779. Ten years later, La Pérouse vanished in the reefs off Vanikoro in the Santa Cruz Islands and it took nearly 40 years to solve the mystery of his disappearance.

Nevertheless, the scientific outcome of these expeditions was impressive. Tahiti, for example, sighted by Queiroz in 1606 but later lost, was rediscovered by Wallis. The tales of mythical lands were repudiated, the legend of an austral continent was definitely discredited by Cook who made four excursions beyond the 60th parallel.

Added to these was the exploration of unknown coastlines, including Cook's proof that New Zealand and New Guinea were, in fact, islands.

Henceforth, all navigators published or at least made known the results of their observations. Their work exerted a considerable influence on literature, philosophy and customs. The logs of Anson and Bougainville were enthusiastically received and provoked the most lively controversies between sailors, scholars and philosophers. The great minds of the age could keep abreast of the latest discoveries which provided the basis for future research. For although the eighteenth century yielded rich rewards, the work of discovery was far from complete and ample scope was still left to succeeding generations.

ÉTIENNE TAILLEMITE

Curator of the Archives Nationales
for the Ministère de la Marine, Paris

THE GOLDEN AGE

After the Napoleonic wars, Western Europe entered
into a period of economic expansion and trade. Ships
from these nations sailed the oceans of the world;
sailors, explorers and scholars came to know the true
face of the globe. These nations' fleets were largely
responsible for developing and maintaining the military,
political and commercial interests of the west in their
colonies spread over Africa, Asia and the Pacific.

THE EVOLUTION IN SHIP DESIGN AND TYPES
FROM 1600 TO 1850

For two and a half centuries, the great sailing-ship was to rule the waves and assert itself as the capital ship of European fleets. Coming to the fore during the first thirty years of the seventeenth century, it was forced into decline only by the introduction of steam propulsion and the revolution in armaments after 1850. During this long reign, the sailing men-of-war and merchantmen underwent several transformations which, although not radically changing their basic design, nevertheless altered silhouettes and sailing qualities.

These ships were, more and more, taking over the work of the galleys which, with oars and sails, had endured for so long. An essentially Mediterranean craft, the galley's range was limited if only because of the frequent revictualling necessitated by its large crew. Low on the water, exposed to all winds, cramped and uncomfortable, the galley was unsuited to long voyages in rough seas. With its beamy, wide open hull and slender, tapering bow, it proved less seaworthy than the sailing-ship whose sturdier construction and better accommodation allowed a far wider radius of action. With more freeboard, the sailer also made less of heavy weather. Increased spread of sail and more diversified and manageable

rigging endowed her with greater speed and manoeuvrability; in battle, the galley was no match for the sailing man-of-war with its heavier armament. Although doomed to retirement, the galley survived until the late eighteenth century.

The great sailing-ships first made their appearance around 1630. The *Sovereign of the Seas* (see page 59), a British ship built in 1627, and the French *Couronne*, completed in 1638, were progenitors of a long line. Apart from the elongated beak under the bowsprit, inherited from the galley prow, and a sterncastle overloaded with galleries and bartizans, these craft already forecast the general lines of the sailing-vessel. Dimensions were little changed with time, apart from a slight elongation made possible by the use of iron fittings. From an overall length of 175 ft. with a beam of 48 ft. in 1698, ships grew to 205 ft. by 53 ft. in 1786 and 210 ft. by 57 ft. in 1847. By contrast, there was a progressive rationalization in design, the number of different types being reduced. At the end of the seventeenth century, variety was considerable, with five classes of vessels having 24 different gun dispositions. By 1786, only three types had survived and on these the gunnery arrangements had become more or less uniform.

DEVELOPMENTS IN DESIGN - THE HULL

Hull shapes underwent notable changes. At the beginning of the seventeenth century, the topsides had a steep "tumble home" while stern and bows showed a marked upward thrust. The disadvantages of this design, however, had been recognized and by the end of this century, hull silhouettes flattened out to assume a practically horizontal line at the beginning of the nineteenth century. There was also a tendency to reduce the "tumble home" at the beam by lowering the bulwarks, despite the general opinion that a round-bellied hull was more difficult to board

under conditions of battle and also weathered heavy seas considerably better than a straight sided ship.

The most marked developments were shown in the stern and the bow. Very low around 1630, the bow lifted up and the beak shortened, curving back in a graceful curl known as the cutwater, projecting from the upper end of the stem. Until the nineteenth century, a kind of wall, the beak-head frame, remained above the cutwater, giving the forecastle a square finish. This beak-head frame was joined to the cutwater and the stem by curved head-boards, varying in

With the wind on her port quarter, the brig has just taken a line aboard from a small cutter and is brailing up her sails, preparing to luff in order to take the pilot aboard.

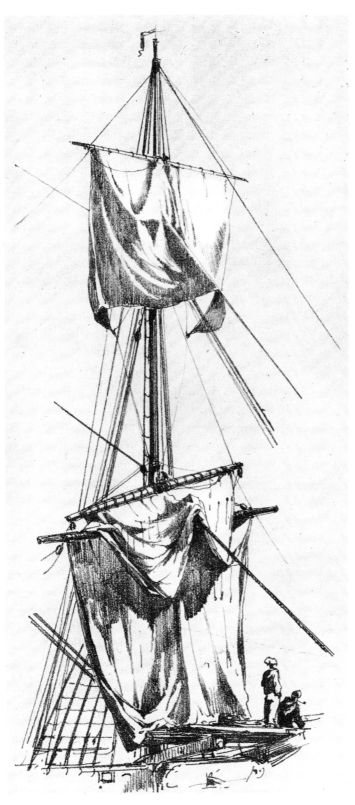

From "The Sea and Sailors" by Antoine-Léon Morel-Fatio (1810-1871), this contemporary sketch shows three sails pathetically limp on the foremast of a ship in port, waiting to regain their majestic, billowing form when she meets the open sea. Two sailors wear woollen caps concealing the flowing hairstyles of this period.

shape according to where and when the ship was built. The bulky forecastles of the sixteenth century were found to occupy space unnecessarily and disappeared, leaving only a modest arrangement used as a crew shelter. Outside, on the lattice formed by the head-boards, were the crew's latrines, called the "heads" in abbreviation of the "beak-head", an appellation which has persisted to this day. All these alterations had been carried out by the end of the seventeenth century, after which only relatively minor changes were made until the end of the era of sail.

Astern, equally important changes came about. Towards 1650, the after deck bore a huge castle, a relic from the previous era. This was composed of three tiers, the lowest extending to the foot of the mainmast and the one above to the mizzen. It was soon realized, however, that all this ostentation blanketed the sails, was cumbersome, heavy and, in short, useless. After 1670, as has been noted, these structures were cleaned up : the two lower tiers disappeared, leaving only a poop level with the upper deck. In the eighteenth century, some ships dispensed even with this anachronism.

Seen from astern, a seventeenth century sailing-vessel appeared broad at the bottom, narrowing towards the topsides, similar in shape to an inverted tuning-fork. But with the lowering of the castle, the height of the hull nearly equalled the beam. Towards 1720, the tuning-fork shape had disappeared and the stern tended to become wider than it was high.

At the beginning of the reign of Louis XIV, the big sailing-vessels such as the *Soleil Royal* (see page 101) commanded by Admiral Anne de Cotentin, Comte de Tourville, had a square, high stern, a broad flat surface that extended even below the water-line. This was scarcely hydrodynamic. From 1675, therefore, the lower frames of the poop became rounder, giving the ship buttocks, to use the technical term, which prevented the hull making eddies in the water and thus decreased resistance to drive. The English had adopted this modification from 1640 but both forms remained in service for a considerable time, flat, square sterns being still seen among fleets in northern waters until 1720. The completely rounded stern was first developed on British vessels about 1817, but it was a long time before this form was generally adopted by other European shipbuilders.

This Greek polacca, the Bella Aurora, *as seen off Marseilles in 1801 by Antoine Roux (1765-1835), has a light, sharp hull and her topsail yards are typically low down on the mast. Standing on the foot-rope, out of sight behind the sail, the duty watch is taking in the mainsail.*

But the stern also carries a very important component, the rudder. In the seventeenth century, the entire steering gear was outside the hull, with even the rudder post attached to the stern-post. In the age of wide, high poops, the tiller, fixed to the top of the main piece, penetrated the hull through a horizontal, rectangular opening, wide enough to allow free lateral movement to the long wooden beam. This aperture could not, however, be placed too high above the water-line, so this primitive arrangement resulted in the helmsman often being drenched. When sterns were rounded at the bottom, about 1710, the poop projected over the water, eliminating this disadvantage since the helmsman could now be inside. The main piece of the rudder passed through a simple hole in the hull, known as a helm-port, rendered water tight by a sealing device, filled with compressed packing, called a stuffing-box.

The problem of protecting the hull against sea-water corrosion and various parasites, such as the alga seaweed and teredo, a mollusc that bores into submerged timber, was tackled in different ways. On British and French ships, the hull below the water-line was often sheathed with extra planks. Alternatively the bottom planking was filled with large-headed scupper nails which, when they became oxydized by the chemical reaction to salt water, formed a kind of protective shell. Lead sheets were also employed but the most logical solution, copper sheathing, was only introduced by British shipbuilders after 1760. The bottom planking was covered with light but strong sheets of copper which had the additional advantage of decreasing the hull's resistance to water and, therefore, slightly increasing speed. British shipbuilders also included a layer of tarred paper under the copper. This new sheathing produced excellent results and was soon taken up by all navies, although its high cost in materials and labour generally limited the extent of its adoption for use on the larger vessels of the growing battle fleets.

MASTS AND SAILS

The various components of propulsion — i.e. rigging and sails — also underwent several notable alterations. From the beginning of the seventeenth century, vessels were generally rigged with three masts, the foremast placed forward, the mainmast amidships and the mizzen-mast towards the stern. Projecting upwards and outwards from the bows over the stem was the bowsprit. The masts, made from pine, were crossed by the yards, which were usually made from fir. It was obviously impossible to find trees of sufficient height to provide a mast of one single piece for the really large ships. Each

Antoine Roux always drew two different views of his ships, in the same way he has sketched this magnificent American three-master. The ship on the right heaves to, backing and filling, in order to drop anchor. Left, the spanker, not unlike a curtain, is clewed up to the mast.

mast was therefore made up of three sections : the lower mast, the topmast and, above this, the topgallant mast, the sections being joined together at the top and the topmast-trestle-trees. The top was a platform originally circular, later becoming semi-circular with the straight side facing aft, built round the lower-cross-trees at the point where the topmast was fitted into the lower mast-cap.

Very few changes were made to the masts themselves, apart from the constant endeavour to strengthen the mast-caps, never really robust joints. Masts were, indeed, lengthened to allow for an increase in sail area. In the eighteenth century, the mast-head, the uppermost extremity of the lower mast to which is joined the base of the topmast, was also lengthened to increase purchase and, by so doing, to strengthen the mast against the wrenching forces of the wind. In this way, colossal structures often resulted, with the truck of the mainmast towering 200 ft. or even more above the water.

On the other hand, many important changes were made to sails. Each mast carried a set of sails comprising, in the seventeenth century, three sails one above the other : the lower, the upper sail and, above that, the topgallant sail. On the mainmast, the lower sail was the mainsail, on the foremast it was called the headsail or foresail. The topmast sails were usually known as topsails. Topsails and topgallant sails were referred to as main topsails on the mainmast and fore-topsails on the foremast.

Time wrought few changes in the cut of the sails, which were usually trapeze-shaped, gradually

Sambre, a 40-cannon Dutch frigate, as shown by Roux, has a painted white band on her hull which, with black deadlights and wales, produces the effect of battlements to make the hull appear longer than it is. No spritsail is carried but the firmly stayed bowsprit takes four jibs.

Ships painted by F. Roux in 1850 in the Hyères roads illustrate the characteristic silhouettes of the first composite ships ; such details as longboats on their davits can be clearly seen. The choppy sea is no mere artistic whim, the rough swell from an easterly gale appears to be patently genuine.

tending to become rectangular. In the seventeenth century, sails were rigged slackly so that they could form a pocket for the wind but, as time passed, they were stretched more tautly to form a flatter surface.

About this time, too, increasing use was made of lateral studding-sails to enlarge the sail surface and also to add to the vessel's speed. These "bonnets" as they were also called, were auxiliary sails rigged, in fine weather, on one or the other side of the yard by the studding-sail-boom which extended the foot of the sail. During the seventeenth century, only the lower sails carried bonnets on occasion, but towards 1690 they were also rigged on the topsails. Very much later, about 1760, a fourth sail was carried above the others, the royal sail, originally on a fourth mast section, the royal mast. Quite soon, however,

in order to restrict the number of mast sections, which shivered too easily, the topgallant mast was lengthened so as to carry the royal sail as well as its own. All these sails were handled by an elaborate system of ropes, the running rigging, which served to hoist the sails, haul aft the sheets and trim the sails. The large fixed ropes, firmly staying the masts to the deck, were known as the standing rigging.

Between the masts, triangular staysails could also be hoisted to enlarge the sail area still further. In practice, however, all these sails whose total area was enormous, as much as 10,000 square feet on a large vessel in the second half of the eighteenth century, could scarcely ever be carried simultaneously as some blanketed the others. Apart from actual drive, a vessel also had to be able to alter course and manoeuvre with maximum efficiency and this led to gradual refinements in sails for this purpose, as much in the forward rig as the aft. At the bows, a sail was essential for tacking and, when getting under way, for casting and catching the wind. To achieve this, the sail had to be as far forward as possible. Even in the Middle Ages, mariners used a spritsail, a low sail which was bent under the bowsprit. Too close to the water, this had little chance of catching the wind as it was often obscured by the swell.

Strangely enough, it would appear that a reasonable solution to this relatively simple problem was not found for many years. In the beginning of the seventeenth century, especially after 1620, a fifteenth-century method was revived in the form of a fore-stay-sail or the sprit topsail. A small vertical mast was placed in the fore extremity of the bowsprit on a miniature "top" and carried a matchingly small sail. Very ineffectual because of its size, this spritsail had the added disadvantage of an extremely delicate mast. However, it was not until the mid-eighteenth century that it was replaced by the vastly more practical and stronger jibs. In those days, development was slow and different methods continued to be used at the same time. The jib, a small triangular sail between the bowsprit and the foremast, was adopted from the middle of the seventeenth century and for many years was used side by side with the bowsprit topsail, which was not finally discarded until the eighteenth century. Jibs were extensively used in the Dutch fleets from about 1745 but were not generally carried by ships of the French navy until some time later, during the Seven Years War. The spritsail survived far longer, up to the nineteenth century.

The use of jibs entailed changes to the gammoning of the bowsprit which, in time, rose from the lower battery to the higher levels until the eighteenth century when the bowsprit was extended by the flying jib-boom. Manoeuvring sails were no less necessary at the stern than at the bows. Although the sails of the mainmast remained practically unchanged, several alterations were made to those on the mizzen. In the seventeenth century, this mast was as loaded with canvas as the mainmast and carried a topsail. The lower sail was a lateen, similar to those used on galleys : a triangular sail bent on a long yard, the loof. Later, the area of this sail was progressively

Morel-Fatio depicts a very unusual sail arrangement. While becalmed, the sails are brailed up instead of being furled around the yards so they can quickly be let go the moment a breeze springs up.

reduced as it tended to obscure the mainsail. Once again, progress was slow. Under the command of d'Estaing, ships setting out for America in 1778 still carried lateen sails. Soon, they were reduced in size to the after half of the sail only, swinging from the mizzen-mast by a fork-shaped piece of wood, the gaff. The years immediately preceding the French Revolution witnessed an evolution towards the fore-and-aft spanker, its lower part bent on a spar called the spanker-boom, or simply, the boom, this also swivelling onto the lower part of the mast. The old triangular lateen sail became quadrilateral, greatly facilitating manoeuvres and tacking, since it was easily trimmed. Above the spanker three square sails rose one above the other on the mizzen-mast : the mizzen topsail, the jigger topgallant and the mizzen-royal. About 1790, the sail balance on most sailing-ships had achieved near perfection, remaining virtually unchanged until the steam-powered ship puffed its way onto the sea lanes. Further developments were made in the case of clippers and steel-hulled sailing-ships which sometimes carried up to five masts and an extremely complex suit of sails.

Roughly sketched while strolling round Marseilles, this illustration by Roux is not strictly accurate although the essential features are correct and show that shipbuilding had scarcely changed since Louis XIV. Rib-bands are being used to support frames during construction.

THE SHIPS

While hull shapes, rigging and sails were going through a period of change during these two and a half centuries, so also were the types of vessels themselves, the most important changes being a reduction in the number of different classes and a tendency towards units of much greater tonnage.

The French navy, according to a regulation passed in 1661, classified vessels into five categories. Those in the first category ranged from 1,400 to 2,400 tons burden and carried 70 to 110 cannon. The second category ranged from 1,100 to 1,300 tons with 64 to 68 cannon; the third from 800 to 1,000 tons with

48 to 60 cannon. The fourth category included vessels from 600 to 750 tons with 36 to 44 cannon; the fifth was reserved for those of 300 to 550 tons with less than 35 cannon. This classification was rapidly outdated as the smallest units were replaced by frigates, so that the other categories were altered accordingly. In the British navy, classification was slightly different and included a sixth category for very small vessels carrying 18 to 26 cannon, this type of light vessel being retained very much longer in the British than in the French fleet. From the end of the seventeenth century, the number of vessels carrying

less than 50 cannon tended to diminish and a fundamental law in shipbuilding trends began to manifest itself : that is, that an increase in power inevitably leads to an increase in tonnage. Towards 1720, the 74-cannon sailing-ship typical to this century made its appearance. The keel of the first French example, the *Sceptre*, was laid at Brest in 1719. Highly successful, extremely seaworthy and with exceptional sailing ability, this ship carried 26 cannon of 36 pounds on its lower battery as well as 28 pieces of 18 pounds, 16 of 8 pounds and 4 of 6 pounds. With a crew of approximately 700 men, it gradually superseded the 50-cannon warship, the last of this French class being the *Sagittaire*, launched in Toulon in 1749. The 64-cannon man-of-war, an economical vessel with good sailing qualities, had been very popular but was considered to be insufficiently powerful after the War of American Independence.

Not every navy followed the same trend. In 1785, the British fleet still had 18 vessels of 50 cannon in commission and another new vessel of this class was completed in 1790. The Spanish navy also launched a 50-cannon man-of-war in 1778 and one of 58 cannon in 1780 but, apart from rare exceptions such as these, all fleets were henceforth composed mainly of 74-cannon vessels. From the seventeenth century, shipbuilders had started on the construction of mammoth men-of-war carrying 100 or more cannon, such as the British *Sovereign of the Seas* and the French *Soleil Royal*. Very costly, few were built, the British fleet having only seven in commission in 1716. Moreover, these giants often proved disappointing.

The French *Foudroyant*, for example, built in Brest in 1724, was never able to put to sea and had to be broken up, a total failure.

During the eighteenth century, improvements in naval architecture and fleet requirements led to a reduction of classes, only three remaining at the end of the *Ancien Régime* in France. These were the 74-cannon ships and the slightly more powerful 80-cannon, which carried 30 pieces of 36 pounds, 32 of 24 pounds and 18 of 8 pounds, the first French ship of this class being the *Tonnant*, launched in 1744. The third type was the 110-cannon, a real dreadnought among warships under sail, marking the limit of wooden ship construction beyond which it was practically impossible to grow. Some navies, nevertheless, did attempt to improve on this size. In 1736, the Russians built a vessel with 114 cannon, the *Impératrice Anne*, and in 1780 the Spanish commissioned eight vessels bearing 130 cannon and no less than four decks; one of these, the *Santissima Trinidad*, was sunk at Trafalgar.

When skilfully constructed in wood that had been allowed to dry thoroughly, and well maintained with frequent and regular repairs, warships of these times proved amazingly durable. The French *Montebello*, launched in 1810, was still considered one of the best ships in service by 1848, and the *Ocean*, designed by Sané and built in 1790, was only condemned in 1855. Nelson's flag-ship, the *Victory*, was nearly fifty years old at the time of the Battle of Trafalgar. Although badly damaged during this engagement, she remained in active service for another seven years.

FRIGATES AND CORVETTES

For all their versatility and variety, these large vessels were not suitable for all missions. So, from the beginning of the seventeenth century, a lighter and faster class of ship appeared : the frigate. In the sixteenth century, the name frigate described a small galley carrying one mast with a lateen sail and six to twelve banks of oarsmen, its principal function being to convey orders to other ships in an age when signal codes were, at best, rudimentary. Until the

beginning of the eighteenth century, "frigate" was also used to designate a type of fast, well-armed merchant-vessel, carrying 30 light cannon. Capable of moving under oars alone if and when necessary, this frigate was first sailed by Breton mariners from St. Malo, Morlaix and Roscoff. Such merchant frigates distinguished themselves in brilliant trading offensives in the Indian, Pacific and Atlantic Oceans, and were also extremely successful as

"Naval Parade at Portsmouth on June 23rd, 1814" commemorates a visit by the King of Prussia and the Emperor of Russia. In an idealized representation, the ship's manoeuvres are shown as proceeding in perfect order, with smooth perfection, unfortunately never the case in actual fact.

privateers in time of war. In the years around 1620, the battle frigate began to show a marked breakaway from its galley origins. The British led with the major changes which became well defined towards the middle of the century. By this time, the frigate had become similar to a sailing-ship in appearance, only much smaller, appropriately rigged and armed with 10 to 15 pieces of ordnance. Such vessels ranged from 100 to 300 tons and were mainly assigned to policing the roadsteads or scouting ahead of their flotillas. However, proving no exception to the law of continuous growth, they lost little time in gaining weight and fire-power so that, gradually, they replaced the smallest class of sailing-ships in many battle fleets.

By the middle of the eighteenth century, the frigate had an overall length varying from 120 ft. to 133 ft.

while her armament had increased to 40 cannon, half in the 'tween decks battery and the remainder on the top deck. Never having more than one battery under cover, she always remained easily distinguishable, even when seen from a considerable distance, from ships of the line which invariably had at least two.

Fast and easy to handle, frigates proved formidable tactical weapons, particularly useful for reconnaissance and settling armed disputes with pirates and enemy merchant-vessels. At the end of the eighteenth century, the frigate had achieved such popularity that by 1785 the British fleet included almost as many frigates as ships of the line, 146 as against 151. Between 1783 and 1791, the British built 40 ships of the line and 41 frigates, most of these armed with 44 cannon. In France, the frigates designed by Sané attained near perfection and acquitted themselves brilliantly during the wars of the French Revolution and of the Empire. Throughout the first half of the nineteenth century, the frigate continued to develop. Its length extended to 183 ft. and the *Terpsichore*, launched at Brest in 1827, was armed with 62 cannon.

Another law in the evolution of warship classes can be defined as follows : when a given type of vessel increases in size to the extent of becoming unrecognizable, its original form reappears under another name. Such was the case of the corvette which, in the seventeenth century, resembled the frigate of the century before. Towards 1750, the name corvette was applied to a vessel that would have been termed a frigate in the preceding century. The corvette, too, became a sailing-ship of the line on a reduced scale, carrying identical rigging. In the eighteenth century, she was armed with approximately 10 cannon which, by 1830, had increased to between 20 and 30.

A class of ship approximately 120 ft. long, 30 ft. in beam and armed with 20 cannon was, therefore, known as a 5th or 6th-rate sailing-ship in 1690, as a frigate in 1760 and as a corvette eighty years later. Although dimensions and armament scarcely differed, hull shapes did. Frigates and corvettes were more finely-built than ships of the line and were also faster, with improved manoeuvrability.

All the developments in hull form described earlier and, especially, in the rigging of sailing-ships, apply equally to frigates and corvettes, allowing for the smaller dimensions of these classes.

MERCHANTMEN

Until the seventeenth century, men-of-war and merchantmen did not display marked differences and this similarity was maintained, to a large degree, until the end of the eighteenth century, particularly in the case of large vessels designed for trading over long distances. Because of the ever-present hazards of maritime routes, even in peacetime, merchantmen were obliged to carry considerable armament, amounting sometimes to 40 or 50 cannon, although of a generally smaller calibre than those employed in men-of-war. This state of affairs lasted until the beginning of the nineteenth century. The large ships commissioned by the Indian companies of the British, French and Dutch were scarcely distinguishable from men-of-war, and this resemblance often led to grievous mistakes on the high seas. Admiral Linois of the French navy discovered this to his cost. Encountering a big British convoy in the China seas in February, 1804, and believing them to be ships of the line, he sheered off, deciding not to attack such a formidable fleet. However, on March 11th, 1806, the situation was reversed and, sighting seven ships which he mistook for merchantmen, he rashly attacked the convoy, and after a losing battle was taken prisoner for his pains.

The big merchantmen were so similar to men-of-war that when the French disbanded their Indian Company in 1769, its ships were partly integrated into the royal fleet. One of them, the *Duc de Duras*, after thirteen years' plying to and fro from China, was refitted by the famous American privateer, John Paul Jones, given the new name of the *Bonhomme Richard* and, in this new guise, successfully served as his flagship during the War of American Independence. Indeed, sometimes the ships of the East India Companies were as much men-of-war as cargo vessels. Averaging only 400 tons burden in the years prior to 1700, their size steadily increased to 1,200 tons in the late eighteenth century. These mighty merchantmen carried up to 56 eighteen-pound guns on the upper deck, the lower deck being reserved for cargo. When circumstances demanded, they could easily be converted into 64-gun warships.

Since they were commissioned for very different purposes, however, the apparent similarity of the merchantman and man-of-war often masked several important divergencies in construction. Whereas a merchantman needed huge holds for cargo, a man-of-war needed, above all, solid decks capable of supporting heavy armaments, and a reinforced hull that

This aquarelle of the American frigate Constitution *was painted by Commodore John Rogers, who had chosen her as flagship during operations against Barbary pirates in the Mediterranean. Dear to the hearts of the American people, the ship was saved from the breaker's yard by the stirring poem of Oliver Wendell Holmes, "Old Ironsides", and restored in Boston with money collected by school children.*

could withstand enemy missiles without excessive damage. On the other hand, the big East Indiamen, as the India Company merchant-ships were known, were extremely robust and could hold their own against frigates. Such units, however, were exceptional and, right up to the nineteenth century, the majority of long-distance and, even more pertinently, off-shore traffic was carried on in ships whose size would appear ridiculously small by today's standards. About 1680, ships of 150 to 250 tons were built at La Rochelle for trading with the West Indies and Canada. The larger of these carried 10 to 12 cannon and a crew of some twenty hands. Ships only scarcely larger were used by the shipowners of St. Malo when, between 1700 and 1720, they engaged in their extremely profitable colonial trade in Spanish America and in the Far East.

In Britain, too, special merchantmen were built for the West Indian trade. In the late eighteenth century, the West Indiamen averaged only three to four hundred tons and had barely increased in size

by the early nineteenth century. These vessels were, however, superior in speed to the East Indiamen.

Another point worth noting is that no passenger ships worthy of that name existed until the middle of the nineteenth century. The vessel called a "packet-boat", a word coming into use from the seventeenth century onwards, was simply a small, light, relatively fast craft, originally serving to carry orders or mail from officers commanding flotillas to the rest of the ships. From the end of the seventeenth century, this term was also applied to boats on postal services, then gradually being introduced, which were the first vessels to serve regular shipping lines, working to schedules as weather permitted. These "packets" also carried a few passengers but, in the majority of cases, the sea-traveller sailed in a cargo-boat or a man-of-war where his accommodation and the living conditions were anything but comfortable. For anyone seeking to make a sea voyage, luck or good connections were of equal importance in securing a berth if a ship could be found for his destination.

U.S.S. CONSTITUTION · "OLD IRONSIDES" 1797

BY PHILIP K. LUNDEBERG

U.S.S. Constitution, one of six powerful frigates commissioned on March 27th, 1794, by the act of Congress which created a permanent American naval establishment, is still that nation's most venerated naval symbol, being the oldest warship retained on the Navy List. This historic 44-gun man-of-war, laid down at Boston as the young Republic responded to attacks on its Mediterranean shipping by the Barbary powers, was designed by the far-sighted Philadelphia shipbuilder Joshua Humphreys, assisted by Josiah Fox and William Doughty. Intended to be superior to contemporary European frigates, with which the British-trained Fox was well familiar, the sharp-lined *Constitution* and her sister ships, *President* and *United States*, represented weapon systems of remarkable sophistication, constituting the practical culmination of a century of warship construction in North America. Their shipwrights who lofted the *Constitution's* massive frames were merely carrying on a tradition reaching back to the fourth-rate ship *Falkland*, built for the Royal Navy at Portsmouth, New Hampshire, in 1695; the 24-gun *H.M.S. Boston*, a remarkable proto-frigate constructed at Boston in 1748; and the 44-gun *H.M.S. America*, completed at Portsmouth in 1749.

Originally armed with twenty-eight long 24-pounders (rather than 18-pounders) on her 175-foot gun-deck, in addition to ten long 12-pounders on her forecastle and quarter-deck, the *Constitution* increased her fire power to 52 guns early in her career, with the result that, like her sisters, she sustained substantial hogging. Launched at Hartt's shipyard in Boston on October 21st, 1797, the ochre-hulled *Constitution* was embellished with a heroic figurehead of Hercules mounting the rock of Independence, grasping the Constitution manuscript in one hand and the classic fasces in the other.

Fitted out under Captain Samuel Nicholson, this Yankee frigate first saw service against the privateers of revolutionary France which, around 1798, were ruthlessly plundering American shipping in the Caribbean. The *Constitution* was initially dispatched to patrol from Hatteras to the Florida Straits, subsequently joining the Dominica-based squadron of Commodore John Barry, one of four squadrons deployed in West Indian waters during the quasi-war with France. Though less successful in engaging Gallic men-of-war, than the 38-gun *Constellation*, the *Constitution* and her consorts clamped such surveillance on privateer havens in Martinique and Guadeloupe that American shipping cruised the Windward Islands with safety by the close of hostilities in 1801.

Taking advantage of growing British preoccupation with the ambitious Bonaparte, American merchantmen had meanwhile expanded their Mediterranean trade, notwithstanding the continued menace of Barbary corsairs. Answering a Tripolitan declaration of war in 1801, Jefferson's Administration dispatched a squadron to the North African coast to institute a blockade of that insatiable Barbary power. The Americans postponed an assault on Tripoli until the summer of 1804, following the arrival of Commodore Edward Preble in the *Constitution*. Undaunted by the loss of frigate *Philadelphia* in Tripoli harbour, Preble initiated a cutting-out operation under Stephen Decatur that succeeded in destroying that unfortunate vessel. With the black-hulled *Constitution* closely supporting, Preble's gun-boats moved inshore on August 3rd, engaging shore batteries and the Tripolitan flotilla in fierce actions, marked by bloody boarding encounters that shattered the Turks' morale. Four subsequent attacks on Tripoli met little opposition from the Bashaw's gun-boats as the *Constitution*, assisted by

brigs *Argus* and *Syren* and schooners *Nautilus*, *Vixen* and *Enterprise*, battered the fortifications at close range. Having sustained but moderate spar damage, the *Constitution* remained on blockade station that winter as flagship of Commodore John Rogers. In her cabin the treaty of peace with Tripoli was drafted in May 1805, terminating tribute payments to the Bashaw and providing ransom for *Philadelphia's* imprisoned crew. Two months later Rogers similarly concluded a demonstration of force off Tunis, bringing the Bey to terms that offered additional security for American merchantmen.

Returning to New York in 1807 for major refitting during the era of Jefferson's Embargo policy, the *Constitution* emerged on the eve of the war of 1812 with a new billet head, dragon-encrusted trail board, star-studded stern decorations and a battery of twenty-two 32-pounder carronades on her spar deck.

The latter improvement, designed to reduce topside weight and improve her sailing qualities, as well as strengthen her broadside power, proved critical from the outset of hostilities. Approaching New York early on July 17th, 1812, the *Constitution* ran afoul of a British blockade squadron in light airs and barely escaped capture. Wetting down a full spread of canvas, Captain Isaac Hull resourcefully lowered his boats and attempted to warp the frigate beyond range with a kedge anchor, finally making off in a squall by daring use of his fore and topgallant sails. Captain Hull replenished at Boston, thereupon heading north for the Gulf of St. Lawrence, where he captured two merchantmen before sighting *H.M.S. Guerriere* on August 19th, off Halifax. Withholding fire as British shot ricocheted off the *Constitution's* stout bulwarks, Hull loosed his first broadside at 6 p.m. toppling his opponent's mizzen-

Length :   204 ft.
Breadth :   44 ft. 8 in.
Draft :   22 ft. 6 in.
Armament :   52 cannon : 30 long 24-pounders
                          22 32-pounder carronades
Crew :   400 men including 22 officers

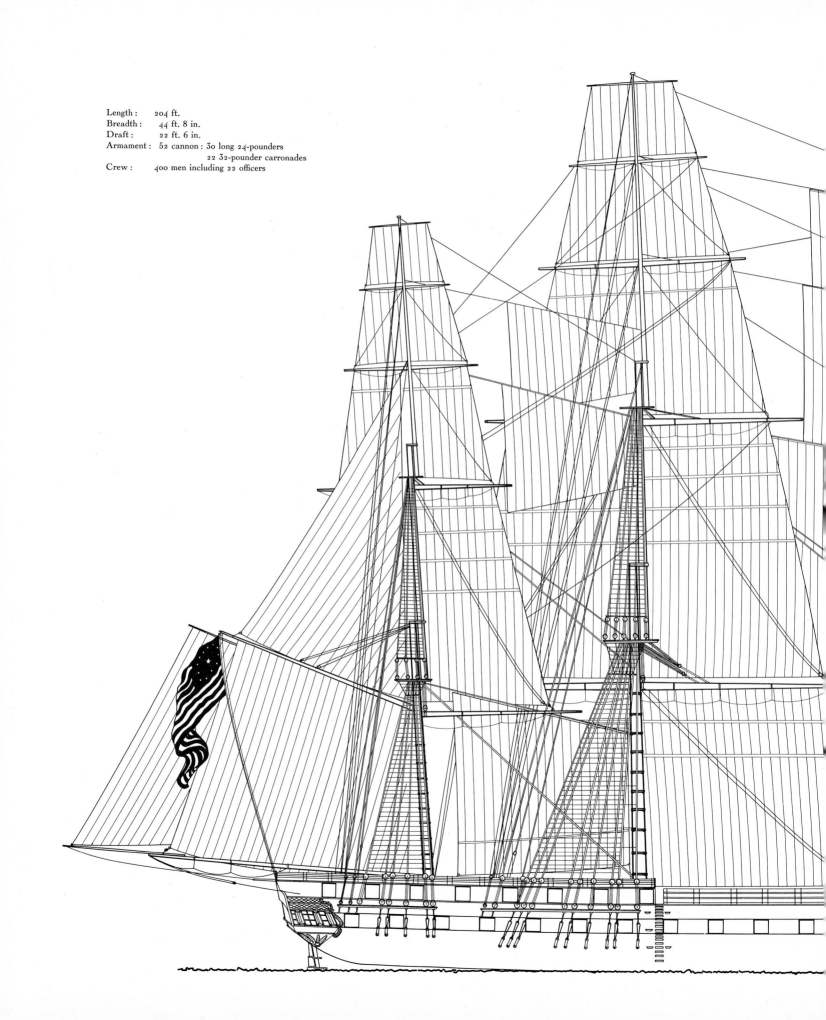

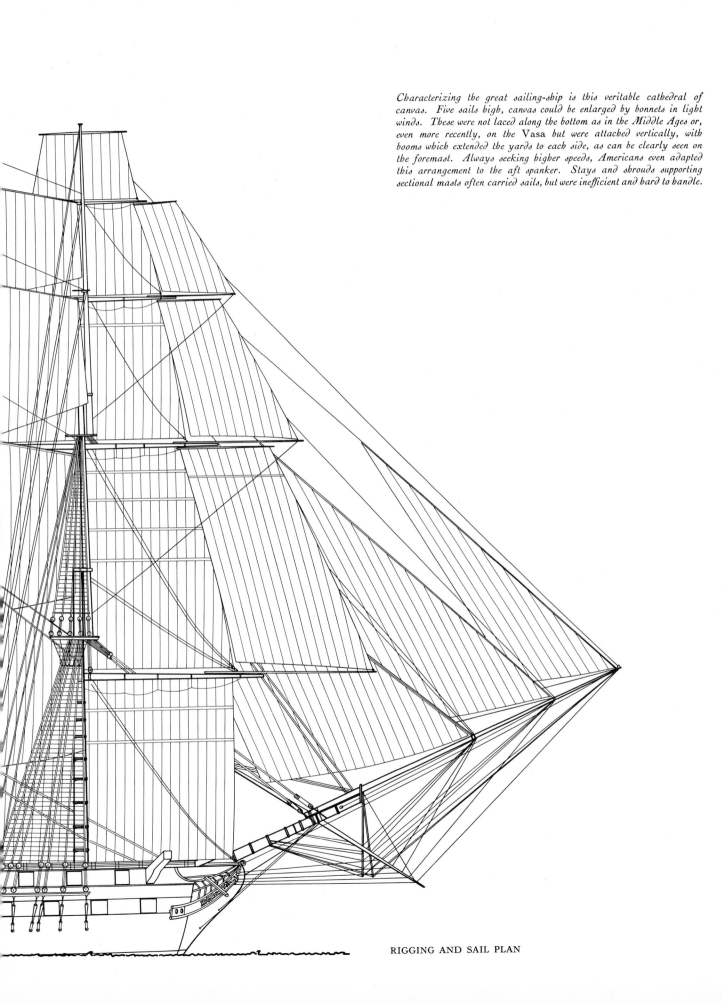

Characterizing the great sailing-ship is this veritable cathedral of
canvas. Five sails high, canvas could be enlarged by bonnets in light
winds. These were not laced along the bottom as in the Middle Ages or,
even more recently, on the Vasa but were attached vertically, with
booms which extended the yards to each side, as can be clearly seen on
the foremast. Always seeking higher speeds, Americans even adapted
this arrangement to the aft spanker. Stays and shrouds supporting
sectional masts often carried sails, but were inefficient and hard to handle.

RIGGING AND SAIL PLAN

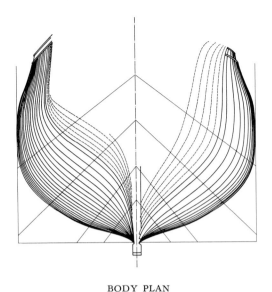

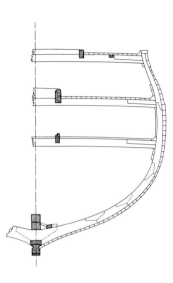

Never designed as a "floating gun battery", speed and manoeuvrability were the qualities most sought after in the frigate. Still a round ship, more or less, the quick-works had fined down considerably, particularly towards the stern, a vital factor in improving the vessel's sailing qualities. The traditional tumble home had not entirely disappeared but was substantially reduced. The waist section drawing of the frigate U.S. Constitution shows that sturdiness was by no means sacrificed for the sake of fine lines. The joints of the futtocks, the sections which comprised the frames, are reinforced by strongly fashioned knees for further support.

BODY PLAN

SECTION AT WAIST

This extremely simplified sectional drawing, as well as that of the hull shown on the adjoining sail plan, reveals one striking innovation : the disappearance of superstructures. The poop and forecastle have but one deck, so low as to be scarcely visible above the bulwarks running along the hull between those two extremities of the ship. Little indeed, remains of the superfluous and cumbersome extravagance of past centuries. At the stern, the ornate galleries are no more and the modest quarter-galleries are corbelled out horizontally. There is also a slight touch of shoreside luxury in the form of the windows, seemingly too fragile and dainty for life at sea. Forward, the cutwater, bending back to the stem, precariously clings to life, soon to surrender to the figurehead. "Battlements" have given way to more functional design and only the masts, yards and rigging still stand helpless, awaiting the time when they, too, must give way to more modern amendments and improvements.

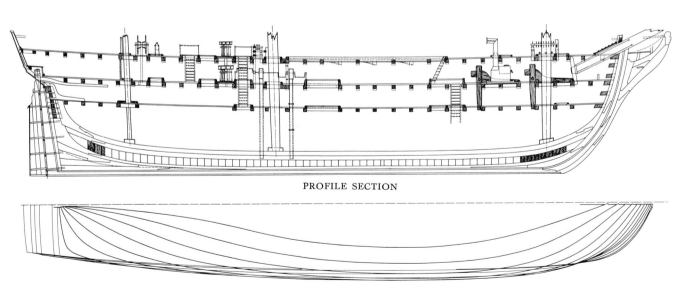

PROFILE SECTION

HALF-BREADTH PLAN

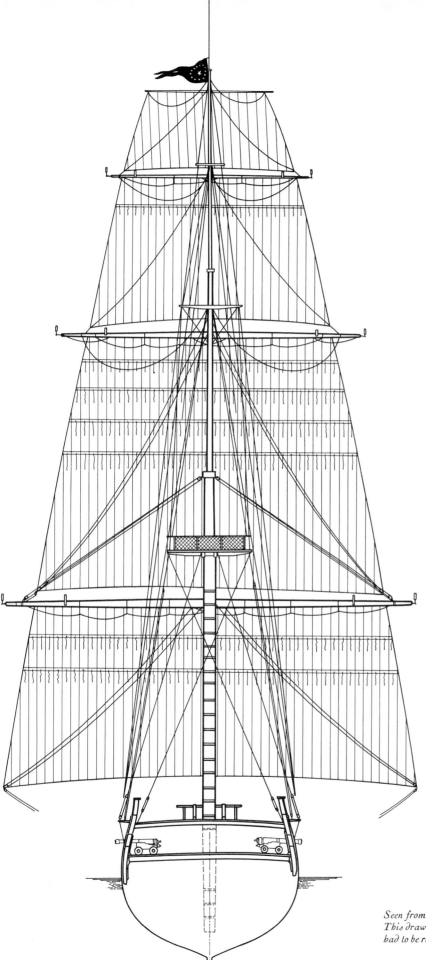

mast within ten minutes. Raked separately and unable to board the American, Captain James Dacres was obliged to surrender, having seen the *Guerriere* completely dismasted in this decisive thirty-minute engagement, from which the *Constitution* emerged as "Old Ironsides" in the plaudits of a grateful nation starved of victory.

Constitution's second notable victory, achieved during far-ranging American commerce raiding operations in the Atlantic, was claimed by Commodore William Bainbridge, former commander of the *Philadelphia*, who brought the 38-gun *Java* to action off the coast of Brazil on December 29th, 1812. Handicapped by a shot that earlier carried away his wheel, Bainbridge was hard pressed to match the British frigate's manoeuvres, nevertheless finally succeeding in dismasting *Java* with accurate fire and obliging Captain Henry Lambert to strike his colours after an engagement lasting two and a half hours. Serious decay of the *Constitution's* timbers had been revealed by battle damage, inducing Bainbridge to return for major repairs at Boston, where "Old Ironsides" temporarily fell victim of the tightening British blockade. Under Captain Charles Stewart, the battle-tested frigate finally slipped out of Boston late in 1814 and cruised eastward to the Madeiras, closing her only fighting career on February 20th, 1815, three days after ratification of the Treaty of Ghent, by simultaneously capturing the 34-gun sloop *Cyane* and the 20-gun sloop *Levant* in a spectacular display of skilful seamanship and gunnery.

Retired from active service in 1828, the *Constitution* was condemned as unseaworthy two years later, but rescued from destruction by the patriotic appeal of Oliver Wendell Holmes' poem *Old Ironsides*. Stout-hearted enough to circle the globe in 1844-45, this gallant man-of-war was rebuilt in 1927-31 at Boston, where she remains the most cherished naval shrine of the American people.

Seen from the front, the canvas is more campanile than cathedral. This drawing shows the lack of proportion in sail area, which often had to be reduced by tying the canvas up to the yards with reef-points.

HULL SECTION AT THE MAINMAST AND SAIL PLAN

The white band girdling a ship's hull, interspersed with black dead-lights, forms a kind of Greek border, and was typical of warships during the First Empire. Romanticism in drawing has yielded to accuracy so that the illustrations on this page are truly lifelike. Above, the ship is shown hit by a squall, bow wave foaming. Below, on the left, she drives superbly before the wind on well-drawn waves. To the right, all is calm after the battle. Constitution has merely suffered a few holes in her sails, while her adversary's rigging is razed to the deck, one mast already adrift. The illustration below, on the right, depicts a dead calm, the sailor's worst enemy. All possible canvas is aloft, to no avail. Constitution escapes, towed by her boats, and covering her retreat by stern fire, a famous episode described in the text.

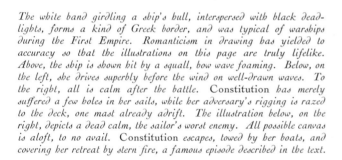

AMERICAN INFLUENCE

Surprisingly enough, prior to the French Revolution, neither naval architects nor those in command of warships or merchantmen displayed any great regard for speed. In a world where everything moved at a generally slow pace, nobody seemed seriously concerned with improving a vessel's speed, and the few isolated attempts that were made generally proved unproductive. Progress in this direction was confined to slightly increasing the sail area on warships, which were already assuming the role of experimental laboratories for naval equipment, this function becoming increasingly important as time went by. Private shipowners, for their part, were obviously not interested in adopting methods which, by requiring larger crews, would have increased the running costs of their vessels. Merchantmen, limited by economic and financial considerations, could not do without the capacious holds, which resulted in lines hardly conducive to speed. Even men-of-war remained very slow. Under optimum wind conditions, a good sailer rarely attained a speed of ten knots. Generally, the average was only five to six knots, with frigates making fractionally higher speeds in short sprints under exceptional conditions.

In the realm of speed, American ships took the lead. At the time of the War of Independence in 1776, American naval construction already boasted a long tradition. In this country, with its immense coastlines, men-of-war and merchantmen had been built from an early date and these were in no way inferior to their European counterparts, shipbuilders liberally interpreting the specifications laid down by the Admiralty in Britain. Shipyards were kept very busy from 1720 onwards. During an era when maritime trade was rigidly controlled and home states assumed, at least in theory, the monopoly of trade with their colonies, there were rich opportunities for smugglers and all kinds of interlopers, who engaged in highly profitable and illicit traffic such as slaves or West Indian spirits. These conditions, combined with the geographical position of the American colonies and the enormous sea distances, induced shipbuilders to design light and fast ships, requiring little upkeep and small crews. It would also appear that American naval architects had closely followed the researches into the theory of naval construction conducted in Europe, particularly from the early eighteenth century. They were familiar with various theories on displacement, research into the mathematical approach to stability, water resistance and other matters, and Chapman's pioneering work on the principles of hull construction (see page 89) undoubtedly influenced their designs.

The schooner, a class of ship entirely American in conception, sailed onto the scene in 1750. Built in considerable numbers in the shipyards around Chesapeake Bay, New York and Massachusetts, these fast little craft with their characteristic silhouette, two masts raked towards the stern, fore-and-aft sails and topsails, were used for fishing and also for smuggling. Capable of carrying several guns, their sail plan endowed them with first-class sailing qualities, particularly when close-hauled in a fresh wind. They soon attracted the notice of the British who bought several before 1776, putting them into service as armed coast-guard vessels.

After war had broken out between the future United States and Britain, a number of schooners were fitted out as American merchant raiders, and British naval staffs were amazed at the ease with which these ships eluded the frigates sent in pursuit, as though playing tag. When the French sailors arrived in strong support of the insurgents from 1778 and onwards, they too were impressed by the excellent quality of American construction and were loud in their praise of the shipyards at Boston and Philadelphia, even proposing that French naval engineers should be sent there in order that they might study American techniques.

Various factors were responsible for the superior turn of speed of these small units, the most conspicuous being the fine, sharp lines of the hull. The square-body, instead of being placed approximately amidships was carried considerably further forward, the topsides were no longer nearly horizontal as in European fleets, but displayed a marked sheer, curving upwards sharply at bow and stern, as in the ships of the early seventeenth century but without the voluminous castles. But the supreme advantage of the schooner was its fore-and-aft triangular sail, which enabled it to beat up to windward with ease.

During their war of independence, the Americans, surmounting formidable obstacles, built frigates which, far from simply imitating their European sisters, represented the culmination of systematic research into speed, based on experience in the use of smaller craft. Certain of these units built between 1777 and 1780 in American shipyards marked an important turning-point in the history of sail. The frigate *Randolph*, launched in Philadelphia, was considered to be a work of near perfection. As for the 32-cannon *Hancock*, even the British with their exactingly high standards and, notwithstanding the political situation, described her as "the finest and fastest frigate in the world".

The American Revolution thus had important naval consequences. Apart from the testing of new weapons, such as the American David Bushnell's submarine, the *Tortoise*, certainly the first submersible to make a dive in time of war, naval tactics clearly proved the importance of speed combined with powerful armament, and established the inadequacy of over-small units, a lesson only too often disregarded thereafter. American shipbuilders discovered that lengthening the hull improved its speed through the water, and succeeded in perfecting a type of frigate of such outstanding qualities, that it soon acquired world renown. Step by step, the course was shaped towards the creation of a craft that can be considered as the almost perfect sailing-vessel, the acme of the shipwright's art : the clipper.

The war also brought about a marked development in every aspect of merchant shipping and the materials used, principally in America. Hitherto, fitting out ships for maritime trade had been a family business, undertaken on a relatively small scale, apart from those few companies financed, more or less, by the government. Many of the shipowners possessed only one vessel and sometimes commanded it themselves. But, across the Atlantic, new ideas were gradually changing the pattern and, moving ever further away from the time-honoured European customs, shipowners in the new-born United States commissioned larger and more expensive vessels whose operation necessitated the substantial backing of finances by the merchant trading companies.

LIFE ON BOARD AND ASHORE

Conditions of life on board one of the big sailing-ships scarcely changed between the seventeenth century and the end of navies under sail. In every respect, life was precarious, full of uncertainty and discomfort. Those on board put their faith blindly in the caprices of the elements. The voyages were long, mostly arduous and fraught with hazards. Mariners were at the mercy of the winds, never knowing when they could set sail and even less when they would arrive. A crossing could take twice its normal time, or even longer, depending on meteorological conditions. Charts and navigation instruments gave only very approximate indications and their development to the point of any degree of accuracy was extremely slow. A rolling ship made readings difficult and errors of a hundred miles or more were not uncommon.

Food was mediocre, often outright bad and crews considered themselves fortunate if, on a voyage longer than foreseen, they were not beset with famine and thirst. Accommodation and hygiene were deplorable, clothing often insufficient, illness habitual and the death rate high. These extremely hard living conditions account for the difficulties encountered by all navies in recruitment, as well as for the insubordination and characteristic mentality of the sailors, which resulted in the harsh discipline meted out on board, coupled with the threat of merciless corporal punishment. These scarcely appetizing conditions under which the sailors were forced to work only showed marked improvements in the nineteenth century. Badly paid, they also had to wait a long time before laying hands on the money due to them.

The chief characteristic of navigation in the age of sail was its uncertainty. It was impossible to arrange a sailing time in advance and sailors were obliged to await a favourable wind in order to clear port, the delay sometimes running into weeks. The duration of a voyage and the date of arrival at any destination were even harder to forecast. A crossing from Western Europe to the West Indies could take from 35 to 60 days and even more. Toulon to Gibraltar could be made in three or four days with a fair wind; it could also take three weeks. The calms encountered in certain regions endured for weeks on end and could retard a ship's passage considerably. In storms, on the other hand, ships were often blown completely off course. Such was the case of the merchant ship which left Hendaye, near Biarritz, in 1717 for the Canary Islands and, running into bad weather, landed finally in Martinique. In August 1778, the Norwegian vessel *Leviathan* left Bergen for Fécamp with a cargo of timber. Eight days after setting sail, she ran into violent west winds in the Dover roads, which blew her right back into the port of Bergen. She set sail again on November 28th and arrived off Fécamp on December 5th but, unable to enter the harbour, fresh squalls forced her back to the English coast. She did not succeed in making her port of destination until December 23rd, after five months of exhausting sailing. This was no exceptional case. Naturally, men-of-war were no less prone to such misadventures. Admiral Hawke, patrolling in a British ship off Ushant in 1755, keeping a watch on the Brest approaches, was blown, helpless as chaff before the wind, as far as the coasts of Spain.

Seafarers thus had little if any control over when they sailed, or where they actually arrived. Winds and currents dictated the actual maritime routes, which had to be followed almost as closely as the land routes and from which it was as difficult and even dangerous to stray. To sail from Europe to the West Indies and back, it was necessary to make an almost complete circuit of the North Atlantic. Outward-bound, the ships had to find the trade winds in the vicinity of the Azores; returning, they hugged the American coast sometimes as far north as Newfoundland, in order to pick up the prevailing west winds towards Europe. A voyage to India first

necessitated a detour to the coasts of Brazil from where the trades helped the ships to double the Cape of Good Hope, after which the monsoon carried them northwards across the Indian Ocean.

Navigation was strictly governed by the calendar. To be avoided at all costs were the severe gales that raged in various regions during certain seasons as, for example, round the Cape from May to June. To sail to India, ships' masters had to time their arrival in the Indian Ocean between May and October, when the monsoon blew from the south, and leave for Europe between November and February when the monsoon came down from the north. If a monsoon was missed, the ship could be laid up for several months. Sailing into the teeth of the monsoon was only attempted experimentally, slightly before the French Revolution, but such voyages were considered as heroic feats. The famous "three-cornered voyages" from France to the African coast returning via the West Indies, which made a fortune for many private shipowners, were conditioned by the movement of the winds and currents, nature-made courses from which there was no escape.

In the age of sail, some voyages were practically impossible. For instance, the Benguela Current which flows up the west coast of Africa made it easy to sail from the Cape to Gabun, but in the opposite direction, an immense detour had to be made as far as the coasts of South America. It was an easy run from Guiana to Martinique and thence to Santo Domingo, but a reciprocal course was practically impossible. In order to cross the Pacific Ocean from the Far East to America, ships had first to sail nearly as far north as the Aleutian Islands. This was the course followed by the Spanish galleons on their "line" between Manila and Acapulco, a crossing taking six to seven months. Up to the seventeenth century, navigation methods remained unscientific and the early mariners had only rudimentary instruments at their disposal. Charts were lamentably inaccurate and led to grievous miscalculations. "... Evil be to him who traces lands on a chart with no foundation other than the whim of his own ignorance. Would that he could share, in some part, the cruel nights that we have passed ..." So wrote Bougainville in the log of his voyage round the world when lost somewhere between the New Hebrides

Two typical wharf-side characters.

Early nineteenth-century sailors.

These sketches of seamen and dockside workers by Roux abound in accurate detail. Taken from his notebooks, preserved in the Peabody Museum at Salem, U.S.A., they evoke the seafaring world in all its familiar forms. Only the soldier wears uniform. Bare-footed or down at heel, fishermen, carpenters or sailors on and off duty are distinguishable only by their headgear, covering their long and lice-infested hair.

This view of the Marseilles harbour is from a series of paintings of French ports by Claude-Joseph Vernet (1714-1789), grandfather of the famous Horace Vernet. Governments might rise and fall, fashions change, but the big sailing-ships continued to come alongside the quays, bringing cargoes and news of foreign parts. And, with each arrival, colourful and vociferous crowds gathered to watch, as they had always done.

A marine of the nineteenth century.

Off duty, and fishing.

Journeymen-carpenters at work.

Fishermen back in the harbour.

Carrying ballast in a basket.

and the Philippines. One of his officers added the rueful rider, "... We sail like blind men, having no notion where we are ..." Certain islands, discovered and inaccurately positioned by one seafarer, were lost to be rediscovered by another. However, never being quite sure if the islands were the same, mariners frequently set sail in quest of phantom continents and archipelagos, with many a voyage courting disaster. In 1741, Anson, a seasoned British navigator, lost his bearings and groped blindly about the South Pacific for a month. The art of navigation in those times was a matter of intuition and this often proved far from infallible. A Portu-

guese ship, sailing towards the Indian Ocean in 1686, her captain convinced that he had doubled the Cape of Good Hope, ran gently aground on the African coast, nearly 200 miles farther north than her estimated position!

Progress in maritime chart-making and seafaring knowledge in general was frustrated by attitudes characteristic of the times. Over a very long period, mariners and scholars worked along strictly separate lines, navigators following their own hunches for better or worse. Conservative at heart and harbouring feelings of jealousy, they tended to scorn the theories of astronomers and mathematicians. Sug-

Throughout the nineteenth century, in London's West India Dock, sailors' shipwrights' and dockers' lives entangled under a forest of masts and yards where the damp smell of the sea mingled with the heady fragrance of tropical spices and the warm, now forgotten odour of horse droppings.

INDIA DOCKS, FROM THE SOUTH EAST.   W. PARROTT

gested improvements were often met with indifference and even hostility. These attitudes did not begin to break down until well into the second half of the eighteenth century, by which time many ships' officers had been able to undergo a much more advanced technical training before receiving their officers' papers.

Another factor delaying progress was the chauvinistic rivalry which, as we have seen, prompted each country to surround its discoveries with the strictest secrecy. Yet another powerful curb was the principle of authority, the bed-rock of the French social system before the French Revolution — an authority reluctant to admit any doubt of the ac-curacy and judgement of ancient geographers, particularly Ptolemy. This gave rise to heated disputes between the ancients and the moderns, the latter only gradually gaining acceptance for their views. The establishment of libraries of coastal maps and charts in France in 1720, and in England and Holland towards 1740, stimulated research by making it possible to catalogue and centralize information and, as a result, to draw up slightly more accurate charts. However, it was not until the nineteenth century that really concrete progress was made in this direction.

The inadequacy in map-making was directly attri-butable to the inaccuracy of navigation instruments.

Although everything is strictly where it should be, the seeming disorder of the dockyard of any age is apparent in a sketch by A. L. Morel-Fatio. A corvette is being refitted while the owner of the small boat in the foreground patiently waits, as others wait today, for masts to be stepped.

Only in the eighteenth century were any serious efforts made to improve their efficiency. The steering compass, a magnetic needle mounted on a centre pin and swinging over a compass-card, had scarcely been improved on since the sixteenth century while, for calculating latitude, the "quarter" invented by John Davis (1550-1605) remained in use until about 1750. In 1731, John Hadley (1682-1744) perfected the quadrant and, about 1750, the sextant appeared allowing more accurate estimation of the height of the sun at noon and thus calculation of latitude.

Serious difficulties, however, were encountered in measuring longitude, which necessitated timepieces of extreme accuracy and an absolutely regular rate, undisturbed by the movements of a ship. In 1714, the British Government offered a reward of £80,000 to anyone inventing an instrument capable of determining a ship's longitude within thirty nautical miles at the end of a six weeks' voyage. About 1760, a Yorkshire carpenter named John Harrison (1693-1776) succeeded in producing a fairly satisfactory chronometer which was the first timepiece designed to counteract temperature changes by means of a "compensation curb", which altered the effective length of the balance-spring in proportion to the expansion or contraction caused by temperature variations. Although deviating by only 1 minute, 54 seconds over 147 days, Harrison's chronometer which, incidentally, won the reward, was a complex, costly and impractical instrument. In 1765, Julien Leroy of Paris (1686-1759), working in close collaboration with a Swiss watchmaker, Ferdinand Berthoud (1727-1807), invented and constructed a marine timekeeper embodying, albeit in a very primitive form, practically all the essential features of the modern chronometer. Its mechanism was so poised as to remain horizontal whatever the inclination of the ship and, instead of the spiral balance-spring and lever escapement of an ordinary watch, it featured a helical balance-spring and the mechanically superior detent spring or "chronometer" escapement, used to this day. These chronometers were thoroughly tested from 1766 onwards during a number of cruises, the best known being that made by the frigate *Isis* which, from 1768 to 1769, made a long Atlantic voyage. The results of the experiments were highly successful although the new invention, being very costly, was not widely adopted until considerably later among the merchant navies of the western world.

As for the ship's speed, this was measured with the log, which had been introduced at the end of the sixteenth century and became standard equipment over the next hundred years. On the whole, navigation remained an art rather than a science until the latter part of the eighteenth century.

Despite all the care taken in their construction, wooden ships remained relatively fragile and were constantly prone to mishaps and damage of all kinds, particularly aloft. Masts and yards frequently splintered if the wind freshened suddenly. The hulls, too, were subject to heavy strain and it was quite common for seams to open up so that the tightness of a ship to sea and rain-water became, to say the least, unreliable. After a few weeks' sailing, most ships were in bad condition, masts shattered or chafed by friction and only held together with makeshift repairs, hull planking working apart, resulting in leaks which often necessitated running for the safety of a harbour in emergency. It was no rarity to see a ship arriving at her port of destination in such condition that she could not possibly undertake the return voyage, and had to be broken up then and there. Shipwrecks were frequent, on long voyages as well as off-shore sailing.

Under such conditions, a sea voyage prior to the nineteenth century remained an adventure full of surprises, sometimes quaint, often tragic. Passengers received scant consideration and miserable accommodation, owing to the constant congestion on board; moreover, they were frequently exposed to the none too gentle chaffing of a crew with little regard for land-lubbers. Designed primarily for transporting merchandise, ships were devoid of any comfort or privacy. A merchant from La Rochelle, travelling in the eighteenth century off the coasts of Brazil, complained bitterly of sleeping on board "... in a lean-to more like a mouse-trap than a cabin. It is impossible to sit and when I lie down my feet stick out of the door ..." Conditions were roughly the same on men-of-war, and although officers were entitled to "individual cabins" these were spaces simply partitioned off with canvas.

Even in times of peace, hazards lurked on every side until the middle of the nineteenth century. On the high seas, in any case, peace was never observed in more than theory. Barbary, Greek, Malayan and Chinese pirates incessantly roved the Mediterranean, the West Indies, the Indian Ocean and the China seas, and they were joined by large numbers of deserters from European fleets, drawn there to try their luck. Political unrest following the emancipation of the Spanish colonies in America led to a renewal of piracy in these waters. In 1826, during the months of June, July and August alone, twenty ships were reported to Lloyds as victims of piracy in various areas. Because of their size and inadequate means of defence, boats engaged in off-shore traffic were especially vulnerable to such predatory attacks, although ocean-going vessels were by no means immune, often suffering the same fate.

Despite all these difficulties and dangers, or perhaps because of them, seafarers found ways to amuse themselves on board, for sailing in those days was often a monotonous affair. When the wind was settled and steady, as in the Atlantic when the ship was borne along by the trade-winds, the sails needed little trimming and the sail changes necessitated by alterations of course were possible from the deck and the tops. On the other hand, when storms threatened and the sails had to be reduced, the crew had to clamber bare-footed up the masts and scramble along the foot-ropes stretched below the yards to take in the sails. These manoeuvres were extremely difficult and called for great agility and strength when the canvas had stiffened with rain and wind. The same held true for the handling of the anchors, which could weigh as much as three tons on a large ship: manning the capstans was no work for weaklings. But there were also quieter moments which gradually acquired a traditional and picturesque maritime character. The forecastle was the ship's "village square", the meeting-place for those off duty. Here the latest gossip, jokes and tittle-tattle were exchanged while sailors came to light their pipes from the wick, closely guarded by a sentry, as the risk of fire was ever-present and it was strictly forbidden to smoke elsewhere than on the upper deck. This daily "news bulletin" of life on board, which must have had its colourful side, came to be called the "Wick Gazette". Games were also organized, with sailors pitting their skill and agility against one another.

Games of chance involving money were forbidden according to regulations but were nevertheless frequently played. On large ships, a few musicians were even taken on board. During his voyage round the world, Bougainville took along two oboe-players who gave concerts and provided music for dancing. On slave-ships, too, the human cargo was made to dance, doubtless with the intention of making them forget their wretched lot or, at most, of keeping them in good market condition.

Catering for crews and the occasional passengers was a difficult task and, here again, no real progress was made until the nineteenth century. On the whole, food served on board a ship remained the same for two hundred years. Cooking arrangements were extremely primitive: on a big ship with a crew of a thousand or so hands, making a meal was no easy matter. An enormous boiler was hoisted on to a stove and held in position by an elaborate system of tackles to offset the roll of the ship. This boiler was installed on the upper deck to limit the risk of fire. For meals the sailors were divided into groups, usually of seven men, each "mess" sitting together and eating out of the same kettle. When the meal was being prepared, a delegate from each mess came and tossed into the boiler his messmates' portion of meat on a skewer, distinctively marked so that, when the meal was cooked, he could identify and recover their property. There was little mutual confidence for after all the portions had been deposited in the boiler, the lid was firmly closed and the master-at-arms padlocked it to prevent any pilfering or surreptitious insertion of foreign objects. At meal-time, the ship's cook fished out the portions of meat with a gaff and distributed them to their rightful owners.

Until 1820, each mess had its communal dixy into which each sailor in turn plunged his spoon. Individual dixies were not used in the French navy until the time of the Restoration; detachable benches and tables fixed to the floor did not appear until the days of the Second Empire. Plates and dishes were confined to the minimum, with dixies and spoons made in wood or pewter, except for the officers who often brought their own silver plate on board ship.

Food was almost invariably atrocious. Salt being the only means of preserving foodstuffs until the late nineteenth century, great quantities of salted meat and fish were consumed. Supplies of fresh meat were quickly exhausted, for it was only possible to take a few live cattle and poultry on board, certainly insufficient for a long crossing; and these, furthermore, were usually reserved for the sick. Towards the middle of the seventeenth century, more attention was paid to victualling on French ships. They actually found space for a sheep pen, sometimes two storeys high, to double the capacity and ensure a longer supply of fresh meat. Fresh vegetables were often grown on the deck if water could be spared. When weather permitted, a trawl net or harpoon was used to harvest fresh fish which enlivened a very monotonous bill of fare, normally based on dry vegetables and biscuit. In tropical waters, large turtles weighing anything from 66 to 110 pounds were eagerly hunted and were very popular for their delicious meat. When captured, these were placed between decks, to one side of the gun-ports, belly to belly on top of each other to immobilize them. By throwing a pail of sea water over their bodies daily, it was possible to keep them in condition without any other food or attention for over a month, and turtle soup as well as meat could be enjoyed by everyone.

Stored down in the hold in wooden barrels, all the staple foods, salted meat, biscuits and vegetables, kept badly in the extremely damp atmosphere which encouraged the development of numerous parasites. Bougainville claimed that rats ate as much as was consumed by one fifth of the entire crew. Worm-eaten biscuits were commonplace but, provisions being scarce, wastefulness was severely curbed. The unexpected prolongation of some cruises forced certain mariners to resort to scarcely desirable expedients. During an arduous Pacific crossing, Bougainville was reduced to eating dogs and even rats which, incidentally, he found "extremely good". It was no time to be finicky and, as he observed philosophically when contemplating the menu, "...one must eat the good with the bad...rotten bread and meat whose stench, when it is put in to soak, sometimes daunts even the least fastidious among us..."

In the navies, food supplies were governed by regulations which were not always strictly adhered

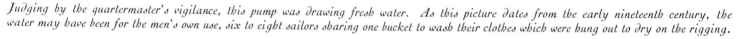

Judging by the quartermaster's vigilance, this pump was drawing fresh water. As this picture dates from the early nineteenth century, the water may have been for the men's own use, six to eight sailors sharing one bucket to wash their clothes which were hung out to dry on the rigging.

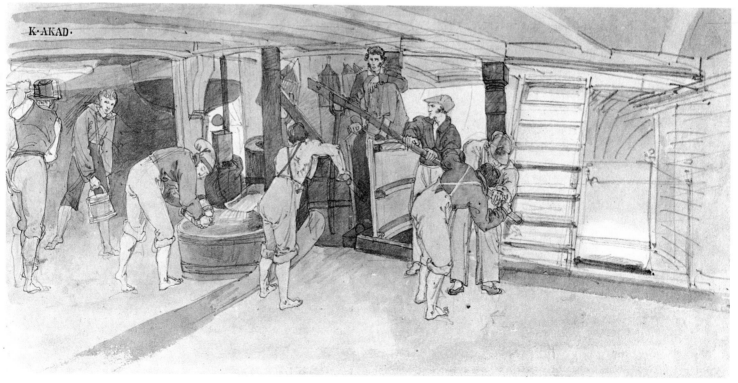

to. A regulation passed in 1669 in the French navy provided for meat, beef or salted bacon three times a week, and fish — cod or herring — on the other days. Meat was flavoured with stock and the fish with oil and vinegar. Each day, the sailor could draw a ration of beans or peas together with ship's biscuit and watered-down wine. In the navies of Catholic countries, cheese replaced meat on fast-days, a custom that was little appreciated by the crews. Naval officers were entitled to neat wine and received an extra sardine or half a herring. Watch-keepers slaked their thirst with vinegar water, claimed to be a remedy against scurvy while, outside the tropics, spirits were issued.

The fatal association between the lack of fresh fruit and vegetables and scurvy was not established until the mid-eighteenth century by a Scottish doctor, James Lind. British crews were then regularly issued with lime juice and, on the voyage in 1772, Captain Cook sailed with a large amount of carrot marmalade, in addition to orange and lemon juices. In the British navy, each man received daily a ration of a pound of ship's biscuit and a gallon of beer; a pound of beef and a pound of bacon twice a week, and an allowance of butter, cheese and half a cod between four men three times a week. The diet was very much the same in the Dutch fleet.

Beverages were always a difficult problem. While the French ships stocked wine, cider and spirits, the British and Dutch favoured beer. During the eighteenth century, British sailors also drew a rum ration. In 1740, Admiral Vernon had the idea of reducing rum consumption by diluting it with water, the mixture taking the name of " grog ", after the admiral's nickname among his sailors. By far the greatest problem was fresh water, which remained the seafarer's nightmare until the end of sailing-ships. Fresh water was cumbersome to carry and difficult to keep fresh. Before the more hygienic metal water tanks were employed about 1825, water was stored in wooden barrels, and as a result it quickly became tainted and most unpalatable. From the seventeenth century on, efforts were directed towards the desalinisation of sea-water and numerous inventors

On the battery deck of the Austria, *sailors bunked down with the cows and sheep, tethered among cannon and other armaments, breathing the foul air throughout such voyages as Trieste to Rio which took 95 days. This sketch was made by Austrian painter Thomas Ender (1793-1875).*

produced methods which, more often than not, proved disappointing or impractical. In the latter part of the eighteenth century, primitive stills were introduced and Poissonnier, a French doctor, invented a still which burned charcoal to accompany Bougainville round the world. Though producing reasonable results, its heavy fuel consumption precluded its constant use. Captain James Cook also had stills aboard but these were hardly satisfactory and Guilleux La Roërie was not greatly exaggerating when he wrote: "The vessels of old were haunted by equal or greater thirst than the Sahara".

The crew's water ration was stowed on the forecastle in a wooden cask called the scuttle-butt, into which the men dipped with their mugs. During protracted voyages, when fresh water became scarce, a sentry was posted day and night to see that none of the precious liquid was drawn off for anything but drinking purposes, and then only in moderate quantities. When the situation became critical, the scuttle-butt was available only between certain hours, this rationing being all the more keenly felt as it inevitably coincided with a preponderance of salted provisions, soaked to no great effect in sea water. Various methods, such as old nails and pebbles thrown into the scuttle-butt, were claimed to prevent fresh water from spoiling but their efficiency was rarely confirmed by experience.

As even in some navies sailors had to provide their own clothes and pay for them, they were frequently inadequately dressed. Life and work on board involved heavy wear and tear and, as a result, crews were only too commonly in rags and tatters. The Russian navy, however, bore the cost of providing clothing for its crews so that each year the sailor received, or was entitled to, two shirts and two pairs of linen drawers, one pair of woollen stockings and a jacket, as well as a pair of canvas breeches, a watch-coat and frock-coat lined with heavy wool,

In a pensive posture, a sailor sits on one of the cages for keeping chicken and ducks on deck, and which also served as life-buoys.

all this sartorial splendour being crowned with a skull-cap and a knitted wool hat for extra warmth.

It was not until the mid-eighteenth century that naval uniforms can be said to have been introduced, but in practice they were not actually worn by sailors, or even by many officers until considerably later.

Only in 1786 did the French navy start providing its seamen with proper clothes and the compulsory outfit then comprised six shirts, two pairs of linen drawers, a hat, four pairs of stockings (two in wool), and two pairs of shoes. A hammock, a blanket and a leather pouch completed the issue. When embarking for cold latitudes, storm coats, boots and gloves were provided for the watch. Every Sunday, officers inspected kit and checked on the cleanliness of the seamen, who were ordered to shave once a week and comb their hair every day. The maintenance of a ship was no easy matter, particularly in view of the intense clutter and congestion that reigned on board, especially at the outset of a voyage. Some of the cargo and provisions had to be stowed on the upper deck, hands and passengers crammed together in the 'tween-decks among the innumerable cases and packages, with little if any room for swinging their hammocks from the heavy beams.

It is to their credit that the navies of those times made heroic efforts to keep their ships clean and tidy. Even then, large quantities of paint were used to protect the ship from salt water corrosion. The Dutch seem to have excelled at keeping their ships clean, regularly sweeping and swilling them down. At sea, twice a week, the ship was cleaned, the sea-mens' chests moved aside and the decks thoroughly swept. Despite all these precautions, however, vermin and, above all, rats soon found their way on board and could never be completely cleared. Towards the end of the eighteenth century, the French navy improved standards of hygiene, holds being washed out every other day in hot climates and

One of the officers of the Geographe, commanded by Nicolas Baudin on his expedition in Tasmania (1800-1804), at his ease.

Thomas Ender was commissioned as official artist during a natural history expedition to the coasts of Brazil from April, 1817 to August, 1818. Also taking part in the expedition was the frigate Augusta which carried the Grand Duchess Leopoldine of Austria. Here is Ender's view of the Austria, looking forward as sailors climb the rigging in order to trim the sails aloft.

every three days in cold regions while, four times a year, the ship's interior was thoroughly disinfected with a powerful, vermin-killing solution of lime wash.

Poor food, constant damp, questionable cleanliness and over-crowding of large numbers of men in confined and badly ventilated quarters were routine. A 74-cannon ship carried 680 hands and manually-operated ventilators were not introduced until about 1780. All these factors combined to form an ideal breeding ground for the various diseases which ravaged those on board until the end of the eighteenth century. Drinking more or less tainted water often caused typhus or, as it was known at the time, "ship fever", while the lack of fresh fruit and vegetables resulted in scurvy and other vitamin deficiency diseases. The death rate remained very high until about 1760. During the campaign in 1690, the Comte de Tourville was obliged to put ashore a third of his complement because of various illnesses, which proved considerably more deadly than enemy cannon fire. In one month's Pacific campaign in 1741, the British admiral George Anson (1697-1762) lost 80 men through scurvy alone, and in 1757, Dubois de la Motte put into Brest after a voyage from Canada with 6,000 cases of typhus in his squadron. The dreaded disease spread to the local population, eventually depleting the total available forces by two thirds.

These epidemics sometimes crippled naval operations, as in the case of the 1779 campaign led by Louis Guillovet, Comte d'Orvilliers (1708-1792) in the Channel, which was abruptly curtailed by sickness among his crews. Obviously, the same fate also befell merchant-vessels on voyages over long distances. The Spanish galleon sea route between Manila and Acapulco regularly cost between 40 per cent and 70 per cent of the ship's hands. In the beginning of the eighteenth century, crew losses of 50 per cent were taken for granted during the two-year voyage to and from Europe and India. Very little was then known about the causes or treatment of these shipboard and tropical diseases.

An embryonic medical service did exist, as rudimentary as medical care ashore. Doctors and surgeons taken on board were hardly conspicuous for their skill and competence, and regulation medicine chests contained little more than old wives' remedies.

No serious consideration was given to health on board by the authorities and no noticeable decline in mortality during long sea voyages was apparent until well on into the second half of the eighteenth century. Even then, improvement was very slow.

Hospital ships did, however, follow the squadrons of the large navies during action at sea. Ashore, hospitals reserved for the navy treated sick seamen who, whilst aboard, were lodged between decks in canvas cradles. When a seaman died, the corpse was sewn into sail canvas, weighted with a cannon-ball, placed on a sloping plank over the gunwales and, while the chaplain intoned the last rites and the crew recited a prayer, the body was slid into the deep.

Extremely arduous conditions on board hardened the men's characters, often rendered them violent, quarrelsome, undisciplined, drunken and depraved. Of necessity, discipline was fearsome to a degree. Basic ideas on discipline varied very little from one navy to another, relying heavily on corporal punishment, the two most severe types being keel-hauling and gauntlet-running. Keel-hauling consisted of suspending the wretched offender on a rope from the tip of the main yard and dropping him sharply into the sea, heaving him up and dropping him again, up to as many as five times. Another version of this punishment took place in the dry dock, without the victim actually being plunged into water. Dutch keel-hauling was even more brutal, the victim being dragged under the ship's keel by a rope. History would have us believe that the Dutch were responsible for the introduction of this punishment. "Running the gauntlet" was gentle by comparison, the offender merely received a beating as he was forced to run between a double row of sailors wielding lengths of rope under the merciless goading of a ship's officer.

A rule passed in the Dutch navy in 1664 laid down that "anyone drawing a knife on an impulse of malice, even though he wound nobody, be nailed by the hand to the mainmast with the knife until he tear himself free . . ." If a sailor killed another on board, the dead and the live man were bound back to back and cast into the sea. If murder was committed on land, the culprit was beheaded. Any rebellion or violence against officers was severely repressed. Each man was responsible for his post and any man falling asleep while on duty was sentenced to deep

An unknown Chinese artist painted this view of the Hong Kong roads where ships from the West coasted alongside Chinese junks, seen on the left. The sea which had separated civilizations now brought them together: this water-colour is similar to contemporary European aquarelles.

keel-hauling, the same punishment meted out to any sailor leaving his post before being relieved. The law also stipulated that none "... be he high or low in rank, make so bold as to admit women or females to the ship on pain of severe punishment ..." This ban was amply justified by the great number of women of ill repute who crowded the ports, sometimes causing the authorities considerable trouble and embarrassment. Needless to say, these regulations were often ineffectual and some officers, Yves-Joseph de Kerguelen (1734-1797) for one, went so far as to embark female stowaways, which invariably caused them considerable difficulties.

A tendency to more humanitarian consideration developed in France towards the end of the reign of Louis XIV and was perhaps responsible for a slight alleviation in the severity of shipboard discipline,

something which Colbert had already attempted without any marked success. The naval ordinance of 1765 aimed at reducing corporal punishment still further, but it is difficult to establish how far this was carried out in practice. At all events, violence only slowly declined and severe corporal punishment was not completely abolished in the French navy until 1848. Discipline was no less severe in the merchant fleets: the ship's company was exposed to the captain's unrestricted and frequently unjustified tyranny which often gave rise to mutinies, some of which have remained among the most famous of the many stories in the annals of sailing history.

The hazards of sea voyages and the harshness of living conditions in the navies of early times made recruitment extremely difficult and sometimes resulted in the use of the most deplorable stratagems to secure crews. Until about 1670, the principal recruiting measure was the press-gang, which conscripted for the king's ships men living on the coasts and engaged in seafaring activities, merchant sailing or fishing. This method entailed so many drawbacks that Colbert tried his utmost to replace it with the more reasonable and enlightened contingent system. All men in maritime activities were registered and divided into classes, serving in turn on the ships of the Royal Navy. In compensation for this compulsory naval service, conscripts received various tax and financial benefits. For many reasons, however, chiefly the Royal Treasury's perpetual penury, this system never functioned satisfactorily until the nineteenth century. In war-time, when the navy's man-power needs were sharply increased, it was always necessary to resort to the press-gangs, and difficulties and obstructions were endless. Sailors, poorly paid and receiving their miserable wages only after considerable delay, either deserted or went into hiding to escape from the conscription gangs. Their families were frequently left destitute as the men were paid only for the time actually spent in service. On merchantmen, the sailor was entitled to take on board a substantial personal cargo for private sale, on which he could make a handsome profit. The same procedure, although strictly forbidden, was just as commonly practised on men-of-war during the eighteenth century, even by officers who were also paid irregularly and had to find some means of their own invention to make ends meet.

But men-of-war were not permanently on active service. During the winter, they were almost always laid up in harbour, retaining only a skeleton crew for maintenance and with all valuable equipment, such as arms, masts, spars and sails dismantled and put into store. The remainder of the crew, put ashore, drew only half-pay, loafed around the ports and lived in billets, naval barracks for their housing being non-existent in France until 1786.

Port and naval dockyard workers fared little better. The working conditions were distressing, as in all industries at that time. Children from the age of six to seven were employed for special jobs such as caulking and preparing tow. They were also taken on board and many a famous mariner started his career at the age of eight or ten as a cabin-boy on his father's ship. Seafaring in those days was very much a family affair, both in the merchant and royal navies, and cabin-boy was the bottom rung of the ladder which could lead to quite high rank.

The British navy employed different recruiting methods. Instead of the contingent or quota system, all the coastal population, river workers and even farmers when necessary, were conscripted into service at sea. For appearances' sake, Acts of Parliament were passed tempting men to come forward as volunteers, and to that end offering the inducement of various privileges. The British had excellent nurseries for sailors: in foundling homes, and in the orphanages at Greenwich and Christchurch a sort of school for cabin-boys existed where about 150 sailors' sons were maintained, receiving basic nautical training. Pupils were admitted between the ages of eleven and thirteen and, after three years, were engaged on board the King's ships or merchantmen. Merchant ship captains also took apprentices on board and gave them instruction. Officers of the Royal Navy, who themselves engaged their crew, were not allowed to employ men having less than three years' sailing experience. Despite these varied sources of recruitment, there was always a shortage of man-power and the British navy, like its European counterparts, frequently had to resort to press-gangs and the recruitment of a wide assortment of foreign mercenaries. The sailor of those times was not renowned for his integrity, readily transferring his allegiance to a higher bidder, so that both Merchant Navy and Royal Navy were constantly plagued by desertion. Shipwrecks and various misadventures sometimes left men stranded in distant parts, bereft of resources, finding work wherever they could, sometimes even on Barbary pirate ships, whose motley crews had deserters from practically every fleet in Europe. But since sailors were always in demand and hard to come by, governments took considerable pains to retrieve them. Consuls and commanders of warships had standing orders to put these so-called "disgraced" sailors on board and to restore them to their motherland. Shaped by a rough and dangerous life, the seaman of those days was a colourful character, capable of amazing feats of strength and endurance and able to extricate himself with great courage from the most perilous situations.

Painted by T. Allom in 1841, this view of Nelson Haven in New Zealand combines the charming delicacy and meticulous accuracy characteristic of this period. Countless such records resulted from expeditions sponsored by the English, French, Russians and Americans.

THE GREAT SCIENTIFIC EXPLORATIONS

The growth of scientific exploration, which made great strides in the years around 1760, was slowed down but not altogether halted by the political troubles which upset Europe from 1789 onwards. Two distinct periods can be recognized; one between 1790 and 1815, when the pace was slackened by European wars ; and the second, extending from 1815 to 1840, which witnessed intense activity. The main protagonists were the French, British,

Russians and the American newcomers. As in earlier voyages, attention was chiefly concentrated on the Pacific Ocean, whose general outlines had been mapped out between 1760 and 1790. But an enormous amount of detail work remained to be done ; it was now less a matter of actual discovery, unknown lands being rare, and more a quest for geographical precision with, above all, the development of branches of scientific knowledge which were then beginning to diversify at a rapidly increasing pace. During the period from 1790 to 1815, seven voyages made history. Two of these were made by Frenchmen, Joseph-Antoine d'Entrecasteaux and Nicolas Baudin ; two in British ships under the command of Matthew Flinders and George Vancouver; another by an American, David Porter, while two voyages were conducted under the Russian flag, commanded by Adam-Ivan Krusenstern and Vassili Golovnine. Another important voyage resulting in notable discoveries was made during this period by a Spanish explorer, Alexander Malaspina.

The disappearance of the French explorer, Jean-François de La Pérouse, from whom no news had been received since early in 1788, had caused a flurry in seafaring and scientific circles and it was decided to organize an expedition which, among other missions, would attempt to find some trace of the lost mariner. The command was given to Captain Joseph-Antoine d'Entrecasteaux, who already had several successful campaigns to his credit, including a brilliant exercise in sailing against the monsoon both in the Indian Ocean and the China Seas in 1786. He sailed out of Brest in 1791 with two frigates, the *Recherche* and the *Espérance*, bound for Australian waters. The last letter from La Pérouse having been addressed from Botany Bay near Sydney, investigations were naturally directed to these regions. After making the first stage to the Cape of Good Hope and Mauritius, d'Entrecasteaux set course for Australia. He discovered that Tasmania was, in fact, an island ; took note of the coasts of New Caledonia which Bougainville had skirted without seeing, and finally put into harbour at Amboina. On the second stage of his voyage, he turned back to the Australian coasts, then sailed northwards and passed, quite unaware, close to the Santa Cruz islands where La Pérouse had been shipwrecked off Vanikoro, a fact that only finally came to light in 1826. By this time, however, the two frigates were in a bad state. D'Entrecasteaux, himself, died from scurvy on July 21st, 1793, and the expedition came to a sad end without ever having achieved its goal. None the less, a wealth of scientific facts was amassed which, after countless misfortunes owing to the existing state of war, finally reached France, being published in 1807 and 1808.

At about the same time, another French expedition was being organized, this time with commerce as the main target. A Marseilles shipowner had decided to try to establish a trade in furs between the Pacific seaboard of Canada and China, where they seemed to be in great demand. In December, 1790, under the command of Etienne Marchand, the three-master *Le Solide* weighed anchor off Marseilles. Primarily commercial, her mission also included a certain amount of scientific exploration, particularly studies of natural history.

After rounding Cape Horn, Marchand made a landfall in the Marquesas Islands, discovering Nukuhiva Island. He then proceeded up towards the North American coasts to buy furs, revictualled at Hawaii and, without putting into port again, arrived at Macao. Here, he discovered the commercial optimism completely unfounded and returned to France via the Indian Ocean, the Cape of Good Hope and St. Helena. Although commercially unsuccessful, his voyage, being devoid of any serious misadventure, was proclaimed by Charliat as "a model of speed and precision, a triumph for scientific navigational methods". So instructive were the lessons learned during this expedition that they were subsequently published in four large official volumes.

Keen rivalry for the fur trade existed between England, France and Spain and was partly responsible for the voyages made by George Vancouver and Alexander Malaspina. A former companion of Captain Cook, and in command of the *Discovery* and the *Chatham*, Vancouver left England in 1791, rounded the Cape and charted the St. Paul and Amsterdam Islands. Reaching New Zealand and Australia, he completed the hydrographic studies begun by Cook. On his way to Hawaii, his ships dropped anchor off Tahiti near the scene of the famous *Bounty* mutiny which had dealt such a blow to the reputation of the British. After visiting Hawaii, Vancouver also coasted along the territory now known as British Columbia, and forced the Spaniards to withdraw from these waters by chasing them out of Nootka Sound. George Vancouver also visited the coasts of Alaska and completely disproved the claim of Captain Meares, an Englishman, to have discovered a North-West Passage between the Atlantic and Pacific Oceans by way of the Juan de Fuca Strait.

At about the same time, Spain dispatched two ships to these regions, the *Discubierta* and the *Atrevida*, under the command of Alexander Malaspina. Sailing from Spain in 1789, he remapped the coasts of South America and established a precise sea route to the Philippines. This Spanish commander crossed the Pacific from north to south and took accurate bearings of the coasts of North America, where he also studied the glacier which now bears his name. In 1795, he returned to Cadiz with a vast amount of scientific information. In spite of his impressive achievements, Malaspina, because of his liberal opinions, was emprisoned and died in obscurity.

The discoveries went on. A few years later, Nicolas Baudin who, between 1792 and 1793 had conducted a campaign in the Pacific and Indian Oceans on behalf of the Emperor of Austria, was entrusted with a scientific mission, which doubtless had political undertones. Baudin sailed from Le Havre in 1800 with the *Géographe* and the *Naturaliste*, bound for Australia. The voyage proved arduous, not only because of exasperating climatic conditions, but especially because of the intense rivalry that sprang up between the scientists on board the two ships. Surmounting innumerable difficulties, Baudin explored the west and south coasts of the little-known Australian continent but died at Mauritius during the return voyage.

Baudin's expedition was probably the first to have brought together such a number and variety of scientists on board. More than twenty botanists, zoologists, horticulturists, astronomers, mineralogists and other specialists sailed on board the two ships. In spite of many and varied misadventures, the expedition was far from a failure and greatly contributed to the knowledge of these inhospitable regions. A fairly comprehensive survey was made of Tasmania. Members of the expedition came into contact with primitive peoples, now extinct, providing invaluable ethnographical details in the notes and drawings brought back by the scientists and artists on board the two ships. Equally important botanical information came to light. Exploration in the Australian outback and on hitherto unexplored islands yielded an abundant harvest of new information, some of which was later included in the *Voyage to the Austral Lands* published by Peron, an anthropologist, and

Louis de Freycinet, a ship's officer, on their return. At about this time, the British mariner Matthew Flinders (see page 181) was also exploring the same regions, taking the bearings of the Tasmanian coast, and the two navigators actually crossed paths. In spite of the war, there was still some semblance of international collaboration on scientific affairs: Baudin had been provided with a British passport and Flinders was granted a similar document by the French government. However, this did not prevent its holder from being interned for seven years on Mauritius in particularly unpleasant conditions.

The United States in turn entered the arena with the voyage of Commodore David Porter, who had cut a conspicuous figure during the campaign against Barbary pirates off Tunis and Tripoli in 1800. At the time of the Anglo-American war in 1812, Porter undertook a long cruise in the Pacific to attack British whalers. Based successively in the Galapagos and Marquesas Islands between 1812 and 1814, he took advantage of his long voyages in the South Seas to pin-point numerous features on the charts of the Pacific Ocean.

Other wartime operations were turned to good account by geographers. The French squadrons of frigates, engaged in vigorous campaigns against the British in the Indian Ocean between 1803 and 1810, also collected a considerable amount of information which contributed greatly to the improvement of charts in this area. Equally useful facts came to light concerning the African coasts and, to a lesser extent, the North Atlantic, where the French Captain Leduc, while on operations against British whalers in 1806, reconnoitred Bear Island and made a further survey of the coast of Iceland. The British were also active in the same waters and, from 1807, William Scoresby (1760-1829) applied himself to interesting studies on glaciology and oceanography while cruising off Greenland on thirty different missions.

The Russians, for their part, sponsored the expedition by Adam-Ivan Krusenstern who, between 1803 and 1806, sailed round the world, concentrating especially on exploring the seas around Japan and Korea. He established that Sakhalin was an island, surveyed the Kuril Islands and revised the charts of these regions more accurately. His research was subsequently continued between 1808 and 1818 by

At sea, fire and ice were worse enemies than any storm, as Dumont d'Urville painfully discovered on February 9th, 1838. His ice-bound Astrolabe was painted by the artist, writer, sailor and corsair, Ambroise-Louis Garneray (1783-1857) who took part in the expedition.

Vassili Golovnine (who died in 1832) in the distant reaches of the North Pacific and Arctic Oceans.

By 1815, apart from the polar regions, men had thus gained a fair knowledge of the general configuration of the earth's surface. Countless details remained to be filled in, a less spectacular and, in many ways, a less rewarding task, requiring increasing accuracy to meet the ever more exacting demands of scientific compilation. While planning a voyage in 1817, Freycinet commented: "Nothing remains but to go back and fill in the details which will clarify geographical knowledge, rather than add to it. Although our predecessors have left us only scraps of archipelagos to explore ... they have bequeathed us an enormous amount of mistakes to correct."

The end of the Empire Wars in France led to a surging renewal of maritime exploration, motivated by fresh objectives. From this period, emphasis shifted away from the interest in natural phenomena to geophysics, magnetism and meteorology, sciences that were all still very much in their infancy.

Between the years 1817 and 1840, voyage followed voyage in quick succession. This new series was launched in 1817 by the Frenchman Louis de Freycinet who had taken part in Baudin's expedition and who now set sail in the *Uranie*. He crossed the Indian Ocean and reached Australia, where he continued the studies started by his old commander. Subsequent exploration took him to Timor, New Guinea, Guam, the Marianas Archipelago and the Hawaiian Islands. He pressed on as far south as the polar regions, bringing back an important collection of scientific specimens, including over 400 unknown plants. Madame de Freycinet, disguised as a

An octant: the eye-glass is folded up.

Matthew Flinders (1774-1814).

matelot, accompanied her husband on the voyage, and the French navy wisely closed their eyes to this infringement of the regulations. De Freycinet's second-in-command, Louis Duperrey, set sail in turn on the *Coquille* in August, 1822, with Dumont d'Urville (see page 181) as his second-in-command, reaching the Pacific via Cape Horn. Two and a half years later, on March 25th, he returned after a voyage of over 60,000 miles without the loss of a single man, and with a wealth of scientific information which filled seven volumes and four atlases.

Unquestionably the most famous navigator of those times was Jules-Sébastien Dumont d'Urville, who brilliantly carried on the tradition of scholarly seafaring initiated the century before. As a young ensign, he had been responsible for the purchase, in 1819, of the recently discovered Venus de Milo. He subsequently took part in the voyage of the *Coquille* and, on his return, his herbarium contained 4,000 plants and his collection of insects amounted to 1,100 specimens, 700 of them completely unknown. In April 1826, he weighed anchor in the *Coquille*, renamed the *Astrolabe*, and set out to circumnavigate the world, a voyage which was to yield rich scientific rewards. In the Pacific, d'Urville plotted more than 2,500 miles of coastline, discovered or corrected the supposed position of over 150 islands and found the time to build up a surprisingly complete collection of 900 rock specimens. This voyage aroused his interest in oceanography, and on return he engaged in lively and memorable controversies with the learned members of the *Académie des Sciences* on various topics, including the maximum height of waves. While in Tasmania, he learned that a British captain, Peter Dillon, had succeeded in finding traces of La Pérouse. D'Urville immediately left for Vanikoro and there collected pieces of wreckage which left no doubt as to the fate of his

Jules-Sébastien Dumont d'Urville (1790-1842).

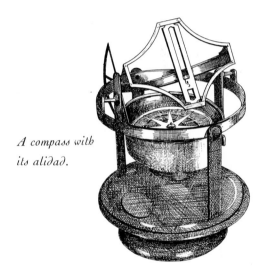

A compass with its alidad.

Charles Wilkes (1798-1877).

unfortunate predecessor in these inhospitable waters. Before leaving, he raised a monument in his memory. The fame of Dumont d'Urville was even more enhanced by his second voyage between 1837 and 1840 with the *Astrolabe* and the *Zélee*, which took him as far as the Antarctic where he discovered the land he named after his wife, Adélie. Ironically, this great mariner who had sailed round the world no less than three times came to an end sadly lacking in glory, in one of history's first railway accidents in 1842.

During these early years of the nineteenth century, the European powers were setting out on a course of overseas expansion, which led to some voyages being concentrated on political and economic goals rather than scientific objectives. Such was the case of the voyage undertaken by Hyacinthe de Bougainville, son of that great navigator of the previous century. Following in his father's wake, he sailed the *Thétis* round the world between 1824 and 1826. Although his mission was primarily devoted to establishing diplomatic and commercial relations with China and Tongking, he also circumnavigated Australia and crossed the Pacific, returning via Cape Horn. Political and economic motives also dictated the voyage of Auguste-Nicolas Vaillant in the *Bonite* from 1836 to 1837. His cruises in the Pacific and Indian Oceans were chiefly to protect the French merchant and whaling-vessels, there being many in the Pacific at that time, but he also carried on board the naturalists Eydoux and Soleillet. The expedition to the Pacific by Abel Dupetit-Thouars in the *Vénus* between 1836 and 1839 was also mainly diplomatic in purpose. Sailing up as far as Petropavlovsk and the Aleutian Islands, he explored the Galapagos Islands and Easter Island. Pierre-Théodore Laplace, commanding the *Artémise* from 1837 to 1840 sailed across the Indian Ocean and the China Seas, visited the Persian Gulf, put into Tahiti, San Francisco and Valparaiso and returned via Cape Horn. Cécille, also protecting whaling-vessels and bringing the royal support of Louis Philippe to the French Catholic missions which were gradually being established throughout the Pacific, nevertheless took the opportunity to inspect the little-frequented islands off the coast of Australia between 1837 and 1839, aboard the *Heroine*. Thus, in all these expeditions, the interests of science were never altogether neglected. Although most of the limelight seems to be focused on the French during this period, the Russians, British and Americans were by no means idle bystanders. Otto von Kotzebue, a Russian, accompanied by the German naturalist and poet, Adalbert von Chamisso, accomplished two missions in the Pacific from 1816 to 1818, and from 1823 to 1826, during which he completed charts of the Bering Strait. Between 1828 and 1829, his compatriot, Fabian Gottlieb von Bellingshausen (1778-1852) explored the Southern Pacific aboard the *Vostok*, discovering the archipelago named after him.

The British organized several expeditions, the most noteworthy being undertaken by Captain Robert Fitz-Roy in the *Beagle* between 1831 and 1836, a politico-scientific mission which led him to the coasts of Patagonia, Tierra del Fuego, Chile and Peru. On board with him, Fitz-Roy had a young naturalist destined for fame who, during the cruise, compiled a scientific record, a model of its kind, in which he began to unfold his theory of the evolution of the species by natural selection, marking an important stage in man's understanding of biology. His name was Charles Darwin.

The American contribution to world exploration during this period was made by Charles Wilkes (see page 181) who surveyed the Antarctic and the west coasts of North America from 1840 to 1841.

The years between 1840 and 1850 saw the great round-the-world voyages draw to a close. Navigation under sail had reached the height of its glory and the steamship was already edging its way onto the sea routes. From the geographical point of view, maritime exploration was practically concluded, with almost all coastlines and contours plotted. For all this work, man's knowledge of the world was still incomplete and the surface of the oceans had only been skimmed for lack of instruments capable of studying their underlying composition. Measurement of depth, water temperature, chemical analyses, investigation and sampling of the ocean deeps were among the questions that remained unfathomed. Oceanography was a completely modern science that received scant attention until the latter part of the nineteenth century and which, even in our era of technological progress, is only just being developed.

THE BELLE POULE · 1834

BY F. LE BIBOUL

It was at Cherbourg, on the 1st April 1828, that the keel of the *Belle Poule* was laid. She was launched six years later, on the 26th March. The long time taken in building was not unusual and, indeed, was necessary in the days of wooden ships. Frames had to be allowed time to weather and the wooden formers gradually drying out under weight gave the hull its desired shape. Towards the end of the eighteenth century the art of shipbuilding had reached a high degree of perfection, not only as a result of scientific research but also because of the work of skilled engineers among whom the most eminent was Jacques-Noël Sané (1740-1831). To this Breton are credited the plans for every new class of warship under the 1786 regulations.

The plans of the *Belle Poule*, an enlarged version of a frigate by Sané, were drawn up by Engineer-General M. F. Boucher and reflected the contemporary trend in naval architecture. Ships of the Louis-Philippe period were, characteristically, very restrained in silhouette having rounded bows, closed in by bulwarks, with the stern similarly treated. The ships were straight-wall sided, "tumble home" eliminated and the decks widened and untrammelled. Low-built, they had three lofty masts, carrying a sail area with a greater spread than usual towards the end of the eighteenth century. However, the poop of the *Belle Poule*, unlike most others of her time, was not rounded but the imposing stern was squared off with sufficient room to allow the fitting out of spacious, comfortable and luxuriously decorated accommodation.

From the first sea trials, the *Belle Poule* showed herself as having exceptional speed and manoeuvrability. She had achieved the ultimate perfection in sailing-ships and was considered as one of the most successful vessels of her time. Consequently, it is not surprising that this frigate was frequently assigned to diplomatic and prestige missions. The main features of the *Belle Poule* were as follows :

Displacement	1,500 tons
Length o.a.	180 feet
Beam	50 feet
Armament	26 30-pound carronades
	28 30-pound cannon
	4 30-pound guns
	2 80-pound guns
Complement	12 officers, 450 crew

Fitted out at Cherbourg, 6th June 1839, the *Belle Poule* was put under the command of Prince Joinville and posted to the flotilla under Admiral Lalande, then on manoeuvres in the Smyrna roads, during August of that year. It was just at this time the Middle Eastern question came to a head as a result of political intrigues by Mohammed Ali, Viceroy of Egypt. After several months of action in the Echelles campaign off the Levant, the frigate sailed for Toulon early in 1840.

On the 7th July she weighed anchor for St. Helena to repatriate the remains of Napoleon I. This mission explains the mourning dress that henceforth characterized the outward appearance of the *Belle Poule*. With the late Emperor's coffin on board, she stood out for France on the 18th October, escorted by the corvette *Favorite*, dropping anchor in the Cherbourg roads on the 30th November.

The royal remains were transshipped to steamers which were to sail up the Seine estuary to Courbevoie. On the 14th December the convoy came alongside at Courbevoie, from where the hearse rumbled away towards Les Invalides, escorted by a guard of 400 marines from the *Belle Poule* and the *Favorite*, with Prince Joinville at their head.

In May 1841, the *Belle Poule* sailed for Newfoundland to protect the French fishing grounds. Her national colours were seen at St. Pierre and Miquelon and again at Halifax. Later she made New York for repairs, before a rough Atlantic crossing to rejoin the Mediterranean Fleet at Toulon.

After the death of the Duke of Orleans in October 1842, the *Belle Poule* sailed from Brest, dropping anchor at Lisbon to put the Duke of Aumale ashore, on his way to the Algerian theatre of operations, then continued her voyage to the French settlements on the African coast. After these colonial inspection duties she headed for Rio de Janeiro where, on the 1st May 1843, the wedding of François de Joinville to Donna Francisca, sister of Dom Pedro II, Emperor of Brazil, was to be celebrated with great pomp and ceremony. The *Belle Poule* carried the young royal couple to France but the crossing was beset by bad weather and her arrival was considerably delayed. Shortly after she dropped anchor in Brest, the Prince was promoted Rear-Admiral and the command of his beloved ship passed to Commander Hernoux. She could not have been in better hands. In 1844, Prince Joinville commanded a flotilla including, among others, the *Belle Poule* and made an effective show force off the African coast. Tangiers was bombarded and Mogador captured on the 17th August 1844, as a reprisal for the assistance brought to Abd-El-Kader by the Sultan of Morocco. Having forced the Sultan to sue for peace, the French flotilla sailed for Toulon, and Prince Joinville was promoted Vice-Admiral.

Commanded by Captain Cunéo d'Ornano, in 1845 the *Belle Poule* was ordered out to the Syrian coasts. Later she reached the Island of Bourbon, when she came under the orders of Captain Romain-Desfossés, who was Governor of the Island. For several years, she cruised the Indian Ocean, periodically returning to Toulon.

At the outbreak of the Crimean War in 1854, the frigate, refitted as an ammunition ship, saw uneventful service in the Black Sea. Already, the days of the sailing men-of-war were numbered. Only three years later, the French Government, after a solemn session of the *Conseil d'Etat*, passed the act of law in 1857 which put an end to the navy under sail.

During the Italian campaign, the *Belle Poule* was stationed at Genoa in 1859 and used as a powder magazine, returning to Toulon at the end of hostilities. In 1861 she was taken out of commission. Reduced to fulfilling the role of a pontoon, the *Belle Poule* was finally broken up in 1888. Throughout her life she had been renowned as one of the most perfect ships of her time.

"Beautiful as a French frigate, and dressed all over..."

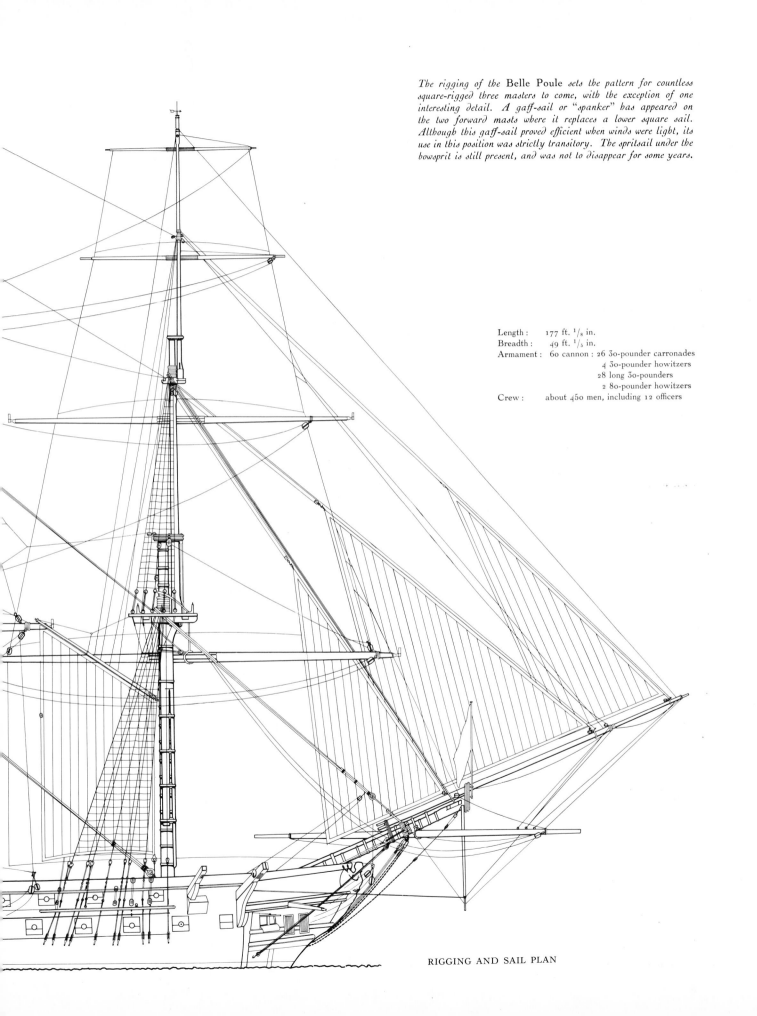

The rigging of the Belle Poule sets the pattern for countless square-rigged three masters to come, with the exception of one interesting detail. A gaff-sail or "spanker" has appeared on the two forward masts where it replaces a lower square sail. Although this gaff-sail proved efficient when winds were light, its use in this position was strictly transitory. The spritsail under the bowsprit is still present, and was not to disappear for some years.

Length: 177 ft. 1/8 in.
Breadth: 49 ft. 1/5 in.
Armament: 60 cannon : 26 30-pounder carronades
                        4 30-pounder howitzers
                        28 long 30-pounders
                        2 80-pounder howitzers
Crew: about 450 men, including 12 officers

RIGGING AND SAIL PLAN

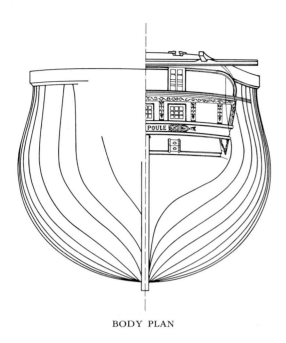

BODY PLAN

So goes the sea-shanty from *Songs of the Sea* by Auguste Dupouy, folksinger of Breton and sea ditties, who is the author of this anthology.

In conclusion, it might be well to note that the illustrious name *Belle Poule* lives to this day. Since 1932 it has been borne by one of the training schooners of the French Naval College. At the launching ceremony, the origin of this name, considered incongruous by the assembled student-officers, was officially explained. They were told that the *Belle Poule* commemorated a woman who, during her lifetime, was reputed as much for her virtue and wit as for her beauty. Paule de Viguier, daughter of a noble Languedoc family, was chosen at the tender age of fifteen by the burghers of Toulouse to recite the town's address to François I, on the occasion of his visit in 1533. The king, dazzled by so much grace, nicknamed the maiden "La Belle Paule" on the spot. However, owing to the indifferent spelling of that era and the vagaries of the local dialect, "Paul" or "Paule" frequently became "Pol" and "Pole" on paper so that she was soon known as the "Belle Poule". During the Seven Years War, a Bordeaux pirate named his ship the *Bella Poula* in memory of this noble Renaissance lady, celebrated for her beauty and whom the High Constable of France, Anne de Montmorency, described as one of the wonders of the world. As for Paule de Viguier, she became the Baroness Fontenilles and was to attain the age of ninety in 1610.

After so long, the deck has become a straight, unbroken line with no trace of the castles of the past. The stern is still rather ornate, in the Restoration style, but no longer juts out over the sides and, instead of being rounded, is flat and square, unusual for this period. The hull section remains almost semi-spherical but with the water-lines extending further and further, they took on more intricate curves, increasingly difficult for shipwrights to fashion. By rule of thumb, they were approaching the shape now determined after experimental tank tests. The cutwater on the stem is no more than a bump and the figurehead now seems to support the bowsprit, as the cutwater once did. This figurehead is the "Belle Poule" herself, the name having no vulgar implications but simply commemorating a beautiful woman from Toulouse. She makes a more decorative support than the cutwater, which often took the form of a sea serpent or the dragoon that traditionally adorned ancient Nordic ships.

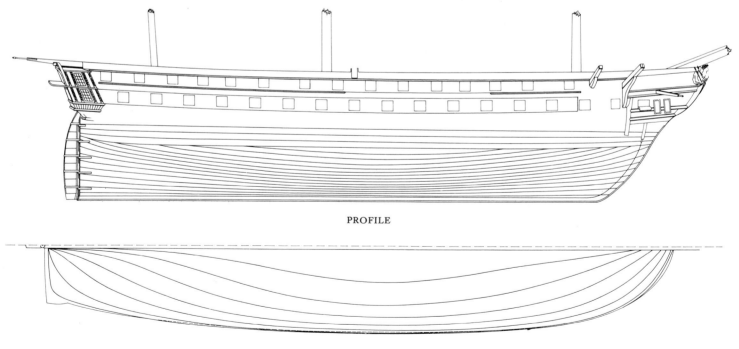

PROFILE

HALF-BREADTH PLAN

The Plans of the *Belle Poule* have been drawn up by the kind permission of the Association des Amis des Musées de la Marine, Paris.

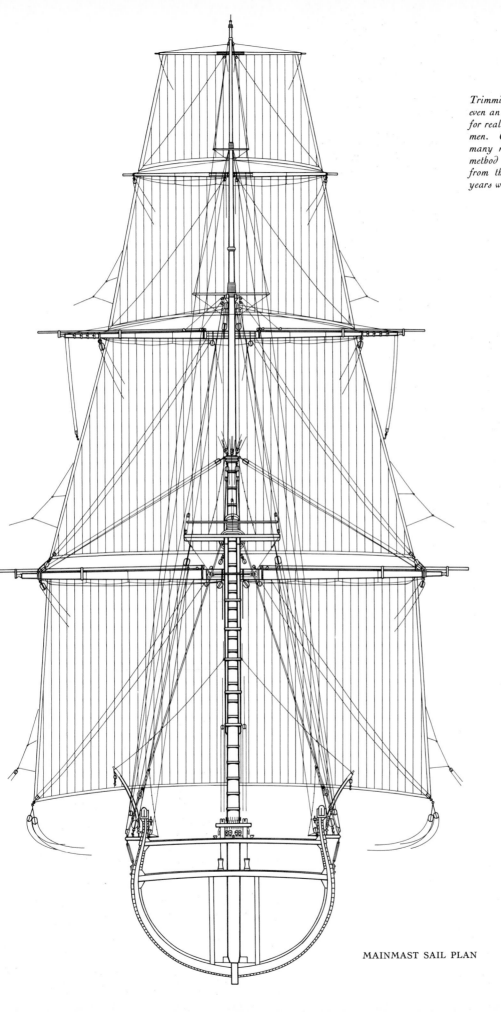

Trimming the upper sails, without the help of even an elementary platform in the top, called for real acrobatic skill on the part of the seamen. One can readily understand why so many naval designers attempted to devise a method whereby the sails could be handled from the deck. Unfortunately, many long years were to pass before they were successful.

MAINMAST SAIL PLAN

Above. *What could be more dreadful than the belching black coal smoke from the steam tug? It blackens and fouls everything within range. And, all the while, its demoniacal steam whistle shrieks like some strange steel animal, drowning human conversation. This is truly the beginning of another era. In the dinghy on the right, oars are raised in salute. The scene is set by the sea wall at Cherbourg. Contrary to general belief, this first really artificial port in the world was not built or even conceived by Napoleon, but constructed under the Restoration. The mainmast of the steamer is actually flying a flag bearing the initial "N" in honour of the mission. These paintings are by Morel-Fatio.*

In the illustration below, on the left, Morel-Fatio simply provides a portrait of the Belle Poule. *The two other paintings on this page are famous, depicting the conveyance of Napoleon's ashes from St. Helena to Cherbourg in this "super-frigate" during the year 1840. Below, the vessel is dressed all over in a very odd fashion, with the national flags of many nations. The topmen are standing to attention, upright on the yards, in honour of the occasion. This is no mean feat, even for them. The* Belle Poule *is under tow while all her cannon are firing.*

The Business Services Group

of

Commercial Credit Company

Cordially Invites You to Join Us

For Cocktails and Hors d'oeuvres

At The Arrival Reception Of

T H E   P R I D E   O F   B A L T I M O R E

At The

Chicago Navy Pier

On

July 23 at 5:00 - 9:00 P.M.

R.S.V.P.

BUSINESS SERVICES GROUP
Sr. V.P. - J. A. Blessing

COMPANIES

AMERICAN CREDIT INDEMNITY
President: H. A. Legge, Jr.

COMMERCIAL CREDIT BUSINESS LOANS
President: F. J. Medeiros

COMMERCIAL CREDIT DEVELOPMENT CORP
President: K. G. Gabel

COMMERCIAL CREDIT McCULLAGH LEASING
President: S. R. Leskovsky

An Authentic Baltimore Clipper

In 1975 the City of Baltimore commissioned the International Historic Watercraft Society, Inc. to design and construct an authentic Baltimore Clipper. The 90 foot topsail schooner, the Pride of Baltimore, was handbuilt, utilizing the same ship-building techniques which fashioned the original Baltimore Clippers.

These schooners made Baltimore and the Chesapeake Bay region world renowned for the design of sailing ships, sporting beauty and speed. From the Revolutionary War until about 1850, these sleek vessels played an important role in the nation's maritime history serving as privateers, merchant ships and revenue cutters.

She is the symbol of Baltimore's proud maritime heritage and present renaissance. In traveling from port to port the *Pride* acts as this City's goodwill ambassador.

Ambroise-Louis Garneray served as a helmsman on the Belle Poule, *was taken prisoner when the ship was captured by the English and subsequently spent eight years in the dreaded prison hulks. His painting of the famous frigate shows Constantinople in the background.*

As she gradually yields her sovereignty to that smoke machine, the steamship, a flag should be dipped in salute to the great sailing-ship which was, to quote Commander Rouch, "one of the most powerful instruments of civilization that mankind has ever had at its disposal". Although only too often adopting a warlike and aggressive role, the sailing-ship played an even greater part in drawing men together and encouraging a mutually rewarding co-operation.

Gradually perfected through much trial and error, navigation by sail, that harsh taskmaster both for men and material, had opened infinite horizons in the realms of economy and science. It was in the days of the sailing-ship that Europeans discovered the world, its true dimensions, and established ever closer and more equable relations between continents, with incalculable consequences in the communication of ideas as well as merchandise. It is said that the sea unites more than it separates. The wisdom of

this adage could scarcely be doubted in the years about 1840, taking into account all the discoveries that had been made. All the blank spaces on the maps were no longer located in the coastal regions but in the hinterlands, which would long resist men's endeavours with more formidable obstacles to overcome than any encountered on the high seas.

The big American three-masted schooner, with her huge spread of sail, held out longest against the competition of steam although the mammoth German sailing-vessel, the steel-hulled *Preussen*, was built as late as 1902. After the First World War, the number of large sailing-ships steadily decreased and, today, only a few can still be seen, serving as training-ships, but even this type of cadet training is under reconsideration, and perhaps has a limited future.

The sailing-ship's swan song was one of triumph. She had played her part nobly and could sail into the legends of the past with all her colours flying proudly.

B.W. BATHE

Curator of the NAVAL SECTION,
SCIENCE MUSEUM, London

THE CLIPPER'S DAY

From 1819, when the *Savannah* made the first Atlantic crossing under
steam in only 16 days, the sailing-vessel had an ever more dangerous
competitor. In 1847 and 1851 when the gold strikes in California and
Australia started the famous « gold rush », sailing was still the fastest
means to get there. In form, these ships were near perfection, but
at the limit of their usefulness. Gracefully, these old ladies of the
sea glided into the past. With them went a special breed of men.

Coleman's California Line,
FOR SAN FRANCISCO,
SAILING REGULARLY AS ADVERTISED
Clipper of **SATURDAY**, March 17th.

THE MAGNIFICENT EXTREME CLIPPER SHIP

STORM KING

CALLAGHAN, Commander,

Is now rapidly Loading at Pier 15 East River.

This celebrated Vessel is well known to the trade as an **EXTREME CLIPPER**, and her uniform RAPID PASSAGES and excellent delivery of cargo, render her at once

THE POPULAR SHIP OF THE PORT,

and insures her PROMPT DISPATCH, as above. She rates strictly first class, and insures at the lowest rates.

WM. T. COLEMAN & CO., 88 Wall St.,

Tontine Building.

Agents in San Francisco, Messrs. WM. T. COLEMAN & CO.

NESBITT AND CO., PRINTERS.

THE ROMANCE OF CLIPPER SHIPS

In the relatively brief period of forty years between 1820 and 1860, the finely designed fast clipper ship of the China Tea Trade was developed, and took the place of the heavily-built slow sailing-vessel of the type previously employed in the East India trade. At no other time in the four thousand years long evolution of the sailing-ship had equivalent advances in hull design and rig taken place in such a short space of time.

In bringing about not only this particular trans-formation, but also the general evolution of the sail-ing-ship, the greatest tribute must be made to the work of the master shipwright and his skilled artisans, who, with little more in the way of tools than the adze, auger and saw, for so many centuries built the trading-vessels and warships of the world. However, honour must also go to the men who by experiments and the application of mechanics, mathe-matics and geometry, developed the theories and rules which became the principles of naval archi-tecture. Unfortunately the practical shipwright was usually slow to take advantage of the work of theoretical writers, although occasionally the quali-ties of the scientific theorist and the practical shipwright were combined.

It is perhaps not generally realised that from the 15th century onwards the major problems of naval architecture — stability, strength of structure, weight calculations and the effect of water resistance to solid bodies — progressively received more and more attention. A 15th century Venetian manuscript lays down the rules and designs for building the best form of hull for the galley and the "round ship" which was the forerunner of the galleon.

In England in 1586, the Elizabethan master-shipwright Matthew Baker produced a manuscript (see page 43-44) which contained elevations, plans and sections of a number of ships. On one of these draughts the shape of the underwater hull of a ship is compared with that of a fish, thus preceding by nearly two hundred and fifty years the 19th century theory of "cod's head and mackerel tail" hull design which gave a vessel a full form near the bows and a fine form at the stern, facilitating movement.

During the 17th and 18th centuries, Dutch, English, French and Swedish writers produced works, many of which were published, dealing with the practice of shipbuilding and the science of naval architecture. In the 17th century experiments were made with small models in tanks of water, and mid-18th century books describe experiments in which various shaped blocks were tested in a tank of water to find out "the form of solid which will move with the greatest velocity through the water". In 1758, the Society of Arts of Great Britain offered prizes for scale models of ships in order to "ascertain by experiment the principles on which a good ship is founded". Six models were produced for this enter-prise and were tested on a pond in the City of London so that water resistance of different hull forms and resistance to rolling could be studied.

The Society for the Improvement of Naval Architecture, founded in London in 1791, offered a number of awards for the best series of experiments relating to the study of the principles of water resistance. Experiments were carried out on the still waters of a London dock where a length of 400 ft. was available. To hoist the towing weights three stout spars were used to form a tripod about 60 ft. high and some nine thousand experiments are said to have been carried out with this apparatus.

Again about 1840, the Aberdeen shipbuilders James and William Hall carried out extensive tests with models on a glass-sided tank 10 ft. in length. On top of the water in the tank a layer of red coloured turpentine was poured. When a model was drawn along by a line led over a pulley at the end of the tank to a weight, the movement of the coloured fluid clearly showed the effect of different bow and hull forms. By using the same weight to provide the motive power with various models, performance comparisons could be made. Thus the tank tests applied to models of ship hulls in present day ship hydrodynamics laboratories are only more elaborate versions of experiments which were first carried out by scientists three hundred years ago.

Early in 1848, the discovery of gold in California engendered the construction of sailing-vessels capable of quickly reaching this new El Dorado from Atlantic ports in America.

EAST INDIAMEN

SHIPS IN SERVICE BETWEEN EUROPE AND THE ORIENT

At the beginning of the 19th century, some of the ships employed by the British East India Company for voyages to India and China were of between 1,200 and 1,500 tons burden and were the finest and largest merchantmen of the period.

From its foundation in the 17th century until 1813, the Honourable East India Company had a complete monopoly on British trade to the East, and even after the monopoly was abolished the company controlled most of the trade, until its trading activities ended in 1833. Most of these large vessels were built at dockyards on the River Thames (see pages 197-199) but occasionally shipbuilders at other ports in England were employed and a number of particularly strong and long-lasting Indiamen were built, almost entirely of teak, at Bombay and Calcutta. The *Herefordshire* shown on page 196 was built at Bombay in 1813. She was of 1,342 tons burden and was armed with twenty-six guns.

A typical Thames-built Indiaman of about 1,200 tons would have been 165 ft. long, between perpendiculars, with a beam of 42 ft. and a depth in hold of 17 ft. The robustness of the construction is shown by the dimensions of some of the structional members, the keel, 1 ft. 3 ins. wide and 1 ft. 4 ins. deep, was made from five pieces of oak scarphed together. The fifty floor timbers — the lowest transverse timbers — were about 1 ft. square and the external lower longitudinal planking was 4 ins. thick.

As a protection against the ravages of the teredo and other marine pests, the underwater part of the hull was sheathed externally with thin sheets of copper. In some constructional features the East Indiamen showed differences and advances over the contemporary vessels of the British Navy. The very great number of new warships built for the Royal Navy during the Napoleonic Wars brought about a shortage of English-grown oak suitable for ship construction. Especially, was there a shortage in the naturally curved wood used for making the angled "knees", used to support and strengthen the deck

beams, and the "breast-hooks", curved pieces used in the bows. The Royal Navy had first call on all timber and the builders of East India Company's ships were forced to find an alternative material for some of the parts of the ships. As a result of proposals by the Surveyor to the Company, after 1800, iron "knees" and "breast-hooks" were successfully used in their ships. Another improvement in East Indiamen at this period was the closing in of the waist. The space between the quarter-deck and forecastle was decked over to form one continuous flush upper deck from bows to stern, an advance not adopted for the Royal Navy until the 1830's.

To provide the maximum cargo carrying capacity the Indiaman was designed with a full body and flat floors, but the excessive sloping inwards or "tumble-home" of the upper-works of the 18th century East Indiaman was greatly reduced. The round bow was built right up to the level of the forecastle deck, and at the stern and quarters two tiers of windows, without projecting galleries, provided illumination to the large cabins. As already stated the waist of an Indiaman was decked over to join the forecastle and quarter-deck and form a continuous deck known as the upper deck. The deck below the upper deck was known in an Indiaman as the middle deck and carried the main defensive armament of about twenty-six 18-pounder guns. Below the middle deck, the deck used for cargo stowage, known as the lower deck, did not usually carry guns and was therefore not normally provided with gun-ports, but many Indiamen had a line of dummy ports painted at this level, externally, to give the appearance that the ship carried a heavier armament. Records show that on occasions the large East Indiamen were mistaken for 64-gun warships. These merchant-ships were all ship-rigged — three masted with square sails on all masts and a fore-and-aft gaff mizzen-sail. Numerous staysails were also set between the masts and between the foremast and bowsprit. In suitable wind conditions studding-sails — small sails set at the sides of the square-sails —

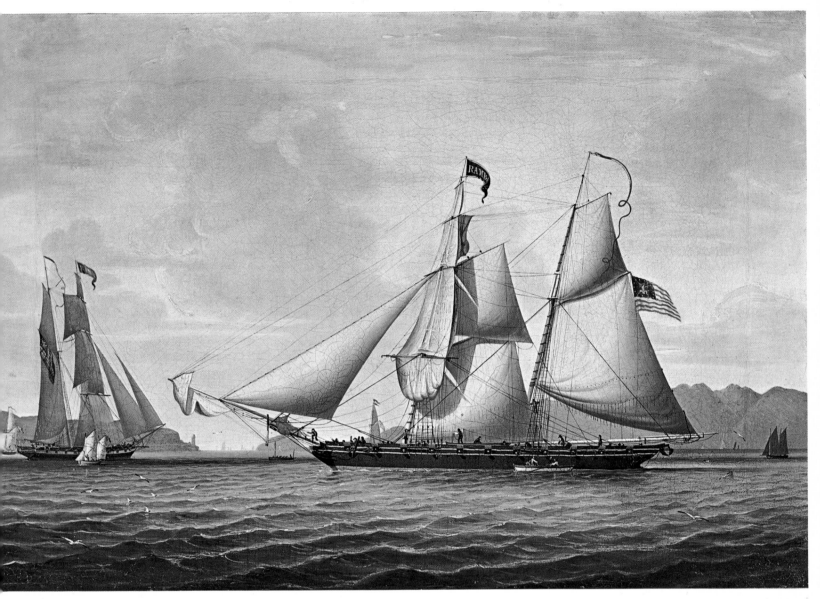

Built in 1812 at Medford, Massachusetts, the Rambler *was one of those fast American "schooner clippers", not to be confused with the great clippers which came later. The long pennant on the mainmast seems to indicate that this vessel was commissioned to give chase to slave-ships.*

and other extra sails were used. The East Indiaman *Essex* is said to have hoisted, on occasions, a total of sixty-three sails! The crew of an East Indiaman were organised and disciplined in much the same way as the crew of a warship, but with a much smaller armament to be served fewer men were required. An Indiaman of about 1,200 tons had a complement of about 130 men which included the commander, six mates, surgeon, purser, midshipman, gunners, boatswain, carpenter, caulker, sailmaker and cook. The East India Company ships bound for the

East, started from Deptford or Blackwall on the Thames and after sailing down river anchored at Gravesend to take on passengers, additional cargo, water and livestock. (Live cows, sheep, pigs, goats and poultry were kept on board to provide milk, eggs and fresh meat for at least part of the long voyage. See illustration on page 169.) The Indiamen then proceeded to the Downs off Deal on the south coast of England. In peace time the mails and last passengers came aboard here and with a favourable wind the real voyage started. If Great Britain was at war and the merchant-vessels had to sail in convoy, a further call was made at Portsmouth where the warships forming the escort were assembled. Convoys sailed at intervals throughout the year and their departures and movements were reported in the contemporary journal *Lloyd's List* published twice a week. A typical entry from this journal, that for February 10th, 1809, notes that on the 8th of the month the East Indiamen: *Lord Duncan, Lady Castlereagh, Baring, Carnatic, Perseverance* and *Nottingham* arrived at Portsmouth from the Downs. Another entry in the List for May 2nd, 1809, reports that on April 28th, the frigate *Lavinia* (a 44 gun frigate built in 1806), left Portsmouth with

the Indiamen *Marquis Wellesley* (for Ceylon and Bengal); *Taunton Castle* and *Dover Castle* (for Bombay); *United Kingdom* (for St. Helena and Bengal); *Surrey, City of London, Retreat* and *Hoppet* (all for Bengal; *Metcalf, Castle Eden* and *Devonshire* (all for Madras and Bengal); *Marquis of Exeter* (for Madeira and Bombay); *Earl Howe* (for Madeira, Madras and Bengal). The *Lloyd's List* for May 30th, reports that the *Lavinia* and the convoy arrived at the isle of Madeira on May 7th, 1809.

The Indiamen were built for cargo-carrying and were not designed for speed, also sail was usually reduced at night, so fast passages were not to be expected. The round voyage from England to China

Off the chalk cliffs of southern England in 1813, the East Indiaman Herefordshire *is shortening sail, caught in a brisk and unexpected sou'wester. It is interesting to note that, even at this time, her three-masted square rig includes only one gaff-sail, the extreme aft spanker.*

and back to England took more than a year. The ships of a convoy for Ceylon and India, as just described, could be expected back in the Thames in about eighteen months from the date of sailing.

However, remarkably fast passages were made occasionally, the *Naval Chronicle* for 1816 notes the arrival of thirteen East Indiamen from China in 109 days and describes the feat as "a combination of nautical skill with good fortune, of which there is no record of an equal exertion". The outward-bound Indiamen for Madras, Bengal and Bombay carried large numbers of Government troops and officials of the East India Company, and a cargo principally comprising manufactured goods, woollen goods and iron. The returning ships, unless specially chartered as troopships, carried fewer passengers but were heavily-laden with a cargo of cotton goods, silk, spices, rice, sugar and more exotic commodities such as sandalwood, ebony, cowries and elephants' teeth.

East India Company ships proceeding by a direct route to China, had very few passengers and no troops aboard. The return cargo consisted almost entirely of tea, a commodity which provided a large profit for the Company. A large Indiaman could carry well over a thousand tons of tea. While dealing with the cargoes carried by East Indiamen it is interesting to note that the 1803 edition of *The Shipmasters Assistant* contains tables giving the

Around 1800, artists enjoyed portraying the weather. One can almost feel the wind in this small cutter's sails. The tall building in the background was a warehouse, serving both as a crane for lifting masts in the dockyards at Blackwall and as a lighthouse for the Port of London.

Custom duties payable on imports into Great Britain. Goods imported by the East India Company were usually subject to a different rate of duty to that of goods from other sources. The lists of goods imported by the East India Company ranged from almond paste to zedoaria (an aromatic substance made from the roots of East Indian plants used in perfumery, medicine and dyeing), and from amber beads to teak wood. The officers and petty officers of the East India Company's ships, in addition to their monthly salary, received valuable privileges. On outward voyages an allocation of freight space for their private trade in certain commodities was granted, varying between 20 ft. for a Commander to 10 ft. for a sailmaker; different amounts of space were allowed on homeward-bound vessels. Other privileges allowed to the Commander included the right to import a limited amount of wine and to fill the spaces in the hold around the cargo with packing material, consisting of woods, such as bamboos or rattans,

and which could be sold on arrival in the Thames. The Commander also received the fares of all passengers but he had to provide provisions etc. for these passengers during the voyage. There were fixed schedules of charges for official passengers on outward voyages and when returning from India. Officers of the British Army and of the East India Company paid according to their rank. For instance colonels of the East India Company paid £200, majors £150 and writers £100, on the outward voyage. For British Army officers the charges were slightly lower. Private passengers and the wives and families of officials had to arrange the charge with the commander, the price to some extent depending on the accommodation they required. An extra charge was made to passengers who wished to have their meals together with the commander.

In the case of a successful round voyage these privileges made it possible for a shrewd commander to make a profit of many thousands of pounds.

BLACKWALL FRIGATES

After 1833, when the East India Company ceased trading activities, with the increased efficiency of the steamship (the first regular Transatlantic steamship service was established in 1838, and a steamship service from the Red Sea to India in 1840), it became evident that the old standardized design previously insisted on by the East India Company for the ships they chartered was no longer good enough and that large sailing-ships, intended for the transport of passengers and freight, would have to be designed to sail much faster to compete with the growing threat of the steamships.

An early vessel of an improved design, of the type which was later to be known as the "Blackwall Frigate", was the *Seringapatam* of 818 tons built in 1837, at the Blackwall Yard of Green and Wigram. This vessel with a length of 148,6 ft. and a beam of 35,6 ft. was of much the same length to breadth proportions as the last of the East Indiamen, but was designed with finer lines and was without the very large poop which on the whole was characteristic

of an Indiaman of the same size, and consequently had only a single tier of quarter and stern windows. The shipbuilders and owners, Green and Wigram launched, between 1837 and the end of 1841, eight further vessels of the new type, ranging in size from the *Madagascar* of just over 800 tons to the *Southampton* of nearly 1,000 tons. In 1842, with the launch from the same yard of the *Prince of Wales* of 1,200 tons the new design was first extended to the largest ships. The *Prince of Wales* was 179,4 ft. long and 39,7 ft. wide showing a definite advance in length to breadth ratio, to about 4,3 to 1 compared with the 4 to 1 proportions of the last East Indiamen. The *Prince of Wales* had the long flush deck which was to become the distinctive mark of the "Blackwall Frigates" and indeed closely resembled in appearance a 50-gun frigate of the period.

In 1843, the partnership between Green and Wigram, the shipbuilders who did so much towards the development of the Blackwall Frigate, was dissolved and the yard divided into two separate

In this delicate painting by Holman can be seen a stretch of the River Thames, near Blackwall docks, busy with nineteenth-century sailing-boats. The ships seen on the stocks still have very rounded hulls and huge flat sterns, differing only slightly from those of preceding centuries.

portions, one operated by M. Wigram and Sons and the other by R. and H. Green. Each firm continued to build and operate large and well-designed vessels.

In 1844, R. and H. Green launched the *Monarch* of 1,400 tons. This vessel was 180 ft. long with a beam of 40 ft. thus increasing the length to breadth proportion of the hull to 4,5 to 1. An account of the launch of the *Monarch* in a contemporary journal states that most of the timbers and planking of the vessel were of teak. On the main deck there was accommodation for passengers in twelve cabins averaging 11 ft. by 10 ft. in size, a dining saloon 36 ft. by 18 ft. and the crew's quarters forward. On the lower deck there were two cabins each 18 ft. by 16 ft. at the stern with windows, and sixteen smaller cabins. The forepart of the lower deck was suitable for accommodation of troops.

Vessels of the Blackwall Frigate type continued to be built on the Thames and also in the north of England at Sunderland and on the River Tyne.

These northern-built vessels are also classified as Blackwall Frigates and in fact some of them were owned by London shipping companies. Two particularly successful vessels, the *Marlborough* and the *Blenheim* were built in 1846 and 1848 respectively, at T. and W. Smith's yard on the Tyne. These two vessels were considered to be the finest vessels in the British Mercantile Marine and won awards at the Great Exhibition of 1851, in London. The *Marlborough* of 1,402 tons, was 175,5 ft. long and 41,5 ft. wide, the *Blenheim* of 1,314 tons only slightly smaller. Both vessels had completely flush decks and were without a raised poop or deck-house at the stern.

Although the Blackwall Frigates, when compared with the Clipper ships which followed them, were built with heavy frames and timbers and had relatively full bow lines, they were much faster than the earlier East Indiamen. The *Seringapatam* was able to reach Bombay from England in eighty-five days. The *Minden* built at Sunderland in 1848, made a passage to Calcutta in a mere total of ninety days. In the 1840's, the best Blackwall Frigates usually made one voyage a year from London to Calcutta. In addition to these "crack" ships, many smaller vessels were also engaged in carrying passengers and freight to India, and many notices advertising the departures appeared in the newspapers of the day. A typical example from the London *Times* of July 9th, 1845, reads as follows: "For Ceylon and Madras, to sail 25th July, having room for passengers and light freight only, the fine frigate-built ship *Hindostan*, A1., 708 tons register, John Bowen Commander, lying in the London Dock. Has a full poop with elegant accommodation for passengers and will carry an experienced surgeon."

Prior to 1844, except for a few Blackwall Frigates, the sailing-ships carrying emigrants to Australia were mostly old and small. Conditions on board were so bad that in 1844, a Report was made to a Parliamentary Committee. After this conditions improved somewhat, but the following advertisement from the *Times* of October 5th, 1850 perhaps provides a rather exaggerated description of the benefits of travelling on this particular ship, but also hints that unscrupulous shippers were still operating: EMIGRATION ON THE NEW PRINCIPLE, carrying one class of passengers only. For Port Adelaide, Port Philip, and Sydney, the fine British-built ship *Anglia*, classed A1. at Lloyds, 570 tons register and 750 tons burden, Charles Gardner, Commander; lying in the East India Docks, and will sail on the 18th of October, calling at Plymouth. This fine ship (having made her last passage in 90 days) has a full poop, with seven feet height in her 'tween decks, and carries neither chief cabin nor steerage passengers, but is fitted with enclosed cabins throughout for passengers of one class only, who have the full range of the ship, and are taken at the uniform rate of £21 per adult, including provisions of the best description, medical attendance, bedding, etc. An experienced surgeon proceeds in the ship. For particulars and dietary scale etc., apply to Hall Brothers, 2, Riches-court, Limestreet; T. B. Mallet, 4, Castle Court, Burchin Lane; or to Hotchkin and Mobbs, 3, East India Chambers, Leadenhall Street, London. N.B. Intending passengers will please compare our dietary scale and accommodation with those of other parties

professing to give as good for £15, and are particularly requested to ascertain the real tonnage of ships before engaging their passages; some being advertised for journeys to the Australian colonies at twice the weight of their register tonnage".

The discovery of gold in Australia in 1850, soon led to a very large increase in the number of people wishing to go to that country and created a demand for fast passenger ships. From 1852 onwards, ships of the Blackwall Frigate type were built especially for the passenger trade to Australia and many of the existing ships were transferred from the India route. The old-established firms of R. and H. Green, M. Wigram and Duncan Dunbar all took an active part in the prosperous Australian passenger trade. Typical examples of vessels built specially for the Australian run were the *Kent* of 927 tons and the *Dunbar* of 1,321 tons, both launched in 1852. The *Kent*, built and owned by M. Wigram of Blackwall, was 186 ft. long with a beam of 33 ft. This vessel made — for a ship of her class — several very fast passages to and from Australia and on occasions was able to beat some of the well-known clipper ships.

The underwater lines of some of the "frigate-built" ships of the 1850's were comparable to those of the "medium" clippers of the period, and it is interesting to see that Messrs. M. Wigram and Sons in an advertisement in the *Times* for April 14th, 1855, describe the *Kent* as "the splendid new clipper ship" and state that the vessel "has performed three of the fastest voyages on record". The *Dunbar*, built at Laing's yard at Sunderland, was 202 ft. long and 35 ft. wide with a poop deck 85 ft. long. This vessel was wrecked in 1857. Other Blackwall Frigates built by M. Wigram and Sons, on the Thames, and employed by that firm, for a regular packet service to Australia were the *Devonshire* and *Cornwall* built in 1848 and 1849 respectively, the *Hampshire* and *Sussex* built in 1852 and 1853 and the *Suffolk* and *Norfolk* built in 1857. Even in the very minute part of mid 19th-century shipbuilding represented by this series of vessels built by Wigram, a progressive increase is apparent in size, and in length to breadth proportions. The *Devonshire* was 156,5 ft. long with a beam of 32,5 ft., the *Sussex* was 174,1 ft. in length and 32 ft. in breadth while the *Norfolk* was 222,5 ft. long with a beam of only 32,7 ft. All these Blackwall Frigates were built of wood and were sheathed with felt and yellow metal (the felt was placed under the thin sheets of yellow metal and was usually applied in conjunction with a coat of tar). With the advent of sailing-ships of the more extreme clipper design, the Blackwall Frigates were generally outclassed for the fast passenger and freight trade. However, many fine wooden "frigate-built" ships continued to be built at yards at Blackwall, Sunderland and on the Tyne. These very strongly built and roomy vessels were frequently used as troopships and for freight, when the speed of delivery of goods or trans-ference of soldiers was not considered essential. In 1866, the firm of R. and H. Green built their first iron sailing-ship the *Superb* at Blackwall, and the iron sailing-ship *Melbourne* was completed in 1875. These vessels were constructed of iron, but they had the long poop and high bulwarks of the frigate-built ship. They also had dummy quarter-galleries at the stern, which were, however, merely planted on the vessel's side, and did not project from the hull as with older wooden ships. *Melbourne* is held to be one of the finest iron passenger ships built, and was probably the last of the famous Blackwall Frigates.

BALTIMORE CLIPPERS

Some of the schooners built on the eastern sea-board of the United States of America, particularly in the Chesapeake Bay area, during the early years of the 19th century, were then among the fastest vessels in the world. Consequently during the war between the United States and Britain, 1812-15, these schooners were in great demand as privateers (see page 195) and blockade-runners, and later were much used by slavers. At the end of the 18th century schooners of this type were generally known as "Virginia-built" vessels, by 1812 as "Baltimore-built" and somewhat later the vessels achieved the title "Baltimore Clippers". The word clipper — a slang term for "a thing excellent of its kind" — which seems to have been applied to fast horses and then particularly to these American schooners, became even more famous later in the 19th century when it was adopted as the usually-phrased name for the very fast sailing square-rigged ships.

The design of these fast American schooners was not a sudden local development, but as with most other advances in naval architecture, was the result of a gradual progress. It would seem most probable that the design of the Baltimore Clippers originated in vessels from the West Indies which, from the beginning of the 18th century, traded between the West Indies and ports on the east coast of America. These vessels were first known as Jamaica sloops but in the latter half of the 18th century were known as Bermuda sloops. The Bermuda sloop was usually about 60 ft. in length and built with a slanting stem and stern-post, a deep heel aft and a somewhat "V" underwater transverse form. The single raking mast carried a gaff mainsail, a square topsail and top-gallant sail, and three fore-and-aft sails forward of the mast. Later in the 18th century, larger Bermuda vessels of similar hull design were fitted out with two masts and were schooner-rigged.

The hull form of the earlier fast American-built schooners was akin to that of the Bermuda sloop. They had the same raking stem and stern-post deep keel aft and the same "rising floors" giving a "V" shaped underwater section. It is possible that this design also owed something to that of the fast sailing French three-masted lugger — *"chasse marée"* — a number of which were employed in American waters during the Revolution.

A typical Baltimore-built privateer schooner of the 1812 war was about 90 ft. long on the deck, with a beam of about 24 ft. Strongly constructed of the finest materials available, usually white oak and pine, the hull, in addition to the features already described, had sharp lines and a long run aft. The long flush deck was kept as clear of fittings as possible, to give maximum working space for the gun crews. A raised forecastle and quarter-deck were not fitted. The armament often consisted of ten to fourteen 6-pndr. guns and sometimes included one long

This whale-fishing scene, by Louis the Breton, a sailor-artist who died in 1866, is set down with rare accuracy and observation. An American whaler is heaving to in British waters, under the watchful eyes of the Royal Navy, while her boats make the most of a quarry so close inshore.

24-pndr. gun — a "Long Tom" — mounted amidships between the masts so that it could be trained as required. One large and three or four smaller hatches, all fitted with gratings, were spaced along the centre-line of the deck, and a large capstan was fitted abaft the mainmast. The two tall raking masts each carried fore-and-aft gaff sails, and on the foremast a square topsail and topgallant sail were also hoisted. A fore-staysail and jibs were extended between the foremast, bowsprit and long jib-boom. In some ships protection for the very large crew — about 120 men for a privateer of the size and armament described — was provided by continuous high bulwarks running the length of the ship from bow to stern.

These privateer schooners were commanded by resolute and skilful seamen and continually harried the British merchant shipping, avoiding action with warships by using their fast sailing qualities. A British newspaper of the period, writing on the menace of the American privateers, comments : "They daily enter in among our convoys, seize prizes in sight of those that should afford protection, and if pursued ' put on their sea-wings ' and laugh at the clumsy English pursuers." The British Navy assembled their fastest frigates and sloops-of-war to use against the commerce raiders and occasionally they were able to capture even the fastest privateers. For instance the famous large privateer schooner

Prince de Neuchâtel made several successful cruises, and in October, 1814 beat off an attack by the boats of the British frigate *Endymion*, which had been sent against her during a calm. However two months later the vessel was captured by fast British frigates after a chase in wind conditions which did little to favour the privateer.

After the end of the Napoleonic and American-British wars a new and terrible employment was found for the American schooners. By 1820 the principal governments of the world had agreed to suppress the slave-trade and patrolling warships were operating off the coasts of Africa and the West Indies. The seizure of slave-ships was usually made in accordance with the various treaties which gave to naval powers the right to search vessels for slaves, of capturing and confiscating vessels engaged in the illegal trade, and punishing those taking part. In these circumstances the large vessels formerly employed for carrying slaves were no longer suitable as they were usually too slow to escape the pursuing naval forces. The Baltimore-built schooner was still one of the fastest vessels afloat and was therefore very suitable for the slave-trade. For some years after the end of hostilities the ordinary privateer schooners were used for transporting slaves, and were so successful that during the period between about 1820 to 1850, schooners were specially designed and built for the slave-trade. Most of these schooners were between 70 and 100 ft. in length and being lightly armed, often with one centrally-mounted carronade, did not require the very large crew of the relatively heavily-armed privateer schooner. For one of the larger slavers of about 200 tons a crew of about 50 men was usual.

The main burden of suppressing the slave-trade fell upon the British Navy, and to overcome the problem of catching the fast sailing slavers, newly armed brigs and schooners were designed and built with some of the hull design features of the Baltimore Clippers, older vessels were altered to make them faster and captured slavers were re-armed and taken into the service of the Royal Navy. The influence of the Baltimore Clipper design was apparent in some of the naval vessels and when Captain (later Sir) William Symonds was appointed Surveyor of the British Navy in 1832, he gave much attention to the problems of improving the hull design of warships to attain greater speed. The vessels designed by Symonds had increased beam at the water-line and steep floors, giving them an even more pronounced "V" underwater section than the Baltimore Clippers. The sloops and brigs designed by Symonds and engaged in the suppression of the slave-trade were undoubtedly much faster than their predecessors — as indeed were the larger warships designed by Symonds — but they all had a tendency to heavy pitching and rolling and were therefore unstable gun-platforms in some wind conditions.

Some of the more spectacular successes of the British Navy against the slavers include the capture in 1829 of the *Josepha* and *Midas*, with 207 and 400 slaves respectively, by the 75 ton schooner *Monkey*, armed with only one 12-pndr. gun. In 1834 the large Spanish slaver *Formidable* carrying 707 slaves, was captured after a nine hour chase by H.M. Brigantine *Buzzard*, 10 guns. In 1837, H.M. Sloop *Snake* of 16 guns captured the *Arrogante* with 406 slaves aboard and the *Matilda* with 529 slaves. These examples are only isolated instances of the excellent work done by the navies of Britain, the United States of America and other nations over a period of about forty years, but they do indicate the large numbers of slaves packed into the small holds of the slaver brigs and schooners.

The design of the Baltimore Clippers, which had produced such successful vessels for the specialised work undertaken by privateers and slavers, was not very suitable for normal trading ships because of the very limited cargo capacity inherent in the design. From about 1850, with the suppression of the slave-trade, the more extreme Baltimore Clipper type of schooner was replaced by fore-and-aft vessels designed with less sharp lines and more rounded sections. However the successful design of the Baltimore Clipper for fast sailing-vessels affected the design of later sailing-vessels. Pilot schooners, Newfoundland fishing schooners and the schooners employed in the fruit trade from the Mediterranean to Britain, a trade in which speed was essential, all show something of the Baltimore Clipper design. Even more important it was basically from the long, fine lines of the Baltimore Clipper that the famous ship-rigged American clipper came to be developed.

ABLE SEAMAN

Such scenes of life aboard as this engraving, made at sea on a sperm whale's "tooth" by an unknown crew member, provide us with valuable records. The sailor, a sail-maker's palm on his hand, is mending the peak of a jib, while a swell obscures the hull of a passing ship.

The location and date of the origin of whaling — that is the hunting and killing of whales to obtain the valuable fat and oil etc., from their carcasses — is unknown, but it perhaps commenced in the prehistoric era with the taking of whales which had been stranded on or near the shore.

In the 9th century A.D., whaling was undertaken from the coasts of Norway and by the 12th century the Basques, particularly from the port of Bayonne, had established regular whaling in the Bay of Biscay. Whaling continued in this area and in more distant waters for the next three hundred years and the Basques became so expert at handling the boats and harpoons, that later when the Dutch and English commenced whaling voyages they employed Basque harpooners. At about the end of the 16th century the Dutch began to send whaling vessels to Spitzbergen and at the same time at Hull, in England, vessels were first fitted out for whaling off Iceland. In 1610, the English Muscovy Company, which had been founded in 1554 for trading from London to Russia, financed a whaling voyage by two small vessels to East Greenland, the first of a series of similar voyages. In 1613, the Muscovy Company obtained a royal charter from King James I of England granting them the sole right to the Greenland whaling grounds with the power to exclude all other ships, English and foreign. This attempt to monopolize the Greenland whaling grounds was the cause of great friction with the Dutch until the Muscovy Company gave up whaling. The Dutch had the greatest number of whalers operating off Greenland and by about 1640, their whaling fleet is said to have consisted of more than three hundred vessels. In the 18th century the British whaling trade fluctuated greatly. In 1725, the South Seas Company sent twelve whalers to Davis Bay. In 1733, the British Government offered a bounty of twenty shillings a ton to encourage the whaling industry, the bounties were increased in 1740, and by 1749 amounted to forty shillings a ton. From this date the British Arctic whaling fleet grew steadily, and by the end of the century, some two hundred whalers were in use. In the year of 1788, the first British whaler set sail for the Pacific Ocean, and a while later whalers of other nations were to follow the now-established route. In America, whaling started from the New England coast during the colonial period, with more distant whaling grounds coming into use throughout the 18th century. At New Bedford, perhaps the most famous of the American whaling ports, the industry started about 1760. After the end of the American-British war in 1815, the American whaling trade employed more and more whalers until in 1846 the record number of seven hundred and thirty-six vessels was reached. In 1857, New Bedford's whaling fleet of over three hundred vessels landed more than one hundred and seventy-five thousand barrels of whale-oil and over a million and a quarter pounds of whalebone. This was a most impressive amount!

The illustration on page 201 shows a typical American whaler of the middle of the 19th century. The whalers of this period were designed with somewhat less beam and finer underwater lines than vessels intended for the merchant service generally. A number of whalers built in the vicinity of New Bedford in the 1850's were built with raking stems and even sharper lines than the usual whalers. The hull design of these vessels had much in common with that of the clippers. In general it can be said that the American whaler had sailing qualities which were disguised by the heavy appearance of the hull above the water, which was emphasized by the deck-houses and the whale-boats carried on strong wooden davits and on skids above the deck.

These American whalers were built of wood, copper sheathed below the water-line and were either ship or barque-rigged. About seven whale-boats were usually carried on each whaler, some slung from wooden davits, ready to be lowered into the water when whales were sighted, and spare boats upside down on thwartship skids. It was in these lightly-built, thirty foot long, double-ended whale-boats that the actual pursuit and harpooning of the whale was accomplished. The dead whales were towed back to the whaler, where they were cut up. To make this operation easier a portion of the starboard bulwarks, amidships, was removed and a "cutting" stage rigged outboard. Men standing on this stage cut the strips of blubber from the carcass laying in the water alongside the ship. These strips of blubber were hoisted inboard by a strong tackle with very large blocks hung under the maintop. On board, the oil was extracted from the blubber — a

"Hey! What's going on, Cookie? You feed me before your blasted pig. It can have what's left over. You and your mate do well enough out of us men." Between watches, sails trimmed and wind fair, this sailor takes it easy, making the most of a welcome respite.

205

process known as "trying-out" — in the "try-works", a brick oven with large iron vats, situated on deck abaft the foremast.

The whaling grounds, areas in which the various kinds of whales were found, included the North and South Atlantic, the North and South Pacific and the Indian Ocean. The duration of whaling voyages varied from about six months to four years. The whaleman spent much of his spare time during the long voyage in carving ornamental and useful objects from sperm whale teeth, scraps of whalebone and tropical woods. These carved and engraved objects were known as "scrimshaw".

In most cases the designs on "scrimshaw" were the original creation of the whaleman but more sophisticated work was formed by pasting pictures from magazines onto whale ivory or bone and then pricking through the pattern. The paper picture was then removed and the lines of tiny holes accentuated by engraving and filling in with black ink. Engraved sperm-whale teeth, typical examples of "scrimshaw" are illustrated on pages 204 and 205. Besides purely decorative objects "scrimshaw" included articles such as "jagging-wheels" for making designs on pastry, "busks" for the fronts of corsets, cigar holders, canes, rolling-pins and paper knives.

THE EARLY CLIPPER SHIPS

The natural desire to build fast sailing-ships, which had already produced the Baltimore Clippers and the Symondite vessels, was later reinforced by the large profits made possible through the high freight rates which could be obtained by transporting specialized cargoes in the fastest possible manner. The trade in opium from India to China, a dangerous undertaking akin to smuggling, required sailing-ships capable of making fast passages to China in all seasons. The trade in tea from China to Europe and America was particularly remunerative, the earliest consignments each season fetched very high prices and importers were prepared to pay high rates of freightage for the first cargoes home. The discovery of gold in California in 1848 and in Australia two years later also brought about an immediate demand for fast ships to carry men and mining equipment as speedily as possible to these remote places.

The non-technical name "clipper" is a generical term and does not define a particular class of ship. The precise design and performance qualities which entitled a vessel to be called a clipper is still a matter of controversy, but the ability to sail at a very fast speed was a constant factor in the identification. Capacity, running expenses and to some extent durability and the comfort and safety of passengers and crew was of secondary importance in the extreme clipper ship which was designed, built, rigged and sailed

for speed, to carry cargoes or passengers from port to port with a minimum of delay and inconvenience.

To summarise briefly, some of the principal features of clipper ship design were : an increased length to breadth ratio, finely tapered bow and stern, rising floors and large sail area. Whether one of the early clippers fell into the category of "sharp", "extreme clipper", "clipper" or "half-clipper" was largely governed by the extent to which these features were incorporated into the design. A clear division between these three classes is not possible, but only a small proportion of the clippers can be classified as the "sharp" or extreme type.

Although the claim to the title of "the first clipper ship to be built" has been applied to both American and British vessels, it is not really possible to particularise to any individual ship, as the design was the result of a gradual process of finely shaping the hull and incorporating successful features from other proven designs. Indeed, when writing on the design of vessels, the eminent American naval historian Howard I. Chapelle states that ". . . the clipper ship introduced no one feature that was entirely new". This opinion is generally accepted.

The *Ann McKim* of 493 tons, with a length of 143 ft. and a breadth of 31 ft. built at Baltimore in 1832, has often been quoted as "the first clipper ship built", but the vessel was actually an enlarged ship-rigged version of the Baltimore Schooner design. Another claimant to the title of "first clipper ship" was the *Rainbow* of 750 tons, built at New York in 1845. The *Rainbow* was, at that time, declared to be the fastest vessel in the world. Her career was brief; she was lost at sea with all hands in 1848.

In Britain attempts to design faster sailing-vessels were also meeting with success. James and William Hall, of the Aberdeen shipbuilding firm of Alexander Hall and Sons, conducted experiments with various scale hull forms in a water tank and in 1839 built a schooner, the *Scottish Maid*, which proved a very fast vessel and has been considered by some as the first clipper ship. The *Scottish Maid*, of 142 tons, was 92,4 ft. long, with a beam of 19,4 ft. and was designed with "a sharpening of the bow by carrying out the stem to the cutwater". This form of bow became known, and famous, as the "Aberdeen Bow". The *Scottish Maid* was employed on the Aberdeen-London service and is said to have frequently made the voyage in forty-nine hours. Other schooners were built to the same design and proved even more successful. The journal *Artizan* for November, 1843 notes: "A few weeks since one of the Leith clippers (which had been built in Aberdeen) performed the passage to the Nore in the astonishingly short period of 33 hours".

In addition to the Halls of Aberdeen, other British shipbuilders were also endeavouring to design fast sailing-vessels. The following advertisement from the *Times* of October 27th, 1840 shows that at least by that date the term "clipper-built" was applied to British-built square-rigged vessels: "For Lintin or Tonkoo ... under engagement to sail on 15th November, having two-thirds of her cargo already engaged, the handsome clipper-built barque *Grayhound*, A1. 2 years, 317 tons register, Henry Hutchinson, H.C.S. commander, who is well acquainted with the China Sea; lying in the West India Dock. Has good accommodation for passengers. The vessel was built expressly for the opium trade, and from her fast sailing qualities and being very well manned and armed, affords an excellent conveyance for specie". The *Grayhound* had been built at the Newcastle dockyards during 1838.

Despite the improvements in some British ships, there is no doubt that in the 1840's and early 1850's the American-built clipper ships were the fastest and most successful. After the discovery of gold in California it was usual for the American clippers to carry gold-seekers westward round the Horn to San Francisco, then to sail across the Pacific in ballast and load tea in China for New York and Boston. Following the repeal of the British Navigation Acts in 1849, making British ports open to the ships of all nations, the great demand for tea in Britain led to American clippers being used to bring tea to London. The first American tea clipper to unload her cargo of tea in the Thames dockyard in December, 1850, was the *Oriental* of 1,003 tons.

In the early 1850's, the demand for ships and particularly for fast ships, brought about a very large increase in shipbuilding in America (see illustrations on pages 209-210). At many places on the north-eastern seaboard of the United States, clipper ships were built which by their performances at sea won world-wide fame. For instance, William H. Webb built at New York in the period 1850-53, the clippers *Celestial*, 810 tons; *Challenge*, 2,006 tons; *Comet*, 1,836 tons; *Sword Fish*, 1,034 tons and *Young America*, 1,962 tons. At Boston the even more famous Donald McKay (see page 211) introduced machinery into his shipyard, including a steam-driven tilting saw capable of cutting the bevels on frames and a lathe for making treenails — wooden pins used for fastening planks to frames and beams. With this machinery cutting down the building time, McKay built in the five years from 1850 such successful and renowned clippers as *Stag Hound*, 1,534 tons; *Flying Cloud*, 1,728 tons; *Flying Fish*, 1,505 tons; *Sovereign of the Seas*, 2,421 tons; *Great Republic*, 4,555 tons; *Lightning*, 1,468 tons; *James Baines*, 2,275 tons; *Champion of the Seas*, 1,947 tons and *Donald McKay*, 2,408 tons.

These American clippers were built almost entirely of wood. They were fastened with treenails, and iron and copper bolts, and were completely sheathed with copper plates below the water-line. Some of the larger ships were strengthened with internal diagonal wood trusses and with iron straps and knees. Some vessels had iron knees fitted later in their service. Perhaps the most celebrated clipper ship launched from the New York yard of William H. Webb was the *Challenge*, and a full description of this vessel is given in the insert to this chapter. The *Comet* and the *Young America* were also particularly fine clippers. Both the vessels were designed with a full midship section with only slightly rising floors, but of course had long sharp bows with concave waterlines and a long run aft. The *Comet* built in 1851 for the California and China trades was 229 ft. long with a beam of 24,8 ft., and on her maiden voyage from New York reached San Francisco in a hundred and three days. Other fast passages by this clipper included San Francisco to New York in seventy-seven days, New York to Liverpool in nineteen days, Liverpool to Hong Kong in eighty-four days and Canton to New York in ninety-nine days. The *Young America* built in 1853 was employed in the California and Australia trade. This clipper was 236,5 ft. long and had an extreme breadth of 42 ft. The *Young America* made consistently fast voyages from San Francisco to New York and reached Melbourne from Liverpool in only eighty-one days.

Most of the fine clippers built at Boston by Donald McKay achieved great notoriety and have been the subject of much writing, so it is proposed, in this chapter, to deal with a few examples only. The largest clipper — and also at that time the largest merchant-ship in the world — built by McKay was the *Great Republic* launched in October, 1853. This vessel was designed for a registered tonnage of 4,555 on a length of 335 ft., a beam of 53 ft. and a depth of 38 ft. Because of the great length of the hull, extra constructional strength was introduced in the form of a lattice-work of crossed diagonal iron straps. Four decks were fitted, the uppermost being a spar deck with an open wood rail. Unlike the other clippers which were three-masted and ship-rigged the *Great Republic* had four masts and was rigged as a barque with square sails on the fore, main and mizzen-masts, and fore-and-aft sails only on the jigger-mast. This four-masted barque rig did not come into general use until some twenty years later. The masts and yards of this giant clipper were of course in proportion to the hull and therefore of great size. For the mainmast, the lower mast was 131 ft. long, the topmast 76 ft., the topgallant mast 28 ft., the royal mast 22 ft. and the skysail mast 19 ft. The main yard was 120 ft. in length and the foreyard 110 ft. long. The *Great Republic* thus

carried an enormous spread of sail and in order that the size of the crew needed to handle these large sails could be kept within reasonable limits the huge topsails were made in two parts, by fitting a type of double topsail invented some years earlier by Captain R. B. Forbes in which each of the topsails were divided into two, an upper and a lower topsail, of no great depth, each set on a separate yard. Another labour saving device was a 15 h.p. steam-engine fitted on deck to facilitate the manipulation of the sails and yards and to work the pumps.

Unfortunately the *Great Republic*, as built and rigged by McKay, was never tested. The completed vessel was towed from Boston to New York and when nearly ready to sail on her maiden voyage, caught fire and was very severely damaged. The wreck was sold and later practically rebuilt with three decks only and a reduced sail plan in which Forbes' double topsails were replaced by double topsails of a different pattern invented by Howe. As rebuilt, the tonnage of the *Great Republic* was reduced to 3,357 tons and her cargo capacity was nearly 2,000 tons less but she remained the largest vessel in the world and a very fast sailing-ship, her maiden voyage from New York to Liverpool being completed in nineteen days. During the Crimean War the *Great Republic* made large profits for her owners, under charter to the French Government as a troopship. Later the vessel was employed in the California trade and occasionally took cargoes of guano and grain to Liverpool. During the American Civil War the *Great Republic* was chartered by the United States Government. After being altered to a three mast rig she was sold in 1869 to a Liverpool firm and renamed *Denmark*, being finally abandoned at sea in a sinking condition in 1872.

In the early 1850's, the demand for fast passenger services from Britain to Australia and the reputation for speed already gained by the American clipper led to a large number of British firms ordering vessels from American shipbuilders.

In 1853-54, Donald McKay built four vessels at Boston for James Baines of Liverpool. These vessels, the *Lightning, Champion of the Seas, James Baines* and *Donald McKay* became part of the Black Ball Line, carrying emigrants from Liverpool to Melbourne, Adelaide and Sydney. The Black Ball Line, created by James Baines, had already become a leading firm in this trade and in 1854 were charging adults £16.16.od. for an "enclosed berth" on their ships for the passage from Liverpool to Melbourne. Those who had doubts of their ability to make their fortunes in the gold-fields of Australia could obtain return tickets at half-fares "allowing 60 days in the colony". In 1852-53, the Black Ball clipper *Marco Polo* — which had been built in 1850 at St. John's, New Brunswick and purchased by James Baines — under the command of the notorious Captain J. N. Forbes, broke all previous records by making two voyages from Liverpool to Melbourne and back in the period of eleven months, twenty-one days, one of the passages to Melbourne being completed in sixty-eight days. The *Marco Polo*, of 1,625 register tons, was 185 ft. long, with a beam of 38 ft., and a depth in hold of 30 ft. Although the lines of a vessel built at New Brunswick in 1850 would have been much less extreme than those of the later American clippers a contemporary description of the vessel states : "Her lines fore and aft are beautifully fine, her bearings are brought well down to the bilge; thus, whilst she makes amidships a displacement that will prevent

In the age of Louis XIV, it was said that a whole forest had to be felled in order to build one vessel. When this daguerreotype was taken in 1855, this still held true. In Donald McKay's shipyard in East Boston, all this wood must dry in the open air before the hulk to the right becomes a fine three-master like that on the left. In this yard, thirty-two sailers, including the Flying Cloud *and* Great Republic *were built.*

unnecessary 'careening' she has an entrance as sharp as a steamboat and a run as clean as can be conceived. Below the draught line her bows are hollow; but above she swells out handsomely." It would seem from the vessel's performance at sea that this description of the design was not as exaggerated as it would appear to be.

The first and most celebrated of the quartette built for the Black Ball Line by McKay was the *Lightning*. This clipper was 244 ft. long, had a beam of 44 ft., a depth of 23 ft. and was 1,468 tons register. The design of the hull was extreme and the *Lightning* is said to have had more "hollow" at her bows, than any other clipper, but as there are no extant contemporary draughts or models of so many of the clippers, claims of this sort cannot be substantiated. The *Lightning*, constructed with white oak knees and pine decks, had two decks, a large midship house with six state-rooms, a poop and an extensive fore-castle for the crew. Between decks there was head room of eight feet and the four large state-rooms were well furnished. According to the advertisement for the first voyage to Australia "the cabin accommodations are unequalled, and supplied with beds, bedding and every other requisite, including stewards atten-dance and a stewardess for the ladies".

On her maiden voyage from Boston to Liverpool the *Lightning* made a day's run of 436 miles and her first passage from Liverpool to Melbourne was made in seventy-seven days. On her homeward voyage with a time of sixty-four days, three hours and ten minutes, the *Lightning* set up a record which was to remain unbroken by other sailing-vessels. The *Lightning* continued on the Australian emigrant ser-vice until 1857, when together with other clippers, she was used to carry troops to India to suppress the Mutiny. After this Government service the vessel was returned to the Australian trade and in 1869 was burnt and sunk at Victoria, Australia.

There was keen competition between the various shipping firms to obtain prospective emigrants as passengers and various inducements were offered in the advertisements of the day. The *Lightning* de-scribed as "the fastest ship in the world" carried "a full band of music", and "bullion safes and will be armed". The Temperance Line of Liverpool, in 1854, with their clippers *Australia* and *California* not-

ed that "a minister and an experienced surgeon will accompany the vessel. Baths and wash-houses will be erected on deck and a library of 300 volumes will be supplied for the gratuitious use of the pas-sengers". This firm which then charged £25. 5. od. for the voyage to Australia, published a testimonial from 200 passengers on the *California* which reads : "The voyage to Australia, has been effected in per-fect health and happiness without the use of alcoholic drinks (except for medicinal purposes) and attribut-ing to these wise regulations in a considerable degree the harmony and good feeling preserved throughout our rapid and prosperous voyage."

The competition provided by the American ships which were bought or chartered by British firms spurred the efforts of the British shipbuilders to produce fast clippers. These efforts were encouraged in 1854 by alterations in the British laws relating to tonnage measurement. Alexander Hall and Sons of Aberdeen, who had already achieved fame with their fast schooners, built, in 1850, the small clipper *Stornoway*. The following year this vessel made the outward voyage to China via India, but returned from Whampoa to London in a hundred and four days. The *Stornoway*, of 595 register tons, was 157,8 ft. long, with a beam of 25,8 ft. The *Chrysolite* launched by the Halls in 1851, was of very similar dimensions to the *Stornoway* and also proved a fast sailing-vessel, continuing in the China trade for nearly fifteen years. In 1852, the Thames firm of R. & H. Green, renowned for their fine Blackwall frigates, built a clipper, the *Challenger*. In 1856, the *Challenger* made an outward passage to China in the relatively short period of a hundred and one days.

By the middle 1850's, clipper ships were being built at many more places in the British Isles. Ship-builders on the Clyde, at Sunderland and Liverpool and indeed at many smaller places, were launching finely designed vessels for the China and Australia services. The firm of Robert Steel and Co., at Greenock on the Clyde, in the period 1855 to 1859, built the clippers *Kate Carnie*, 576 tons, *Ellen Rodger*, 585 tons and *Falcon*, 794 tons, all excellent ships. It was probably partly from the experience gained from building these small clippers that Robert Steel and Co. were later able to produce such master-pieces as the *Taeping*, *Ariel* and *Sir Lancelot*. The

Crest of the Wave, Spray of the Ocean and Spirit of the Age were built between 1853 and 1854, the first two by William Pile at Sunderland and the other by his brother John at West Hartlepool. The fastest of these three clippers seems to have been the Spirit of the Age. In 1856 this barque-rigged vessel made the voyage from Whampoa to London in a hundred and one days. Another successful clipper, the Fiery Cross, was designed by William Rennie and built in 1855 by the Liverpool shipbuilders Rennie, Johnson and Rankin. This clipper was one of the faster vessels in the tea trade for some years, making several of her passages in under a hundred days. These few examples of mid-19th century British clippers have been quoted because they represent the type of vessel which, although usually

Wearing a top hat, back to camera, Donald McKay casts a critical eye over the launching of the Glory of the Seas, *the last of his clippers, in October, 1869. She sailed the seas until 1908 and, after serving as a fish cannery, was destroyed in 1923.*

Donald McKay (1810-1880) of East Boston built some of the finest clippers ever known in the nineteenth century.

smaller than the typical American-built clipper, competed successfully in the important and profitable Australia and China trades. The ships described are well-known vessels built by eminent shipbuilders, most of whom in the 1860's continued to build clipper ships with even greater success, while in America the financial depression of 1857 and the effect of the Civil War led to a serious decline in shipbuilding.

After describing the design, construction and sailing qualities of the early clipper ships, it is perhaps appropriate to mention something of the hard life of the seamen who manned the sailing-ships of the 1850's. The following extracts from the *New York Tribune*, published in the London *Times* on June 11th, 1857, provide a contemporary account of the treatment some American sailors received ashore and afloat : "In the latter part of April last the packet ship *Cultivator* arrived at this port of Liverpool. Her crew of 24 men, lame and stiff, covered with sores and bruises, presented a frightful appearance. Immediately on arrival they made complaint against the officers of the ship for cruel treatment on the voyage home. On this complaint the captain and the first and second mates of the ship were arrested, the third mate escaping over the ship's side into a boat when the United States Marshal came on board to make the arrests. After a brief examination of the prisoners, which has recently been concluded before the United States' Commissioners Court in this city, the complaint of the seamen was dismissed on the ground that there was not sufficient evidence to sustain it. We have no disposition to carp at the decision of the Court on this particular case. But in view of the remarkable fact that nearly every case of a like character which has ever come under our observation has been dismissed just as this was, we cannot help asking what is that 'sufficient evidence' which is necessary to establish a complaint of this kind ? ... We hear from every quarter of cruelties practised upon seamen on board American ships. The cases on board the *Guy Mannering* and the *James L. Bogart* which were recently investigated by the Liverpool courts and which were not dismissed, as similar cases have been dismissed here, by that subterfuge about 'sufficient evidence' but which were prosecuted to the just punishment of the offenders, are yet fresh in our memory. ... Nearly every ship from Liverpool that drops anchor in this port brings home a crew whose persons have been bruised, battered and mauled on the high seas. These cruelties have been inflicted either by the sailors themselves upon one another, or by the officers of the ship. ... It is true in nearly every one of the cases complained of — and in the case of the *Cultivator* there was ocular demonstration of the fact — that the complainants have been most inhumanly treated by somebody — a treatment which we cannot suppose they inflicted on themselves. They describe minutely the various methods in which they were tortured; how they were bayed by bulldogs, stunned by slung shot, battered with belaying pins, hammered with steel knuckles, maimed with pistol balls; how their naked bodies were scoured in salt water with coarse canvas until the skin was chafed away and the raw flesh appeared ; how their limbs were smeared with slush, their heads shaved and dressed with tar ; how every man in the forecastle was kicked and cuffed, racked and starved day after day on the voyage — by somebody. They show their scars and wounds yet bleeding, and they affirm unanimously that all these barbarities were perpetrated by the officers of the ship, with whom, as the crew of the *Cultivator* said, 'it was nothing but knock down and knock down and maul the whole voyage'. Yet strange to say, these half-murdered men obtain no redress at the law. Their complaint is dismissed for want of 'sufficient evidence' and they are carried back to their hospital, while their brutal bullies return to their ships to enact the same tragedies upon another crew, to be arrested on other complaints and to be again set free. For, in the judgement of our tribunals, there appears never to be any 'sufficient evidence' to convict masters and mates of our packet ships for the barbarities which they may happen to practise upon their men...". Despite the grim facts of this extract, which doubtless contained more than an element of authenticity, it must not be forgotten that strict discipline aboard ship was vital, and it was often necessary to deal harshly with a violent, unruly crew. The *Guy Mannering* mentioned in the above report, was a well known Atlantic packet ship, of 1,419 tons, built by W. H. Webb at New York in 1849. Claims have been made that the *Guy Mannering* made "land to land" Atlantic passages in less than ten days.

THE COMPOSITE CLIPPERS

All the clipper ships so far described were built of wood, although in some cases internal iron knees and strengthening straps were used. Iron-hulled ships were first built in the early years of the 19th century, and the material was gradually used more and more for steamships for it enabled the weight of the hull to be reduced by about a third. For sailing-ships, however, wood remained the most favoured material. For vessels intended for long ocean voyages in tropical waters there was no method of effectively protecting the iron underwater hull from the marine growth which so adversely affected the speed of the vessel. The clippers intended for such voyages, built of wood, were normally protected by copper sheathing — or from about 1840 by sheathing with plates of "yellow metal", an alloy of copper and zinc. These forms of sheathing would remain clear for as long as ten years. It was not practicable to sheath an iron vessel with copper or "yellow metal" owing to the corrosive galvanic action set up between the iron and copper when in contact with salt water.

The difficulties of obtaining suitable hardwood and the obvious constructional advantages of iron ships in due course brought about a form of construction known as composite building, in which all the interior framework of a ship — that is the frames, deck-beams etc. — were of iron, but the external planking was of wood which could be sheathed below the water-line with copper or "yellow metal."

The first composite-built vessel is said to have been a steamship *Assam*, built in India in 1839. Between that date and 1860 there were more than thirty applications to the British Patent Office for patents relating to the use of iron combined with wood in the hulls of ships. The earliest patent, that of William Watson of Dublin, dated the 12th June, 1839, describes "an improvement in the construction of ships" in which the ribs (traverse frames) were formed of iron angle or "T-iron" bars bent into suitable shapes. The skin or outer casing of the vessel was to be of timber planks which were fastened to the ribs by means of rivets or screw bolts and nuts. Other early applicants for the patents relating to

composite ship construction were: in 1841, Thomas Ditchburn, a shipbuilder of Blackwall; in 1844, James Kennedy and Thomas Vernon, shipbuilders of Liverpool; in 1845, Otis Tufts of Boston, Massachusetts, U.S.A., and also in 1845, James Boydell, an Ironmaster of Dudley in Worcestershire.

During this period it would seem probable that composite-built ships incorporating some of these designs were built, but details are not available.

In November, 1849, John Jordan of Liverpool applied for a patent for a more advanced composite system which included, among other improvements, an iron plate running the whole length of the vessel, with a wood keel fastened to its underside. The iron keel plate was continued up the bow and stern to support the wood stem and stern-post. Bolted to the iron keel plate were iron transverse frames "adapted to a covering of wood for the sides, bilges and bottom, and combining with the frames a timber stem, a timber keel and a timber stern-post. Iron plates were used to strengthen the wood deck beams".

The evolution of the composite-built ship is well illustrated by three vessels, incorporating the principles laid down by John Jordan, which were built by the Liverpool shipbuilders Henry Jordan and John Getty. The first, launched in July, 1850, was the *Excelsior*, a small schooner 50 ft. long and of only 33 tons. The second, launched in January, 1851, was a three-masted, barque-rigged vessel, the *Marion Macintyre*, 115 ft. long and of 283 tons. The third, the *Tubal Cain*, also launched in 1851, was a ship-rigged vessel of 788 tons, with two decks and a length of 155,2 ft. The builders of these vessels later made further proposals for composite construction. In 1855 John Getty suggested "the employment of copper bolts for holding the planks in place, the main object being to avoid all contact between the iron and the copper bolts, and consequently to prevent a destructive galvanic action being set up between the two metals". Henry Jordan, in 1858 and 1860, proposed improvements to the construction of the hull which included "an internal transverse framing formed of inverted T-shaped iron". During this period

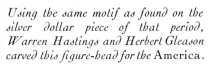

Using the same motif as found on the silver dollar piece of that period, *Warren Hastings* and *Herbert Gleason* carved this figure-head for the America.

Ornamenting the prow of the Lancaster, this eagle in full flight by *John Bellamy* (1836-1914) is carved with such care that each feather stands out in relief.

Apart from mythical subjects, ship's figure-heads also portrayed famous past or contemporary people. The bows of the Salomon Piper were, apparently, graced by carved renderings of her owner's image.

Florence Nightingale's selfless devotion to duty during the Crimean War (1853) made a deep impression on everyone, and her effigy proudly adorned the prow of at least one ship sailing the world's oceans.

other improvements in the method of composite building were introduced, and more ships were constructed in this manner, including the clipper *Red Riding Hood* built by Thomas Bilbe in 1857, for the China tea trade. Bilbe had taken out a patent in August, 1856 for a composite system employing a form of compound frames. These frames were made by bending two angle irons to the correct mould, placing them a suitable distance apart from each other and then filling the space between the projecting edges of the angle irons with wood.

The composite form of construction, however, did not really come to the fore until the 1860's when it was employed for famous sailing-vessels, among others the *Taeping*, *Wild Deer*, *Ariel*, *Sir Lancelot*, *Titania*, *Sobraon*, *Lahloo*, *Thermopylae*, *Cutty Sark*, *Norman Court* and *The Caliph*.

In 1861, Lloyds Register Committee granted a higher classification for composite ships and the firm of Alex. Stephen & Sons, Glasgow, began a new era of composite building with the clipper *John Lidgett*, launched in 1862. Robert Steele and Co. of Greenock on the Clyde continued this series of celebrated clippers in 1863, when they built their first composite ship, the *Taeping* of 767 tons. This vessel was 183,7 ft. long with a beam of 31,1 ft. and could load over a million pounds of tea. In 1866, the *Taeping* reached London from Foochow in the Strait of Formosa, in ninety-nine days.

In 1864, the Committee of Lloyds Register of Shipping recommended suggestions to be adopted when building composite ships, if these vessels were intended for classification in the Register Book. Four years later the Committee published suggested Rules for the Construction of Composite Ships. These Rules — prepared by B. Waymouth, a Lloyds Surveyor and naval architect, who designed several famous composite clippers including the *Thermopylae* — attempted to standardize existing methods of composite construction and were widely adopted. Most of the composite ships built after 1868 were constructed in accordance with the principles laid down in the Rules. The drawings for the Rules — produced by another Lloyds Surveyor, H. Cornish, were exhibited at Paris and Moscow and awarded bronze and gold medals — show constructional features for a vessel with two decks, of 800 tons and

measuring 193 ft. long with a beam of 32,5 ft. The drawings include sketches of alternative methods of constructing the iron keelson and show "box", "intercostal" and "vertical centre plate" forms. Views of the midship sections of the proposed vessel include details of the iron transverse frames of "Z" form, and show longitudinal braces of crossed diagonal iron plates, straps fitted in pairs and extending between the iron sheer strake, just below the upper deck, and the bilge plates. Iron deck beams, pillars and deck stringers are also depicted.

The *Ariel* and *Sir Lancelot*, both launched in 1865, were perhaps the most beautiful clipper ships built by Robert Steele and Co. The *Ariel*, of 886 tons, had a length of 195 ft., a beam of 33,9 ft. and a depth in hold of 21 ft. The *Sir Lancelot* was of almost similar dimensions; in fact, except for some differences in the arrangement of the deck fittings, the vessels were sister ships. Both vessels were constructed with iron frames, planked with teak and elm, their hulls being sheathed with "yellow metal", and the lower masts were of iron.

Two of Steele's composite clippers, the *Taeping* and *Ariel*, together with the *Serica* (built of wood by the same firm in 1863) and the *Fiery Cross* (the second clipper of that name, designed by William Rennie and built of wood by Chaloner, Hart and Co., at Liverpool in 1860), were concerned in one of the most famous incidents of the China Tea trade — "The Great Tea Clipper Race of 1866". On the 30th May of that year these four vessels left Foochow, loaded with tea, within a few hours of each other. With a bonus waiting in London for the first ship to arrive, there was naturally keen rivalry between the captains who made every effort to get the utmost speed from their ships. For the first part of the voyage the *Fiery Cross* led, with *Ariel* and *Taeping* close behind and the *Serica* further away. At St. Helena the *Taeping* was the leader, with the *Fiery Cross*, *Serica* and *Ariel* following in that order. At the Cape Verde Islands the *Ariel* was foremost, a position she still occupied when the English Channel was reached. However, the *Taeping* was then in sight and the two clippers sailed up the Channel together. Finally both ships docked at London on the evening of the 7th September with the *Serica* arriving later the same night, and the *Fiery Cross* the next day.

The special prize of £100 and the premium of 10/- a ton of tea were then consequently divided between the *Ariel* and *Taeping*, as joint winners.

Of the four vessels which took part in this race, only the *Fiery Cross* had a long life, finally sinking in the Medway in 1889. The *Serica* was wrecked near Montevideo in 1872; the *Taeping* was lost in the China Seas in 1871 and the *Ariel* disappeared on a voyage from London to Sydney in 1872.

The shipbuilders Alexander Hall and Sons of Aberdeen, already famous for producing well-designed and fast ships, also built a number of composite clippers. The *Sobraon*, of 2,131 tons, built by this firm and launched in November, 1866, was constructed with teak planking, copper-fastened to iron frames and beams. With a length of 317 ft. overall, a beam of 40 ft. and a depth in hold of 27 ft., the *Sobraon* was the largest composite vessel to be built. Rigged as a ship, the *Sobraon* had iron lower masts with double topsails and later in her career was also fitted with double topgallant sails. The vessel was first owned by Lowther, Maxton and Co., but was chartered to the well-known firm Devitt and Moore, who eventually purchased the vessel in 1870. For twenty-five years the *Sobraon* was employed as one of Devitt and Moore's regular Australian packets, sailing each year to Sydney or Melbourne. In 1891, the *Sobraon* was sold to the New South Wales Government for £12,500 and was converted to a Reformatory ship. In 1911, the Australian Government bought the vessel for use as a training-ship for boys entering the Royal Australian Navy and renamed her *H.M.A.S. Tingara*. When the vessel was at last broken up at Sydney in 1941, the iron beams and frames and the teak planking were found to be in good condition — a tribute to the shipwrights employed by Alexander Hall and Sons when the vessel was built seventy-four years earlier.

The *Sobraon* was designed with particularly commodious passenger accommodation. The first-class saloon was two hundred feet in length and the second-class cabins were on the same deck. The first-class fare to Australia was about £60, and in 1867 the second-class fare was £35, with room for a few "intermediates" at £21 each. Rather more than a hundred passengers were carried on the outward passage with somewhat fewer on the return voyage,

when a large cargo of wool or wheat was stowed in the hold. Her crew usually numbered about seventy, and it is to their great credit that in her whole sea-going career the *Sobraon* only suffered minor damage from the forces of wind and water. The passengers were well provided with food as livestock was carried on each voyage, and she had an icebox with a capacity of ten tons of ice. The *Sobraon* was also fitted with a condensing plant to provide fresh water from salt water. Her outward passages usually took about seventy-five days, but the fastest voyage to Sydney was seventy-three days and to Melbourne sixty-eight days. Homeward passages took longer as the *Sobraon* always returned via the Cape of Good Hope, calling at Capetown and St. Helena.

Further alterations and improvements in the methods of constructing the hulls of composite-built vessels were introduced in the 1860's, and more than forty-five specifications for patents relating to this type of shipbuilding were published between 1860 and 1866. A number of these patents related to methods of protecting the copper fastenings of the hull from corrosion where they passed through iron frames, beams or plates.

From about 1863, the angle iron transverse frames of a composite vessel were usually strengthened by a reverse frame which was also formed of angle iron, the two together thus forming a very strong member of "Z" form. The reverse frames extended from the floors up to the lower and main decks alternatively. Towards the end of the decade a typical composite vessel, of about 1,000 tons would have had a rock elm keel about 16 inches square, with a teak stem and stern-post of about the same dimensions. The keelson of box-frame construction was formed from 9/16 inch thick iron plates and the transverse frames constructed from 3 3/4 inch x 4 1/2 inch x 9/16 inch angle iron, with reverse frames of slightly smaller section. The deck beams would have been made from 9 inch x 6 3/4 x 9/16 inch bulbed T-iron. Externally the bottom planking would be rock elm and the remainder teak. This planking would have been fastened to the frames with copper or "yellow metal" screw bolts and nuts, suitably protected from corrosion by contact with the iron frames. Copper or "yellow metal" sheathing, applied in plates about 4 ft. x 14 inches in size, over a layer of tar and paper, completely covered the underwater body of the vessel. The lower deck would probably have been laid in yellow pine planks 3 inches thick and the upper or main deck and quarter-deck composed of teak planking 3 1/2 inches thick. The bowsprit and fore and main lower masts would have been made of iron, while the mizzen lower mast, all the topmasts and all the topgallant masts would be of pine. The lower yards would be of steel and the remainder of the spars pine. Much of the rigging would have been composed of iron wire.

Scaffolding as of a cathedral surrounds the future glory of the fine wooden sailing-ship to be, when her masts are stepped and rigged. With scarcely any other tools than the adze, shipwrights practically carved out their ships. Donald McKay was the first to use power tools, installing mechanical saws and turning lathes in his Boston shipyards.

The interior of this capital sailing-ship's hull under construction in the Newington shipyards is not unlike a ball-room. On the frames to the left can be seen huge wooden treenails, not yet fully wedged. The shoring timbers are placed in temporary supporting positions on both sides.

THERMOPYLAE AND CUTTY SARK

The last two years of the 1860's saw the construction of two composite clippers which have always created great interest and about which more has perhaps been written than any other ships of the type. The *Thermopylae* was designed by Bernard Waymouth, a successful naval architect, built at Aberdeen by Walter Hood and launched in August, 1868. The vessel was 212 ft. long, with a beam of 36 ft. and a depth of 20,9 ft. and was designed with a raking stem and rounded fore-foot. A deep false keel gave more grip on the water and assisted the ship when sailing to windward. *Thermopylae* was painted green with white lower masts and yards. The sail plan was particularly notable in that the emphasis was on width rather than height and the main yard was 80 ft. long. The *Thermopylae* was built for the Aberdeen White Star Line and on her maiden voyage reached Melbourne in 63 days from Gravesend. Proceeding to Shanghai the *Thermopylae*, after loading with tea, returned to London in 91 days. While in the tea trade, this vessel usually made the outward passage to Australia with a cargo of manufactured goods and raw materials, returning to London, via Shanghai or Foochow, with tea. The *Thermopylae* remained in the tea trade until 1881 and during this period the average time taken on the outward passage was 69 days, while the homeward voyage averaged just over 101 days. In 1882, the Aberdeen White Star Line, which still owned the vessel, put her into the Australian wool trade, where her best time from London to Sydney was 75 days in 1887. In 1890, she was sold to a Canadian firm and was employed bringing rice from Rangoon to Vancouver. Five years later the *Thermopylae* was sold to the Portuguese Navy, converted to a training-ship and renamed *Pedro Nunnes*, finally being made a target for torpedo practice and sunk by the Tagus Estuary in October, 1907.

Always intended as a rival to the *Thermopylae*, the *Cutty Sark* — a vessel which is mentioned whenever clippers are discussed — was designed by the then almost unknown naval architect, Hercules Linton and built at the Dumbarton yard of Scott and Linton.

This firm went bankrupt before the *Cutty Sark* was finished and the vessel was completed by another Dumbarton firm, Denny Bros. In the *Cutty Sark* Hercules Linton succeeded in designing a clipper which incorporated the best features of other successful vessels. The bows were extremely sharp, but a full midship section with square bilges, a fine underwater body at the stern with a pronounced counter and an almost right angle fore-foot gave the *Cutty Sark* not only great speed through the water — she is said to have sailed at 17 1/2 knots on one occasion, and made a day's run of 363 miles — but excellent qualities when sailing to windward and buoyancy at the stern in a following sea. The *Cutty Sark*, with a length of 212,5 ft., a beam of 36 ft. and a depth of hold of 21 ft., was six inches longer than the *Thermopylae* but her tonnage was 963 gross compared with 991 tons for the latter. The length of both these vessels was 5,9 times their beam compared to the 5,5 to 1 length to beam proportion of the American clippers of the 1850's, and 4,3 to 1 for some of the earlier Blackwall frigates. The *Cutty Sark* had two complete decks extending the whole length of the vessel, a raised quarter-deck thirty-seven feet long and a forecastle twenty-eight feet long. A deck-house between the fore and main-masts accommodated the crew and galley and another abaft the mainmast was used by the apprentices. The *Cutty Sark* was planked with rock elm to the level of the upper deck beams and above that with teak. The iron structure was of malleable iron capable of bearing a longitudinal stress of twenty tons per square inch. She was ship-rigged, heavily sparred and carried a very large spread of canvas, and it has been stated that, at the time she was built, there was no ocean-going vessel afloat, steam or sail, which could keep up with her in good, strong, steady wind. The *Cutty Sark*'s first voyage from London to Shanghai, made during a period of light winds, took 104 days. In 1872, the *Cutty Sark* and the *Thermopylae* left Shanghai on the same day, and the prospect of a race between the rival vessels aroused great interest. The *Cutty Sark* carried 1,303,000 pounds of tea and the *Thermopylae* 1,196,460 pounds, both at a freight of £3. 10. 0d. per ton. At the beginning of the voyage the *Cutty Sark* took the lead, but when 28 days from Shanghai, the vessels passed Anjer, in the Sunda Strait, the *Thermopylae* was about a mile and a half ahead. Strong winds then favoured the *Cutty Sark*, enabling her to obtain a lead of some four hundred miles. Unfortunately, during a gale the *Cutty Sark* lost her rudder and although a jury rudder was made and fitted, the *Cutty Sark* arrived at London a week after the *Thermopylae*, which had completed the voyage without mishap in 115 days.

The *Cutty Sark* became an Australian wool clipper in 1880, and while in this trade made some of her fastest passages. In 1887-1888, she made the record time of 71 days from Sydney to London. In the same season the *Thermopylae* completed the passage in 79 days. Between 1888 and 1895, all the *Cutty Sark's* Australian passages, both outward and homeward, were accomplished in less than a hundred days. In 1895, the *Cutty Sark* was bought by the Portuguese, and renamed *Ferreira*. In 1916, after being dismasted, she was re-rigged as a three-masted barquentine. In 1922, the *Cutty Sark* was bought by Captain Dowman, reconditioned and restored to her clipper rig. She remained at Falmouth until 1938, when she was presented to the Thames Nautical Training College and towed round to the Thames. In 1953, the vessel was taken over by the *Cutty Sark* Preservation Society, and on the 10th December, 1954, she was moved into a specially constructed dry-dock at Greenwich where, as the only surviving example of a tea clipper, the *Cutty Sark* is today preserved as a national monument.

The composite-built ship was not a definite stage in the development from wood to iron ships but a side step which at that time was particularly suitable for the conditions of the China tea trade. Although first produced in 1839 it was not until the 1860's that the composite ship became really popular, with a gradual decline until the type of construction was discontinued for ocean going vessels at the end of the 1870's. Composite construction was expensive and required a technique of its own, but at its height it produced strong vessels well able to stand the strain of hard sailing, which were much lighter than a wood-built vessel of the same dimensions.

One of the last large composite sailing-vessels to be built was the *Torrens* which was launched in 1875 from James Laing's yard at Sunderland. This vessel was designed specially for the passenger trade to Australia and was managed by the Elder Line. The *Torrens*, of 1,276 tons, was 222,1 ft. long, with a beam of 38,1 ft. and a depth in hold of 21,5 ft. Although designed without the extreme lines of the China clipper, she was a beautifully proportioned ship and a fine sea-boat. The vessel was rigged with a main lower mast 67 ft. long, from the deck to the cap, a main topmast 52 ft. long, a main topgallant, royal and skysail mast which together was 60 ft. in length. The main lower yard was 90 ft. long, the spanker boom 50 ft. and the spanker gaff 36 ft. long. Stunsail booms were provided for the lower, topsail and topgallant yards on the fore and mainmasts. The *Torrens* cost £27,257 when complete and ready for sea.

Until 1890, the *Torrens* was commanded by Captain Henry Angel, a part owner of the vessel, and the first fifteen annual round voyages to Adelaide, in Australia, and back to London were accomplished without serious mishap. Captain Angel exploited to the full the remarkable ability of the *Torrens* to run before the seas without shipping water and to sail at a relatively fast speed in light winds. During the next thirteen years the *Torrens* continued most successfully in the Australian trade, although in 1890, she lost her foremast, main topmast, topgallant mast and mizzen topgallant mast and had to put into Pernambuco for repairs. In 1899 she was damaged when she ran into an iceberg.

Joseph Conrad, the well-known author, served as second mate on the *Torrens* from November, 1891 for nearly two years and described the vessel as "a ship of brilliant qualities". Conrad prepared many notes for his later works while serving in the *Torrens* and made the acquaintanceship of another famous writer, John Galsworthy when the latter was a passenger aboard the ship. The *Torrens* was not an emigrant ship and normally did not carry more than about 90 passengers in very comfortable quarters. Her fastest passage from Plymouth to Adelaide was 65 days in 1880-81, and her best day's run 336 miles. In 1903 the *Torrens* was sold to an Italian shipping company which continued to operate for a few years, however, in 1910, she was eventually broken up.

THE LARGE AMERICAN SCHOONERS

The schooner rig almost certainly originated in Holland in the late 16th or early 17th century and probably evolved from the Dutch *jacht*, a small two-masted craft used on the inland waters of that country. Although small two-masted fore-and-aft rigged vessels were employed by the English early in the 18th century, the schooner is essentially American in its later development, and when the rig became common in the British Isles and the Baltic, it was from the American schooners that their design was copied. The fore-and-aft rig was particularly suitable for coasting work under variable winds, and after about 1800 a very large proportion of the ships employed along the Atlantic seaboard of North America and in the West Indies were schooners. Until about the middle of the 19th century, the American schooners — apart, of course, from the Baltimore Clipper type employed in specialized trades — were usually under a hundred feet in length, of rather bluff form with full bow lines and rigged with two masts. In addition to the fore-and-aft sails some schooners carried square sails on the foremast.

About 1850, due to the increased number of steam vessels employed in the American coasting trade, a change occurred in the type of cargo available to the schooners, and brought about the need for larger schooners more suitable for the economic conveyance of bulk cargoes, such as grain, lumber, coal, cotton, bricks, etc. The three-masted fore-and-aft rig used for these larger schooners had first appeared towards the end of the 18th century and had been used occasionally during the first half of the 19th century.

In the 1850's, the hull design of these three-masted schooners was influenced by the form of the American square-rigged clipper ships which at that time were being built in large numbers, and many of the schooners were given sharp bows and rising floors. This type of vessel was gradually replaced by schooners with a fuller hull form and therefore greater cargo capacity. A typical example of these vessels during the later years of the 19th century would have been of about 600 tons, with a length of about 150 ft. and a beam of about 34 ft. These schooners were often designed for specific localities and trades, some with deep hulls and keels, others of shallow draught with one or more centre-boards. The comparatively low cost of building a schooner, with easily obtained timber — oak, chestnut and pine, and the low operating costs with small crews and no fuel requirements, enabed these sailing-vessels to compete in certain coastal trades with steam and motor vessels. The schooners were successful and profitable as coasters, and a very great number were built and employed on the Great Lakes and the Atlantic and Pacific seaboards of North America over a period of nearly a hundred years. The *Frank A. Morey*, built in 1917 at Rockland, Maine, is an example of one of the later three-masted schooners. This vessel, of 574 tons, with a length of 163 ft. and a beam of 35,4 ft., was employed in varied trades, including carrying timber to Cuba and sugar back to the United States. The *Frank A. Morey* was lost in 1941 after striking a reef in the Bahamas. The last of the commercial types of the three-masted schooners were built in the third decade of the 20th century.

It had become apparent in the 1870's that even larger schooners could be profitably employed and four-masted schooners were introduced. It is said that the first four-masted coasting schooner was the *William L. White*, of 995 tons, built in 1880 by Goss, Sawyer and Packard at Bath, Maine. Very many of these four-masted schooners were built between 1880 and about 1920, some with a gross tonnage of more than 2,000 tons. The *Frank A. Palmer*, launched in 1897, also at Bath, Maine, was 275 ft. long with a beam of 43 ft. and of 2,105 gross tonnage. These schooners were usually well built and designed and were not so prone to accidents as

"No good before the wind", and a sad shake of the head was the old salts' reaction to five masts with no yards and only cross-trees for shrouds, rising up above this magnificent schooner Governor Ames. *But how much better she sailed to windward, and with fewer men!*

the five and six-masted schooners which were produced over almost the same period. The *Annie C. Ross*, a four-master built in 1917, was one of the last sailing-vessels to survive in the coasting trade and continued in service until the beginning of the Second World War, finally sinking at her moorings in 1955.

During the 1880's the size of American schooners was increased even further and the first five-masted schooner, the *David Dows*, was built in 1881 at Toledo on Lake Erie. This vessel, at that time the largest schooner in the world, was of 1,418 tons with a length of 265,4 ft. The *David Dows* was first rigged with square sails on the foremast but these were later discarded and the fore-and-aft sails only used. The *Governor Ames*, illustrated on page 222 was the first five-masted schooner built on the Atlantic coast. This vessel, of 1,778 tons with a length of 245,6 ft. and a beam of 49,6 ft., was built at Leavitt Storer's yard at Waldoboro, Maine, in 1888. Despite the fact that it was generally accepted that the fore-and-

For all its jumble of spars and ropes, new techniques enabled the three-masted ship Agenor *to be sailed more easily and by fewer men. Anchors seem to have changed shape but little since Roman times.*

In the course of its working life, a sailing-vessel was often rigged several times. Either the original rigging proved unsatisfactory or rough weather on long sea voyages severely damaged masts and yards.

aft rig was not suitable for long ocean voyages, large schooners were occasionally sent from American ports to China, Australia and West Africa. They also took part in the coffee and hide trades with South America and were used in the West Indies sugar trade. The *Governor Ames* was specially built for the overseas trades and the booms and gaffs of her five masts were somewhat shorter than those used on a four-masted schooner. The *Governor Ames* was fitted with a centre-board. On her maiden voyage she was dismasted and when rounding Cape Horn during a voyage to San Francisco suffered much damage. She was employed on the Pacific coast for a time, but returned to the east where she was later employed in the coastal coal trade of New England.

The last, and smallest, five-masted schooner, the *Edna Hoyt*, 1,512 tons, was built at Thomaston, Maine, in 1921. Her dimensions were: length 224 ft., beam 41,1 ft., depth 20,8 ft. For her first eight years, the *Edna Hoyt* was employed in the coal trade. From 1929 to 1936 she brought fertilizer from Venezuela to Boston and other east coast ports. After further voyages with coal cargoes, the vessel sailed in 1937 from Halifax, Nova Scotia, with a cargo of lumber for Belfast, Ireland, and after receiving severe damage during a storm put into Lisbon where she was condemned as unseaworthy.

The first six-masted schooner, the *Eleanor A. Percy*, 3,401 tons, was built in 1900 by Percy & Small at Bath, Maine. This vessel was 323 ft. long with a beam of 50 ft. She was employed principally in the coastwise coal trade, but foundered while making an ocean voyage, about 500 miles off the coast of Ireland in 1919. Later in 1900 the second and slightly smaller six-master, the *George W. Wells*, 2,970 tons, was built by R. L. Bean at Camden, Maine, and was also used in the coal trade. Other six-masters followed and in 1907, the *Wyoming*, 3,731 tons, was built by Percy & Small. This vessel, with a length of 330 ft. was the longest wood sailing-vessel ever built. The hull was strengthened with diagonal iron cross strapping and the planking was of six-inch thick pine. As with other large schooners, several steam winches were fitted on deck to assist a crew of eleven men to handle the sails. All the American schooners were built of wood, with the exception of the five-masted *Kineo*, 2,128

tons; the six-masted *William L. Douglas*, 3,708 tons; and the only seven-masted schooner ever built, the *Thomas W. Lawson*, 5,218 tons. These three vessels were built of steel. The *Kineo* with a length of 259,5 ft., was built by Arthur Sewall & Co., at Bath, Maine, in 1903, and intended for ocean trading. But a voyage from Norfolk, Virginia, to the Philippines, Australia, the Hawaiian Islands and back to the United States in 1905-1906 proved so disastrous with the loss of sails and spars, that the vessel was confined to the coastwise trade until she was sold in 1916, converted to a motor vessel and given the new name *Maryland*.

The *William L. Douglas* was built in 1903, by the Fore River Shipbuilding Co. at Quincy, Massachusetts. This vessel was 316 ft. long with a beam of 48 ft. and was not considered very satisfactory even for coastwise trade. In 1912, she was rebuilt as a bulk oil-tanker and renamed *Delaware Sun*. She was lost in a collision in 1917.

The *Thomas W. Lawson*, the only seven-master, was also built of steel by the Fore River Shipbuilding Co. The hull of the vessel, 395 ft. long and with a beam of 50 ft., was fitted with three steel decks throughout its length. To increase stability bilge-keels were fitted for a considerable length amidships. The seven masts were all of the same height, and each consisted of a steel lower mast 135 ft. long with an Oregon pine topmast 58 ft. long. All the work of hoisting and trimming the sails was done with steam-power. Two large winches were fitted, one under the forecastle and the other in the after deck-house, and to these were led the halyards, topping-lifts and sheets of the forward and after sails respectively. The lighter work of handling the topsails etc., was accomplished with the help of four hoisting winches fitted amidships. With this very complete mechanised equipment, this 5,000 ton vessel required a crew of only 16 men. After a number of coastwise voyages in the oil trade between Texas and Philadelphia, the *Thomas W. Lawson* was chartered in 1907 for a voyage across the Atlantic with case oil. She encountered bad weather in the Atlantic and later fell into serious difficulties when in amongst the Scilly Islands. She anchored in an endeavour to ride out the storm, but during the night of December 13th, 1907, however, she was to capsize.

THE DOWN EASTERS

The last large, wooden, square-rigged sailing-ships were built at Maine and Massachusetts — "down east" in the United States of America — during a period from about 1870 to 1895. These vessels, which became known from their building place as the Down Easters, were designed with moderately sharp lines, a pronounced sheer, large cargo capacity and a reasonable spar and sail plan. They represented the highest development of the American square-rigged ship and were capable of a good turn of speed, with an ease of handling which allowed a small crew and consequently low operating costs.

The trades of the Down Easters included lumber and coal cargoes carried between the American east and west coasts and in the Pacific Ocean, carrying grain from San Francisco to New York and Liverpool, sugar to Honolulu and the Chilean nitrate trade. Two vessels built after the end of the American Civil War by Donald McKay can perhaps be accepted as early Down Easters. These, vessels designed for the California grain trade, were the *Sovereign of the Seas* (the second ship of that name to be built by McKay) launched at East Boston in November, 1868, and the *Glory of the Seas* launched at the same place in October, 1869. The *Sovereign of the Seas*, 1,443 tons, was 199,5 ft. long with a beam of 41 ft., and the *Glory of the Seas*, 2,009 tons, had a length of 240,1 ft. and a beam of 44,5 ft. Both the ships were very strongly built of oak, the frames of the larger vessel were 11 in. square and fitted only 4 in. apart, with longitudinal side planking 6 in. thick on the outside and a ceiling of 4 in. thick planks on the inside of the frames. The *Sovereign of the Seas* did not possess very good sailing qualities and her average westward passages to San Francisco were not less than 150 days. The *Sovereign of the Seas* was eventually cut down to a towing-barge and finally sank off New York in 1902. The *Glory of the Seas* was designed with lines almost like those of a medium clipper and was a fast and successful cargo-carrier. On one occasion, in 1873-74, she made a voyage from New York to San Francisco in 96 days. The *Glory of the Seas* also made several fast voyages from

British ports to California. The earlier Down Easters were usually of under 1,600 tons, and the *Agenor*, shown on page 224, is a typical example of the Down Easter of the 1870's. She was of 1,487 tons, was 202 ft. long with a beam of 39,2 ft. The *Agenor* was built at the Curtis yard at East Boston in 1870, and in 1881 made a passage from Japan to San Francisco in 22 days. She also reached San Francisco from Callao, Peru, in 30 days. On the whole her crew consisted of only 18 men.

In the 1880's, larger and particularly successful vessels were built. Included among this group of Down Easters, all launched in the 1880's, were the *Charles E. Moody*, 2,003 tons; *S. P. Hitchcock*, 2,292 tons; *Henry B. Hyde*, 2,583 tons and the *A. G. Ropes*, 2,460 tons. The *S. P. Hitchcock*, illustrated on page 225, was built in 1883 by Isaac F. Chapman & Co. at Bath, Maine. The vessel was 274,4 ft. long with a beam of 44,3 ft. She was sheathed with "yellow metal" and fitted with three transverse bulkheads. On her maiden voyage, the *S. P. Hitchcock* sailed from New York on the 22nd December, 1883, and arrived at San Francisco 104 days later. On another occasion she completed the same passage in 101 days, a remarkable feat for a ship with the full lines of a Down Easter and comparable with the performances of the clipper ships. The *S. P. Hitchcock* was lost at Hong Kong during a typhoon in 1906.

Considered by some to be "one of the very finest of all full-rigged ships sailing the Seven Seas at any time and under any flag", the Down Easter *Henry B. Hyde* was designed and built by John MacDonald at Bath, Maine, and launched in November, 1884. She was 267,9 ft. long with a beam of 45 ft. and a depth of 28,8 ft. Built with heavy white oak frames and hard pine planking, sheathed with "yellow metal" below the water-line, the *Henry B. Hyde* was strengthened with internal diagonal cross-bracing of iron. The vessel traded between San Francisco, New York and Liverpool, usually with grain cargoes. In 1886, the *Henry B. Hyde* reached Liverpool from San Francisco in 96 days, six hours, and returned to New York in 22 days. Other good passages included sailing from New York to San Francisco once in 105 days and twice in 108 days. Later the *Henry B. Hyde* sailed with cargoes of coal from the American east-coast ports to San Francisco, Honolulu and South Africa. On two occasions she had to put into port with her coal cargo on fire. In 1904, the *Henry B. Hyde* was stranded on Damsbek Beach, Virginia, was refloated, but went ashore again and was abandoned as a total loss.

The *A. G. Ropes*, launched in 1884, was also designed by John McDonald but was built by Isaac F. Chapman & Co., at Bath, Maine, for their own service in the California trade, where she spent most of her career. The *A. G. Ropes* completed ten west-bound passages from New York round the Horn to San Francisco in the average time of 120 days, the fastest passage being 104 days and the slowest 138 days. The vessel was converted into a towing-barge after serving for twenty-two years.

Over a period of some 20 years, the Down Easters carried very much more cargo per registered ton than the American clippers of the 1850's, at an average speed, on long distance passages, which was very little less than that of the clippers. In their period the Down Easters made good profits for their owners but the competition of steel sailing-vessels and steam vessels — the tramp steamers — proved too strong for them and brought about their end.

The last Down Easter, and the last deep-sea, square-rigged, wooden vessel to be built anywhere in the world was the *Aryan*, of 2,124 tons, built by Minotts at Phippsburg near Bath, Maine, and launched in July, 1893. This vessel was lost by fire in the Pacific in December, 1918.

Although they really cannot be classified as Down Easters it is perhaps not inappropriate to deal at this point with four famous American sailing-vessels — the *Rappahannock, Shenandoah, Susquehanna* and *Roanoke*. These vessels, known as the "Big Wood Four", were built in 1889-92 by Arthur Sewall & Co., at Bath, Maine, in an attempt to provide wood sailing-vessels with large cargo capacity and low operating costs which could compete with the steel sailing-ships and the steam vessels of the period. However, the challenge of the steel ship was too strong and even the builders of the "Big Wood Four" had turned to steel construction by 1893. But

despite their limited reaches of success at that time, these were four fine wooden vessels with shapely lines. Perhaps the best-known among them was *Shenandoah*.

The *Rappahannock* was the first of the four wooden giants and was launched in January, 1890. This vessel, of 3,185 tons and 287,2 ft. long, with a beam of 48,9 ft., was the largest full-rigged three-masted ship ever built. The *Rappahannock* was not a success as she was too large for a three-masted rig, which was itself too large to be handled by a small crew. On her maiden voyage she carried 200,000 gallons of kerosene oil in cases from Philadelphia to Japan, returned to San Francisco and took on a cargo of grain for Liverpool. She left Liverpool on July 28th, 1891, with a cargo of coal for San Francisco, but fire broke out in the cargo hold after heavy weather off Cape Horn and the ship was abandoned and became a total loss.

The *Shenandoah*, 3,406 tons, launched in November, 1890, was given a four-masted ship rig and proved much more seaworthy than the *Rappahannock*. She served in the grain, lumber and coal trades, with passages of 111 days from New York to San Francisco and 116 days from Liverpool to San Francisco. In 1910, the *Shenandoah* was stripped of her masts and converted into a towing coal barge; in 1915 she was rammed and sunk near New York.

The *Susquehanna*, 2,744 tons, the smallest of the quartet, was launched in September, 1891. This vessel was also rigged as a four-masted ship and her passages included seven voyages from North Atlantic ports to San Francisco at an average of 129 days each. The *Susquehanna* was lost at sea in 1905. The *Roanoke*, the last and the largest of the "Big Wood Four", was also the largest wooden square-rigged sailing-vessel ever built. The *Roanoke*, 3,539 tons, launched in September, 1892, was 311,2 ft. long, with a beam of 49,2 ft. Like the other three ships of the "Big Wood Four", she was built with a frame and keel of white oak, hard pine planking and was copper-sheathed. Rigged as a four-masted ship this huge vessel was manned by a crew of only thirty men. (The *Great Republic* of 1853, when first rigged had a complement of more than 120 men.) The *Roanoke* was not a fast sailing-vessel but she carried a very large amount of cargo. She was destroyed by fire in an accident at Nehoue, New Caledonia, in 1905.

THE CHALLENGE · 1851

BY ROBERT H. BURGESS

The year 1851 saw the birth of two of the most famous American clipper ships and, of these, the *Flying Cloud* is probably the better known for her speed in sailing. At that time, she was also the largest merchant-ship afloat until another vessel, the *Challenge*, built that year, was launched. She was renowned as the largest and most expensive merchant-ship ever built. She also had the most extreme rig and the sharpest bow of any clipper afloat.

Built for N. L. and G. Griswold of New York, by W. H. Webb of the same city, the *Challenge* was launched on May 24th, in the presence of the largest number of people that ever attended such an event in America. "I have seen many launches, including that of the *Ohio*, but never have I witnessed such interest and excitement before, as attended this launch," wrote one of the spectators afterwards.

Her very appearance exemplified strength and speed. Of 2,006 registered tons, she measured 230 feet in length and was the first sailing-ship in America braced with iron. At her plimsoll line, her sides were 20 inches thick. Her backbone consisted of 11 feet of solid, built-up timbers from the bottom of her keel to the top of her keelson. She was the first American sailing-ship built with three decks.

Her mainmast was 30 inches in diameter and, with the topmasts and sky-sail poles, measured 230 feet from heel to truck. A complete suit of sails comprised 12,780 square yards of cotton canvas. Her graceful hull was painted black with a gold band that terminated at the bow with a figure-head of a gilded eagle.

Just as the *Challenge* was eye-catching from the exterior, inside she was equally finished in good taste. She had two cabin decks. Under the poop, the accommodation was fitted out for the ship's officers. This was also the entrance to the spacious cabin deck below where six state-rooms were

arranged. The oak and rosewood panelling was set off with arches and enamelled cornices, decorated with exquisite carving. Even the edges of the beams were carved and picked out in gold. And each state-room, as well, had its own ceiling light and port.

The main deck paintwork was white with blue waterways. Stanchions, hanging knees, ledges and lower squares of the beams were left in natural colour and varnished while the waterways of the lower deck were painted bluish-grey. This handsome ship was designed for trading between California and China but her appointments and passenger accommodation were as fine as could be found on any first-class European packet ship.

Great expectations were held for the *Challenge*. It was hoped that she would prove to be the fastest sailing-ship in the world. Her very name manifested her goal and, to help her achieve it, a famous commander, Captain Robert H. Waterman, a navigator who was known to have made the shortest passages on record from China, was put in command of this magnificent sailing-ship.

With a complement of 64 the *Challenge* set sail from New York on July 13th 1851, on her maiden voyage bound for San Francisco, California. It was reported that all but two of her crew were foreigners and few of them good seamen. With so many large ships requiring more men, and the California gold fields enticing others, there was a severe shortage of good sailors when the *Challenge* was ready to recruit the men she needed.

One source of information stated that only six of the crew were capable of manning the wheel. The shortcomings of the seamen and the necessary but persistent goading of the officers probably accounted for the mutiny which occurred when the *Challenge* was off Rio. In a letter to a friend in Boston, Captain Waterman told what

happened : "The truth is, when in the neighbourhood of Rio, about fifty of the crew fell on the mate with the intention of killing him and afterwards me, by their own confession. I was on the poop taking observations while the mate stood forward at the gallery. They stabbed him and had beaten him shockingly before I could get to him. I struck down three of them, rescued the mate and quelled the mutiny. I flogged eight of them. Off Cape Horn, three men fell from the mizzen topsail yard and were killed and after a few weeks, four more died of dysentery".

Shorthanded and with a largely incompetent crew, the *Challenge* finally arrived at her destination on October 20th, 108 days out, and delivered her $60,000 cargo in good order. But Captain Waterman failed to receive the $10,000 bonus promised him if he made the run in 90 days.

Captain Waterman, castigated for his harsh treatment of the crew, although it later transpired to be well warranted, was replaced by a Captain Land who made his first passage in the ship to Hong Kong in 54 days. From there the *Challenge* sailed back to San Francisco in 34 days, one day longer than the record standing at that time.

Her next outward passage again took her to Hong Kong where Captain Land died, to be replaced by a Mr. Pitts, former mate of the clipper *Witchcraft*. On August 5th, 1852, the *Challenge* left Whampoa with a cargo of tea for London and made the shortest passage of the season, 105 days to the South Downs surpassing the runs of the American clipper ships *Surprise*, *Nightingale*, *Race Horse* and the British clippers *Chrysolite*, *Stornoway* and *Challenger*. In England, the clipper was so admired that while she was in dock her lines were sketched for possible future use by the Admiralty.

Then the *Challenge* started for another voyage to China, taking the

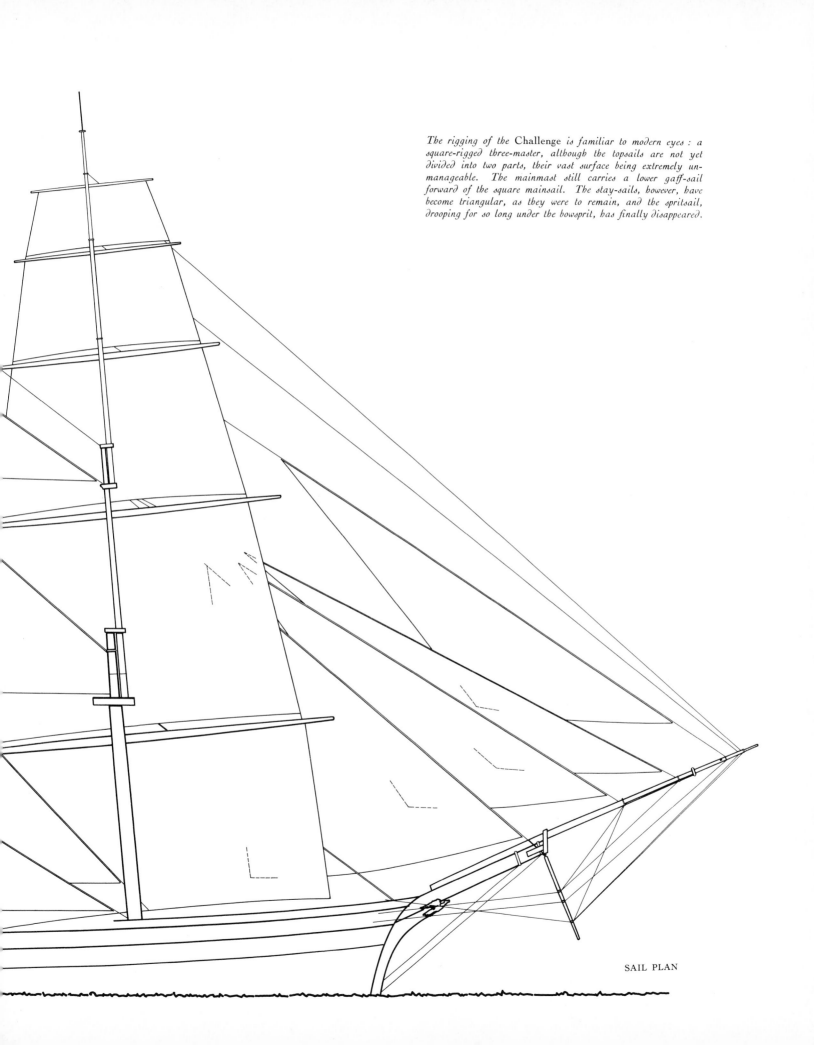

The rigging of the Challenge is familiar to modern eyes : a square-rigged three-master, although the topsails are not yet divided into two parts, their vast surface being extremely unmanageable. The mainmast still carries a lower gaff-sail forward of the square mainsail. The stay-sails, however, have become triangular, as they were to remain, and the spritsail, drooping for so long under the bowsprit, has finally disappeared.

SAIL PLAN

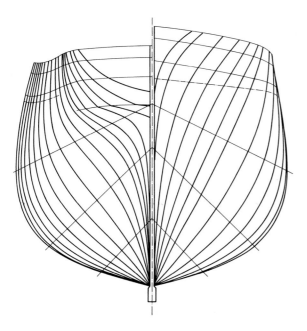

BODY PLAN

lead of all other clipper ships. Her return voyage, however, was less fortunate. Suddenly water entered the ship's hold, grave damage having occurred. In order to save the ship, the passengers had to assist the crew at the pumps. Eventually they reached Faial, one of the Azores' islands, where she left her damaged cargo and went on to New York.

Her next voyage took her to San Francisco, this time under the command of Captain J. Kenney. The *Challenge* reached her port of destination in 118 days, and after a short interval, she crossed the Pacific Ocean and sailed on to Shanghai, in 58 days.

Having returned to New York she set sail for Australia and China with 800 coolies on board. Then she left Swatow for Havanna with 900 coolies. This proved to be another unhappy voyage, not only a mutiny broke out and one man committed suicide, but the captain, 7 men of the crew and 150 coolies fell ill, the *Challenge* was thus forced to make quickly for the next port to get medical assistance. After finally reaching New York once more, she embarked cargo for San Francisco, and later made several crossings between San Francisco and China. On her last voyage under her original owners she lost her topmasts in a

The deeply curved water-lines of the Challenge *were not altogether successful. The thickness of the hull below the foremast, being carried so far back from the stem, created a bow wave which in itself limited the vessel's speed. This "challenger" therefore did not turn out to be a champion among clippers. Her most remarkable feature is the overhanging stern, which can be seen more clearly in the first illustration on page 234 than on the plans. This was the genesis of those excessively raked sterns which so caught the imagination of yacht designers at the end of the nineteenth and the beginning of the twentieth century. Another interesting feature is the very small stern "counter" which is now, of course, free of all ornamentation, the quarter-galleries previously used for officers' accommodation and the fragile windows of the past. This part of the stern follows the lines of a fishing-vessel, except for its sloping and slightly rounded shape, heralding the "Norwegian" stern or "double stem", and can be seen on the left section of the body plan above. The figurehead has now been mounted directly on the almost vertical stem.*

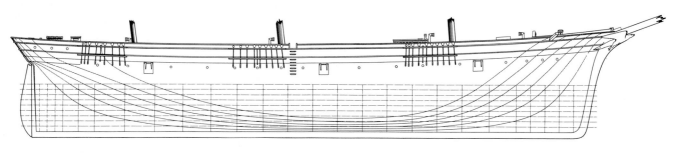

PROFILE AND HALF-BREADTH PLAN

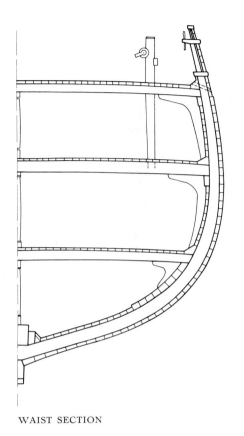

WAIST SECTION

Length :   23o ft.
Breadth :   43 ft.
Depth of hold : 25 ft.
Crew :   64 men

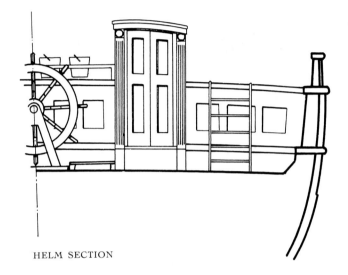

HELM SECTION

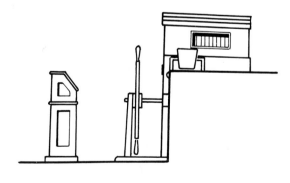

PROFILE OF THE HELM

severe storm, and completed the passage under jury rig. She was then laid up and finally sold for $9,35o.

During the latter part of 1861, the *Challenge* arrived at Bombay, leaking and in bad condition. She was sold, refitted and renamed *Golden City*. Hong Kong became her home port and she was employed for several years trading between China and India.

In 1866 she again changed ownership, this time to Wilson and Company of South Shields, England, who used her in the Java and Bombay trade. On a subsequent voyage to Java, in a gale off the Cape of Good Hope, a heavy sea broke over the quarter, sweeping seven men off the deck and killing all the officers except for the second mate who was to survive.

Some of the virtues that were responsible for the fame of the *Challenge* also helped to decide her fate. Her extreme sharpness is considered to have been the principal error in her design. When sailing under a press of sail this sharpness created a curling of the sea beneath her bow which tended to slow her down. Her lofty rig, reduced three times during her career, made her a dangerous ship to stay and this contributed to her demise when she lost her rudder and grounded off Ushant, on the French coast, in 1876. A French gunboat went to her aid but she hit a reef and broke up. Thus ended the career of the *Challenge*, an ill-starred vessel but one which can fairly be said to be characteristic of the medium clippers of her time.

I

These four illustrations of the Challenge, from the Peabody Museum in Salem, U.S.A., are rather on the formal side, providing merely broadside views of the famous clipper. The era of great marine painting has ceded to that of photography and it is, unfortunately, well nigh impossible to photograph a ship at the dramatic moments of her career. The sea, too, is scarcely photogenic, invariably appearing flat and lifeless. Below, the Challenge has most of her bonnets aloft, rigged to each side and making the square sails appear more or less rectangular. She also carries two large staysails, at variance with the sail plan. The square mainsail is partly clewed up, probably because it is being blanketed by the gaff-sail aft. In the background can be seen a composite steamer-sailer, paradoxically chugging before the wind.

THE IRON SAILING SHIPS

In the 1860's, steam vessels had not been able to compete successfully in the profitable China tea trade, because the enormous amount of coal they required for the long voyage, round the Cape of Good Hope, would have necessitated the provision of a large number of coaling stations on the route, at great expense and loss of time spent in coaling. When the Suez Canal was opened in 1869, the situation was radically changed. The voyage was shorter for steam vessels and only a limited number of coaling stations were required, while the route to the Orient via the Mediterranean and the Suez Canal was not suitable for sailing-ships. The effect of these changed conditions was soon apparent, and by 1880, despite great efforts by the sailing-ship owners, the tea clipper was no longer an economic proposition and these vessels were withdrawn from the tea trade. A number of the former tea clippers were employed

A four-masted barque passing close under full canvas has one mast rigged for fore-and-aft sails. She carries double topsails and topgallants and even staysails set, but her fore-royal is backing. Mute praise for the crew and terse commentary on the captain in the "Wick Gazette"!

in the Australian wool trade. On these Australian passages such famous clippers as the *Cutty Sark* and *Thermopylae*, even with reduced sail plans, were able to make record times and were faster than any of the normal wool clippers. In the case of the *Cutty Sark*, it was after her transfer to the Australian trade that she would earn her greatest reputation. An iron sailing-ship had been built as early as 1838, and in the years following, the number of sailing-vessels of this construction gradually increased. In the later years of the 1860's, iron clippers were built for the Australian trade at various places including the dockyards of Aberdeen, Glasgow and Liverpool. The 1870's saw the virtual end of wood and composite shipbuilding for large vessels except in America. Elsewhere, with the introduction of a

To the left, a three-masted wooden schooner ; behind, without topsails, a four-master in wood ; to the right, a square-rigged vessel on tow. Although playing a utilitarian role in its early days, steam power was not destined to remain the servant to sail, and soon became master.

reasonably efficient anti-fouling paint, the iron-hulled sailing-vessel became more and more numerous. The design of the iron clipper differed from that of the wood and composite vessels. With the extra strength but reduction in weight of iron construction, the vessels were built longer and narrower, with less freeboard. The earlier iron-built clippers had a length of about 6,3 times their beam and in the 1870's

and 1880's the proportion was increased to about 6,6. The increased length to breadth proportion in iron ships when compared with wood ships is evident in the *Salamis*, an iron ship built by Walter Hood & Co. at Aberdeen in 1875. The hull design of the *Salamis* was based on the lines prepared by the naval architect Bernard Waymouth for the famous *Thermopylae*, but while retaining the same beam — 36 ft. — as the

Alongside the huge steel hull of the Scottish Glens *in San Francisco harbour at the end of the last century, a small wooden schooner is employed as a lighter. Even today, these ships ply between islands and little ports, serving small communities with their mixed cargoes.*

237

Thermopylae, the length of the iron ship was increased by nearly 10 ft. to 221 ft., with a small increase in depth. These dimensions gave the *Salamis* a gross tonnage of 1,130 tons compared with the 991 tons of the *Thermopylae*. Owned by G. Thompson & Co., the *Salamis* formed part of their Aberdeen White Star Line and was employed in the Australian trade, particularly as a wool clipper. Carrying a cargo of some 5,500 bales of wool the *Salamis*, over many years, averaged 87 days for her passages from Melbourne to London, and her outward passages to Australia, carrying general cargoes and coal, averaged 77 days, an average time unequalled by other iron sailing-ships. In 1899 the *Salamis* was sold to a Norwegian firm and used for the South American guano trade. In May, 1905 the ship was wrecked on Maldon Island in the South Pacific.

The iron four-masted ship-rigged vessels *Reliance* and *Pegasus*, sister ships built by W. H. Potter & Sons at Liverpool in 1884, are more extreme examples of long, narrow iron ships. The *Reliance* was 313,7 ft. long and the *Pegasus* 314 ft., but both vessels had a breadth of only 42.3 ft., and built with a raised bridge deck, 58 ft. long, amidships. This type of midship construction, which seems to have been first used in sailing-ships built by W. H. Potter & Sons, became a common feature in the later steel sailing-ships. The *Pegasus* was broken up in 1912 but the *Reliance* remained in service until 1924. The use of iron for construction also brought about an increase in the size of vessels. Until 1870, only a few sailing-ships over 1,000 tons were built, but after that date the size increased rapidly to as much as 2,000 tons. A comparison between the iron clipper ship *Cedric the Saxon* built in 1874 and the *Loch Torridon* built seven years later well illustrates this increase in size. The *Cedric the Saxon*, said to have been the most beautiful iron clipper ever launched, was built by John Ried & Co., at Port Glasgow. Her dimensions were: length 260,2 ft., breadth 40,7 ft., depth in hold 23,5 ft. and 1,626 gross tonnage. Built for the Australian trade, the vessel was provided with excellent cabin accommodation and was rigged as a ship. The *Loch Torridon* built by

This view from the poop of the Preussen *illustrates the bewildering complexity of her standing and running rigging. However, winches, seen here, were used to work the braces of several yards at the same time, always keeping the yard-arms level athwartships and holding them fast.*

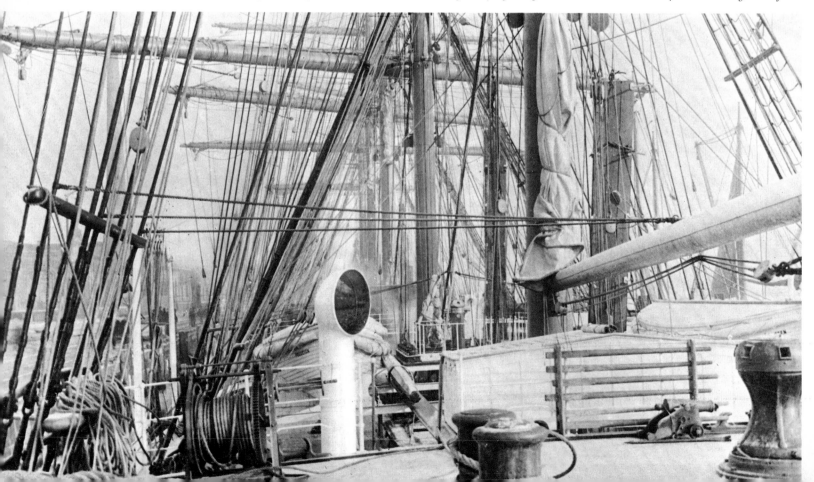

Barclay, Curle & Co., at Glasgow was 287,4 ft. long, with a beam of 42,6 ft., a depth of 24 ft. and of 2,081 gross tons. The increased length of the vessel enabled a fourth mast to be fitted and the *Loch Torridon* and her sister ship the *Loch Moidart* are generally considered to be the most perfect examples of four-masted barques.

The 19th-century four-masted rig which was first introduced in the *Great Republic* of 1853, already described, was not used again until about 1875, when a four-masted ship rig was first used, with square sails on all masts. Three years later the four-masted barque rig appeared. The large iron ships with their iron masts and yards were at first given higher sail plans than the earlier ships. As a result, a number of dismastings occurred. Between 1873 and 1874, eleven large sailing-ships were dismasted, nine of the vessels concerned being on their maiden voyages. Because of these accidents, Lloyds Register Committee directed their chief surveyor and his assistants to examine the circumstances of the dismastings and to study the whole question of the dimensions of the

At work high on a yard of the Pangani *in calm weather, seamen are poised on the foot-ropes, stomachs against the spar : to quote the old saying, "one hand for the ship and one for yourself".*

Lengthwise along the deck of the Preussen, *catwalks allow the men to move about in heavy seas with less fear of being swept off.*

Under the gangways, similar to those which run the length of modern tankers, this view of the deck of the Preussen *might easily be mistaken for that of any cargo ship at sea today.*

masts and yards of large sailing-ships. Some eighty ships and barques of varying sizes were closely examined and all the features of the masts, yards and standing rigging compared. Trials were made of the elasticity and rigidity of wire shrouds when set up with wood dead-eyes and hemp or wire lanyards. Calculations were made to determine the support required for masts and standing rigging under the wind pressure and rolling of the ship. The result of the enquiry was published and contained suggestions for masting ships, which fixed the minimum size and strength of iron and wood masts and spars as well as the rigging for various sizes of vessels.

Iron sailing-vessels gradually took the place of wood ships in the merchant service of most major maritime nations. The *Union*, 2,183 tons (see page 242), the first four-masted iron sailing-ship owned by the famous French shipping firm A. D. Bordes, was built by the British shipbuilders Russell & Co. at Greenock and launched in 1882. The *Union* was at first equipped with two small steam engines driving two propellers, to be used as auxiliary power when the vessel was becalmed, or on entering or leaving harbour. Although the propellers could be raised when the ship was under sail this auxiliary machinery does not seem to have been a success and was later removed. After an uneventful career, the *Union* was captured and sunk at the beginning of the First World War, by the German armed merchant cruiser *Kronprinz Wilhelm*.

In the latter half of the 19th century, in contradiction to the general trend towards increased mechani-

Splicing hemp rope is not such an arduous job, depending on the size of the ropes to be joined. Splicing a wire cable is another story: one of the few more painful tasks overlooked by progress on board ship.

sation at sea, a number of wood and iron vessels built as steamers had their machinery etc. removed and were converted into sailing-ships. Probably because of their high length to breadth ratio these converted steamers were often capable of fast sailing. As an example, the steam-paddle frigate *Punjaub* built at Bombay in 1854, was converted into a sailing-ship in 1862, renamed *The Tweed* and proved very successful in the Australian trade, making a passage in 1875-76 from Sydney to London in 69 days. Again, the iron steamer *Pereire*, built by R. Napier & Sons at Glasgow in 1866 for the Compagnie Generale Transatlantique, after 22 years' service as a mail, passenger and freight steamer, mainly spent on the Havre-New York route, was sold to the British and converted into the sailing-ship *Lancing*. As a steamer the vessel was registered as 3,150 tons gross, but after being converted to a sailing-ship, her gross tonnage was reduced to 2,678 tons. The *Lancing* sailed under the British flag for 27 years ; in 1893 she was purchased by a Norwegian firm and in 1896 passed into Canadian ownership. In 1901, the *Lancing* was bought by J. Johnson & Co., of Christiania, Norway and remained in Norwegian hands until finally sent to Italian shipbreakers at the end of 1924. While owned by J. Johnson & Co., the *Lancing* had a remarkable sailing record and is reported to have made a passage in 1907 from Christiania to Melbourne with a cargo of timber in 75 days. On another passage, between New York and Melbourne, she recorded an amazing speed averaging 18 knots for 72 hours running, a splendid achievement. The *Lancing* is said to have been the last four-masted ship-rigged vessel in normal commercial service, and was by far the most successful of the many conversions carried out from steam to sail. She transported cargoes to ports in each of the five continents, and her length of service totalled nearly sixty years.

The *Scottish Glens*, 2,115 tons (see page 237), an iron three-masted, ship-rigged vessel built by Oswald Mordaunt & Co., at Southampton, England, in 1885, was one of a group of seven similar iron full-rigged ships built in 1883-1890 for W. H. Ross & Company's "Scottish Line" of Liverpool. The *Scottish Glens* was sold to a Norwegian shipping company in 1909. Her new proprietors employed her in the timber trade between the Baltic Sea and Australia.

STEEL SAILING SHIPS

During the 1870's, with the advent of Siemen's production methods, good quality mild steel became readily available to British shipbuilders, and in 1877 Lloyds Register Committee laid down rules for the tensile strength and thickness of steel to be used for ship construction. Ductile mild steel was specially suitable for bending into the various components required for a ship's form, and Lloyds agreed that plates and angles of steel could be one-fifth thinner than those made of iron. Thus by using mild steel plates, which were much thinner but of equal strength to that of iron plates, the weight of a ship could be reduced by about 15 per cent. By the end of the 1880's, iron plates were rarely used for ship construction. The substitution of steel for iron also brought about a further general increase in the size of sailing-ships to about 3,000 tons, and after 1890 a few giant square-rigged vessels were built of more than 5,000 tons. Another effect of the introduction of cheap steel for shipbuilding, and of the economics achieved thereby, was a very marked increase in the number of large sailing-ships built, particularly in the period of about 1888 to 1894. These vessels were not designed for speed but as cargo carriers, with small crews and many mechanical aids, to compete with the ubiquitous steam "tramp-ship". Because of the all-important cargo-carrying factor the steel ships were given very full midship sections and sharp bilges with nearly flat floors. By comparison with the earlier clippers they have been contemptuously described as "steel boxes", but in actual fact many of the sailing-ships of the 1890's had fine sailing qualities and even when heavily-laden could make fast passages. On occasion their mean effective speed — which is what really counted — over long ocean voyages was only a few knots less than that of renowned clippers. During this period the barque rig — three and four-masted — was the most commonly used. With this rig the absence of square sails on the after mast of the rig still allowed sufficient sail to be carried to drive the vessel at a reasonable speed in normal wind conditions, without requiring a large crew to handle the sails. To further reduce weight aloft tubular steel masts and lower yards were fitted,

and in the early 1890's it was usual to make the lower and topmast in one continuous tube. Labour saving devices were gradually introduced ; the adoption of first the double topsail and later the double topgallant sail has already been noted. Between 1860 and 1870, some British ships were fitted with Cunningham's patent self-reefing topsails. By the use of this contrivance the sail could be rolled round the yard without sending men aloft. This invention never became very popular and was superseded by the divided sails of the double topsail and topgallant sail. Flexible steel wire rope was used for the standing rigging and for much of the running rigging. The greatest labour saving innovation was the substitution of winches for tackles. The topsail and topgallant sail halliards were worked by crank winches and the sheets and tacks of the lower sails by rail winches. The Jarvis brace winch, introduced in the 1890's, operated the braces of the lower yard and the upper and lower topsail sails. With the old system of brace tackles more men were required, as each brace had to be slacked away or hauled upon for the different yards, a difficult and dangerous job in bad weather with the lee rail under water and seas breaking over the crew. With the brace winches, two men for each mast, working amidships, could control the port and starboard braces of the three lower yards simultaneously, paying out one

The sail-maker in his den, fragrant with the ship smells of hemp and tar, plies his needle. Unlike the housewife's nimble fingers, all his palm is used ; always hard at work but always behind, of course !

"His giant wings prevent him walking", said Baudelaire. A kind of albatross, this unhappy malamok is pitifully helpless on the slippery deck of the Union. *A bearer of bad luck, he will soon be set free.*

and winding in the other with the yards in any position held by the braces. Brakes were provided to control the winch and to lock it when the yards were correctly placed in the required position.

As the length of sailing-ships increased, alterations were made in the deck lay-out. The use of flying gangways or bridges connecting the poop and forecastle via the roofs of the deck-houses was one method of providing a way to move about the ship in heavy weather, when seas swept the main deck. About 1884, a midship structure, known as a bridge deck, was introduced for the larger ships. This bridge deck, extending across the width of the vessel, not only gave the hull increased longitudinal strength but also provided good accommodation for the crew and a safe, centrally-placed position from which the vessel could be easily controlled.

A study of *Lloyd's Register of Ships* for the later years of the 1880's clearly shows the increase in the number of new sailing-ships built of steel, but in this chapter, it is only possible to describe representative examples of the hundreds of large steel sailing-ships built in British yards during the period 1882-1905. The *Pinmore*, 2,358 tons, launched in 1882, was one of the earlier types of steel four-masted barques.

This vessel, 310,1 ft. long with a beam of 43,7 ft., was built by J. Reid & Co. at Port Glasgow for J. Kerr & Co., and made several fast passages, in 1890 reaching Calcutta from Liverpool in 101 days, and in 1893 sailing from San Francisco to Queenstown, Ireland in 96 days. The *Pinmore* was sunk in 1917 by the German armed decoy sailing-ship *Seeadler* commanded by the famous Count of Luckner. The *Seeadler* herself was originally the British full-rigged steel ship *Pass of Balmaha*, 1,571 tons, built at Port Glasgow in 1888, by R. Duncan & Co. She was captured by the Germans in 1915 and fitted with auxiliary engines, wireless and two concealed 4,2 inch guns. During a seven month cruise the *Seeadler* captured fifteen Allied ships, including the French *La Rochefoucauld* (see page 247). Fourteen of the captured vessels were sunk but the French barque *Cambronne* was sent into Rio de Janeiro with prisoners from the other vessels. The *Seeadler* was lost on a reef off Mopelia Island while Count von Luckner was attempting to careen the ship.

The barque *Archibald Russell*, 2,385 tons, has been selected to represent the final stage in the development of the British four-masted barque. This vessel, with a length of 291,4 ft. and a beam of 43,2 ft., was launched from the yard of Scotts Shipbuilding and Engineering Co. at Greenock in 1905, and was the last large square-rigger built on the Clyde. Despite her full lines, to be expected in barques of this period, the *Archibald Russell* had a very handsome appearance with considerable sheer from the high forecastle to the poop. The *Archibald Russell* was not built with the midship bridge deck, as were so many of the larger barque, but flying bridges connected the 41 ft. long poop with the 36 ft. long forecastle via three deck-houses. The crew's quarters were in compartments on each side of the forecastle, the petty officers were accommodated in the foreward deck-house with the apprentices in the after deck-house — known as the half deck. The midship house contained the galley and a steam engine and winch. A wheel-house on the poop gave shelter to the steersmen. As was usual in the later sailing-ships, the fore, main and mizzenmasts of the *Archibald Russell* were of equal height while the jigger-mast, without square sails, was shorter. The sail plan included royals, double topgallants and double topsails. In her earlier days, the

Archibald Russell's fast passages included Sydney to Falmouth in 93 days ; New York to Melbourne in 92 days and Cardiff to Rio de Janeiro in 45 days. In 1924 the vessel was bought by Captain Erikson of Mariehamn and formed part of his famous grain fleet until the outbreak of war in 1939. While in Captain Erikson's fleet, the *Archibald Russell* made a fine voyage of 93 days from Melbourne to Queenstown in 1929. This steel barque was seized by the British authorities and went to the shipbreakers in 1949.

Very few steel sailing-ships were built in the United States of America but the *Astral* was one of three steel square-rigged vessels built, during 1900-1902, by Arthur Sewall & Co., at Bath, Maine, for the Standard Oil Co. for use in the case oil trade to the Far East. Launched in December, 1900, the *Astral*, 3,292 tons with a length of 332 ft. and a beam of 45,4 ft., was four-masted and ship-rigged with double topgallant sails and royals on each mast. Her main yard was 96 ft. long and she carried a crew of thirty-three men. The sailing qualities of the *Astral* and her sister ships the *Acme* and *Atlas* were not outstanding. In 1909, the *Astral* took 159 days to reach San Francisco from New York. In 1910, she was sold to the Alaska Packers Association of San Francisco, the last American firm to use square-riggers, renamed *Star of Zealand* and employed in the Alaska salmon canneries until about 1929. After being laid up for a number of years the vessel was bought by the Japanese in 1935 and saw further service as the *Star of Zealand Maru*.

Of the many hundreds of steel sailing-ships built in the last twenty years of the 19th century, the *Balclutha* is of special interest because, after a long and varied career, the vessel has been restored to her original condition and is now preserved at San Francisco. The *Balclutha*, 1,629 tons, was built by Charles Connell & Co. at Glasgow in 1886. (They had also built the well-known four-master *Glencova*.) With a length of 256,5 ft. and a breadth of 38,6 ft., the vessel was rigged as a three-masted ship and her mainmast, 145 ft. high from deck level to truck, carried a lower yard 86 ft. long. The *Balclutha* remained in British ownership for her first thirteen years and during this period took part in many of the deepwater trades of the time — coal, grain, timber, wool, guano, nitrate, rice and case oil.

In 1899 she was sold to an American firm and employed in the timber trade and the Alaska salmon trade. In 1904 the *Balclutha* was wrecked near Kodiak Island but was purchased by the Alaska Packers Association, salvaged, and sailed back to San Francisco. After repairs, she was renamed *Star of Alaska* and continued in the salmon trade until 1930. Laid up until 1933, the ship was then renamed *Pacific Queen* and for nearly twenty years was used as an exhibition ship on the Californian coast. Finally, in 1954, the old *Balclutha* was bought by the San Francisco Maritime Museum Association and carefully restored to her original state.

On the perfectly clear deck of his Luzifara, *the captain is quite the townsman with his frock-coat, waistcoat and bowler hat, landlubber's clothes disguising a sailor. His wheel-house is quite an innovation.*

THE EUROPEAN FIVE MASTERS

French and German ship-owners were responsible for the building of some very large sailing-ships in a period when the competition of steam vessels was making it increasingly difficult to operate deep-sea sailing-vessels at a profit. The six large, five-masted, square-rigged steel ships built between 1890 and 1912 were intended to provide cheap trans-oceanic transport for bulk cargoes. These vessels, equipped with mechanical aids to assist in handling sails and cargo and in some cases fitted with auxiliary propelling power, were capable of carrying huge cargoes with a small crew, but must be regarded as not very successful experimental ships.

The first of these giants, the five-masted barque *France*, was built for the French firm A. D. Bordes in 1890 by D. & W. Henderson & Co., at Glasgow. She was launched the same year. The *France*, 3,784 tons, with a length of 361 ft., a beam of 48,8 ft. and a depth of 25,9 ft., was constructed with two steel decks and a cellular double-bottom with a capacity for 2,000 tons of water ballast.

The use of water ballast, generally considered as somewhat dangerous for sailing-vessels, was developed particularly for the sailing colliers, trading between the Tyne and London, because of the lack of return cargoes from London. From about 1880, a number of large sailing-ships for French owners were built with double-bottoms and tanks for water ballast. The iron four-masted ship-rigged *A. D. Bordes*, 2,384 tons, was built at Glasgow in 1884, with a double-bottom holding 450 tons of water, and the steel four-masted barque *Cap Horn*, 2,675 tons, built in 1888, at Glasgow, had a capacity of 600 tons of water in the double-bottom and another 1,200 tons in tanks. The *Cap Horn* is said to have been the first sailing-vessel to round Cape Horn, which depended solely on water ballast for stability.

To revert to the *France*, this vessel was designed especially for the South American nitrate trade and could carry 6,200 tons of cargo. Special facilities were provided in order to ensure rapid loading and discharging, and four steam winches were installed at each hold. On her maiden voyage, with a cargo of 5,900 tons of coal, she reached Rio de Janeiro in 32 days from the English Channel, returning from Iquique with 6,000 tons of nitrate. In 1901, while outward-bound from England to Valparaiso, the *France* was lost at sea after being abandoned by her crew. This was reported by the barque *Josepha*.

The second of the European five-masters was the barque *Maria Rickmers*, 3,822 tons, built by Russell & Co., at Port Glasgow in 1891, for Rickmers Reismühlen Reederei & Schiffbau A.G. of Bremerhaven. With a length of 375,7 ft. and a beam of 48 ft., the *Maria Rickmers* was the largest sailing-ship ever built in a British yard. She had two complete decks and 1,236 tons of water ballast could be carried in the main tank and double-bottom. Auxiliary propelling engines were fitted which developed 750 h.p. and could give the vessel a speed of seven knots in a calm sea. The *Maria Rickmers* was built

(Right) Apprentices climb hand over hand: scramble up to the lofty yards set athwart the masts on Grossherzogin Elisabeth.

(Below) Deck-hands in the Pangani *are ready for a laugh and a joke, even when about to heave on the capstan hand-spikes. They take the rough with the smooth in life at sea. And what the devil can this be? A photographer? "Well now, blow me down!"*

for the rice trade between the Far East and Germany, and on her maiden voyage reached Singapore in 82 days. On her return voyage with a full cargo of rice and a crew of forty men, the *Maria Rickmers* having passed Anjer, Sumatra, in July, 1892, disappeared and is believed to have capsized with the loss of her crew, said to be incapable of handling her.

R. F. Laeisz, of Hamburg, ordered the next five-masted barque, the *Potosi*, from German shipbuilders and the vessel was built of steel at the Geestemünde yard of J. C. Tecklenborg A.G. in 1895. The *Potosi*, 366,3 ft. long with a beam of 49,7 ft., was employed in the nitrate trade until the outbreak of war in 1914, remained at Valparaiso during the war years and in 1918 was allocated to France as reparations, being finally lost at sea by fire in 1925.

The *Preussen*, 5,081 tons, launched in 1902, the fourth five-master, is fully described in an insert to this chapter. In 1906 Rickmers, despite their unfortunate experience with the earlier five-master *Maria Rickmers*, built the *R. C. Rickmers* at Bremerhaven, Germany. A five-masted barque of 5,548 tons, she was 410,5 ft. long with a beam of 53,6 ft. Steam-engines developing 1,000 h.p. were fitted for auxiliary propelling power. Bunkers for 630 tons of

coal were provided and under steam power alone a speed of six to eight knots was possible. The propeller, used in conjunction with this auxiliary machinery, had moveable blades which could be so adjusted as to offer less resistance in the water when the vessel was proceeding under sail only. On deck many mechanical aids were available to assist the crew to handle the sails and cargo. In addition to the usual large capstan on the forecastle, eight capstans were fitted — four to port and four to starboard — along the length of the vessel. Each mast was provided with special winches for the halliards and braces. A deck-house, somewhat forward of midships, was connected by gangways, forward to the forecastle and aft to the 180 ft. long poop. The first, second, third and fourth masts, of almost equal height, each carried a lower course, double topsails, double topgallant sails and a royal sail. The much shorter fifth mast carried a spanker gaff and gaff topsail. The usual fore-and-aft stay-sails and head-sails were hoisted as required. A funnel, 25 ft. high, for the steam engines, together with engine-room skylights and cowl ventilators, all fitted between the third and fourth masts, gave the *R. C. Rickmers* the appearance of a steamship, particularly when the

Even a sailing-ship had its office work. Red tape was beginning its reign. With a weary sigh, captain and mate reluctantly settle down to write up reports and fill out forms in the tranquility of the ward-room.

sails were furled. Typical examples of the ocean passages made by the *R. C. Rickmers* include : Newcastle-upon-Tyne to San Francisco, Burma to Bremen and Australia to Valparaiso.

The *R. C. Rickmers* was probably the most successful of the European five-masters and was employed in carrying many types of bulk cargo, including case oil, rice, wheat, coke, coal, cement and nitrate. Her carrying capacity was about 7,000 tons. The *R. C. Rickmers* was at a British port when war was declared in 1914 and was seized by the British, renamed *Neath*, and later sunk by a German submarine. This was a sad mischance for the ship.

The last of this group of steel five-masters was also called the *France*. The second five-masted barque of that name, she was built at Bordeaux, France, by C. & A. de la Gironde and launched in November, 1911. The *France*, 5,633 tons with a length of 418,8 ft. and a beam of 55,8 ft., was the largest sailing-vessel ever built. The ship was fitted with auxiliary propelling machinery consisting of internal combustion oil engines developing 295 h.p., driving twin screws. Many mechanical devices were fitted to assist in handling the sails and an electric lighting generator and wireless were carried. Although

specially built for the nickel ore trade from New Caledonia, the *France* also carried huge cargoes of coal and wool. Her cargo capacity was about 8,000 tons of nickel and 7,000 tons of coal, and she carried a crew of about 50 men. In July, 1922, the *France* drifted onto a reef near Coya, New Caledonia, and was a total loss. The auxiliary machinery which might have saved the vessel had been removed prior to the commencement of the last voyage.

Auxiliary propelling machinery was fitted to many large merchant sailing-ships during the latter half of the 19th century and in the early 20th century, in order to try and make the vessels more efficient in all wind conditions and therefore better able to compete with the steamer. However, the large sailing-ship with auxiliary power was rarely successful. The drag of the propeller through the water impaired the sailing qualities of the vessel and if the engines were powerful enough to be of real economic value to the speed of the vessel, they required a large amount of fuel and trained engineers to look after them. This necessitated a consequently large increase in running costs from fuel bills and wages. However, much was still to be said for sailing-ships, just as the steamers in their turn had drawbacks as well as advantages.

Taking a sight on the poop or, to be more precise, waiting for the sun to reach its noon height before aiming the sextant. In the background, the helmsman takes it easy, enjoying a spell of good weather and calm seas.

Bending the sail to the yard when it's fine is no problem — except for dizziness. A minor detail, it's part of the job.

Judging by their thick wool caps, they are somewhere in northern waters. This "scrum" is all work and no play but it warms the men up. In the top of the capstan nearby can be seen the square sockets into which fit the wooden hand-spikes — deadly weapons in the hands of mutineers!

Working right out on the lip of the bowsprit is no picnic when she's pitching, in spite of the safety net underneath.

Bending over a yard, steadied by the foot-ropes, sailors are furling up a square sail while, far below, the seas look rough and stormy. On the left of the photograph, a topsail has been half-reefed, to partition its surface area, and the tack strains in the high wind, bent to a yard.

THE LAST OF THE DEEP SEA MERCHANT SAILING SHIPS

One of the last large scale commercial activities of the large sailing-ship was in the nitrate trade from South America to European ports. For many years before the First World War the French firm of A. D. Bordes, with financial help in the form of bounties from the French Government, had an average of about 36 large sailing-vessels employed in the nitrate trade. During the war 22 of A. D. Bordes' sailing-vessels were lost, and economic conditions in France after the war did not permit the maintenance of a subsidised fleet of sailing-ships. The four-masted barque *Valparaiso*, 3,250 tons, which had been built for A. D. Bordes et Fils, in 1902, was the last sailing-ship employed by the firm until this vessel too was sold in 1926.

The German firm R. F. Laeisz, with their famous "P" line, owned undoubtedly the finest and fastest fleet of nitrate carriers. The "P" Line commenced with the ship-rigged iron vessel *Polynesia*, 1,010 tons, built at Hamburg in 1874. Over the years, the fleet was expanded and the individual sailing-ships became larger. In the 1880's the first 1,400 ton vessels were acquired. By the early 1890's, 2,900 ton ships were

in the fleet, and these were followed by the giant five-masters *Potosi* and *Preussen*. The "P" Line nitrate carriers *Pangani* and *Pamir* (see pages 239, 244, 254) are typical examples of the fine four-masted steel barques owned by R. F. Laeisz in the early years of the 20th century. The *Pangani*, 3,054 tons, was built by J. C. Tecklenborg A.G., at Geestemünde in 1903. This vessel, with a length of 322,2 ft. and a beam of 46,2 ft. was constructed with three transverse bulkheads. The poop was 31 ft. long, the midship bridge deck 62 ft. long and the forecastle 37 ft. long. The *Pamir* 3,020 tons, built in 1905 by Blohm & Voss at Hamburg, with a length of 316 ft. and a beam of 46 ft., shipped nitrate until 1914.

One of the largest four-masted barques owned by the "P" Line, the *Peking*, 3,191 tons, with a length of 322,1 ft. and a beam of 47,2 ft. was built by Blohm & Voss at Hamburg in 1911. The *Peking* survived the First World War and in 1933 was purchased by the Council of the Shaftesbury Homes and *Arethusa* Training-Ship, renamed *Arethusa* and anchored at permanent moorings, off Upnor, on the river Medway, to form a training-ship for deprived boys who seek a career at sea in the Royal Navy or Merchant Navy.

After the First World War, the remaining sailing-ships of the Laeisz "P" Line were allocated to various nations as reparations but in the early 1920's, Laeisz bought back six of the vessels, including the *Pamir*, and the German sailing nitrate fleet was again in being. The *Pamir* was sold in 1931 to Captain Gustav Erikson of Mariehamn, Finland, and formed one of the Erikson grain fleet, trading between Australia and Europe until 1939. After the Second World War, the *Pamir* was employed by a New Zealand firm and traded between Wellington and San Francisco. Later, the *Pamir* was chartered as a training-ship for the West German merchant navy and was lost in a hurricane in the Atlantic in 1957. This catastrophe greatly moved the German people.

Bell-bottoms and bare feet, like sailors the world over, these naval apprentices are busy with their domestic chores, washing their dirty laundry on the deck of the training-ship Prinzess Eitel Friedrich.

Ratlines are as good a place as any: hang out the wash unless a squall comes to blow it all away! An officer of the watch looks on.

Between 1913 and 1939, Captain Gustav Erikson built up a fine fleet of sailing-ships based on Mariehamn, in the Aland Islands off the coast of Finland. In addition to his fleet of schooners and barquentines, Captain Erikson acquired over the years a number of fine old steel sailing-vessels. The Erikson fleet included the *Lawhill*, 2,816 tons; *Archibald Russell*, 2,354 tons; *Herzogin Cecilie*, 3,242 tons; *Olivebank*, 2,795 tons; *Penang*, 2,019 tons; *Pommern*, 2,376 tons; *Viking*, 2,952 tons; *Pamir*, 3,020 tons; *L'Avenir*, 2,738 tons; *Passat*, 3,183 tons; *Hougomont*, 2,428 tons and *Moshulu*, 3,116 tons. The Erikson fleet was principally employed in bringing grain from South Australia to the ports of Great Britain. The outward voyage to Australia was usually made in ballast but occasionally cargoes of timber were carried from Finland to South Africa. The grain-ship "races" of the 1930's attracted a great deal of attention and in 1937 no fewer than eleven of Captain Erikson's large sailing-ships took part in the event. During the four years from 1925 to 1929, the four-masted ship-rigged *Herzogin Cecilie* averaged 100 days for her passages from Australia, giving a mean effective speed of just under six knots. The *Herzogin Cecilie* is said to have won the grain-ship race eight times before she was wrecked in 1936.

THE TRAINING SHIP

Until recent times many maritime nations would only grant an officer's certificate after a man had served for a certain number of years in a sailing-ship. Therefore, it is appropriate, as a final note, to describe some of the sailing training-ships which have played such an important part in producing fine merchant seamen and officers.

In 1900, the sail training organisation Deutscher Schulschiff Verein was founded in Germany by ship-owners and merchants. Two of this association's training-vessels, the *Grossherzogin Elisabeth* and the *Prinzess Eitel Friedrich* are illustrated on pages 245, 250, 251, and 253. The *Grossherzogin Elisabeth*, 1,260 tons was a steel, three-masted, ship-rigged vessel specially designed for a training-ship and built by J. C. Tecklenborg A.G. at Geestemünde in 1901. The *Prinzess Eitel Friedrich*, 1,566 tons, also designed as a training-ship for merchant marine cadets, was built at Hamburg by Blohm & Voss in 1909. This steel vessel was also three-masted and ship-rigged and was handed over to France at the end of the First World War. In 1929 she was bought by the Polish Government, renamed *Dar Pomorza* and again fitted out as a training-ship. The *Herzogin Cecilie*, already mentioned as a grain-ship, was built by Rickmers in 1902 for the North German Lloyd Line to be used as a training-ship for their own officers.

Argentine, Belgium, Brazil, Chile, Denmark, Finland, France, Italy, Japan, Norway, Poland, Portugal, Russia, Spain and Sweden have all been in possession of sail training-ships.

The latest of the sail training-ships, the British three-masted topsail schooner *Sir Winston Churchill*, 235 tons, was completed in 1966 for the Sail Training Association and, for many years to come, will provide the opportunity for a number of boys to "take an active part in the working of the ship and to learn to take practical responsibilities".

The interest aroused by the "Tall Ships' Race" which takes place occasionally between some of the world's remaining sailing-vessels is proof of the great attraction these splendid ships still have, not only for shiplovers but also for the general public.

The "Tall Ships' Race" in 1966 started from Falmouth and entrants from Denmark, France, Great Britain, Holland, Norway and Sweden completed the course, which totalled a distance of 800 miles and finished off the Skaw, on the Danish coast.

All the busy sailors of the Grossherzogin Elisabeth *are up aloft. On the deck below, it is peaceful and even the sturdy, clinker-built ship's boats seem to enjoy quietly basking in a spell of hot sunshine. The great 1,260 ton vessel was the German merchant navy's first training-ship.*

Dipping behind the swell, with all sails set, the Pamir *seems so steady as she rides the waves. But one day in 1957, this proud training-ship ran into a ferocious gale and foundered at sea, in the Atlantic Ocean.*

THE PREUSSEN · 1902

BY CAPTAIN HELMUT GRUBBE

Until the opening of the Suez Canal in November, 1869, the sailing-vessel was a much more successful proposition over long distances than the steamer, economically at least.

The steamer only eventually became more profitable than the sailer when the boiler was perfected and with the introduction of the expansion type engine, which gave a much higher yield per ton of coal.

However, the owners of sailing-vessels did not easily give up the struggle and answered the challenge with larger vessels of greater cargo capacity. These were made possible by a new shipbuilding material — iron plates began to be used for hulls. In 1870, a 2,000-ton sailing-vessel was considered large, but only shortly afterwards her successors were to reach 3,000 tons and over. However, even if vessels could not be lengthened indefinitely, they could at least be more broadly built.

Sadly, clippers with slim, sharp lines were succeeded by vessels constructed to yield the maximum speed for the maximum tonnage. Finally, in the nineties, the "bald-headers" made their appearance. Despite their heavy tonnage, the average duration of the voyages was not appreciably increased.

The keeping of meteorological records on board ship was first suggested by the American naval officer Maury. Their analysis in books of sailing instructions and their use in special "pilot charts" drawn up for different seasons and regions, meant the spread of universally accessible knowledge, enabling ships' captains to benefit from the experience of others.

Life on board became ever more arduous for crews. Whereas a clipper of approximately 900 tons still carried a crew of up to fifty hands, a 4,500-ton barque signed on a mere 33 men, sometimes even fewer. Stringent economy had to be constantly observed; a clipper of 900 tons cost almost as much as one of the huge 2,000-ton sailing-vessels ten years later.

Towards 1890, this tendency resulted in the appearance of ever larger vessels which enjoyed considerable economic success. So much so, in fact, that some steamers were even converted to sailers, as in the case of the famous Norwegian square-rigged, four-masted *Lancing*, which remained in service until 1924.

About this time, the first five-masted barques were built. *France I* came from French yards, and the 6,000-ton *Potosi* was built in Germany, both vessels designed for the shipment of nitrates. Outward-bound *en route* to Chile via Cape Horn, they carried assorted cargoes or coal, returning to Europe with nitrates which were used, depending on the political situation at the time, for the manufacture of fertilizers or nitroglycerine. The "nitrate route" was a punishing one, each voyage rounding Cape Horn twice. Despite seamen's and shipowners' ingrained resistance to change, the need for technical improvements, especially simplification of the rigging, could no longer be ignored. Some of these modifications proved highly profitable. This was certainly true of the installation of winches for working the braces, enabling all the yards to be turned according to the wind direction, parallel to the three lower ones. This could now be accomplished in a single operation from amidships and a more or less sheltered position — a great improvement on the old fashioned capstans, which necessitated the crew's standing often chest-high in the water pouring over the vessel's sides. Similarly, with these winches for halyards and sheets, less manpower and fewer ropes were needed for capstan work.

The limit of growth seemed to have been achieved with the world's only square-rigged, five-masted vessel, the *Preussen*. She was built in 1902 in the Geestemünde shipyard for the Hamburg ship owner F. C. Laeisz, by Johann C. Tecklenborg, shipbuilders, and was designed by their director W. Claussen.

The rigging of the *Preussen* sported all the latest innovations. These were also applied to the hull which was reinforced in such an unusual manner for the period as to arouse world-wide curiosity and admiration.

The *Preussen* could carry 8,000 tons burden while, crewed and fully laden, her displacement was 11,150 tons. The last tea clipper, the *Cutty Sark*, with her crew numbering 35, had carried 28 tons of cargo per man. *Preussen*, with 48 officers and hands, increased this ratio to a staggering 106 tons per head. In spite of her impressive size and capacity, the vessel was not completely successful economically because of the difficulty of finding 8,000 tons of freight at the outset of the voyage. Out of fourteen voyages, including twelve round trips to Chile, the *Preussen* weighed anchor with holds full only twice.

Among sailing-vessels, the four-mast barque of approximately 4,750 tons proved the most economical to run. After the loss of the *Preussen*, she was replaced by two such vessels, the *Peking* and the *Passat*. The last four-mast barque was the *Padua*, built in 1926. These three ships are still in service, as can be seen from the list of great sailing-ships.

Usually, these ships took aboard 1,000 tons of coke and approximately 3,500 tons of sundry cargo at the port of departure, returning with 4,500 to 4,800 tons of nitrate. In all, they carried between 9,000 and 9,500 tons of freight with 33 men whereas the *Preussen*, with her crew of 48, carried only 8,000 tons. Naturally, maintenance costs of both vessel and rigging were also lower, even though the construction cost per ton burden was higher than that for the *Preussen*.

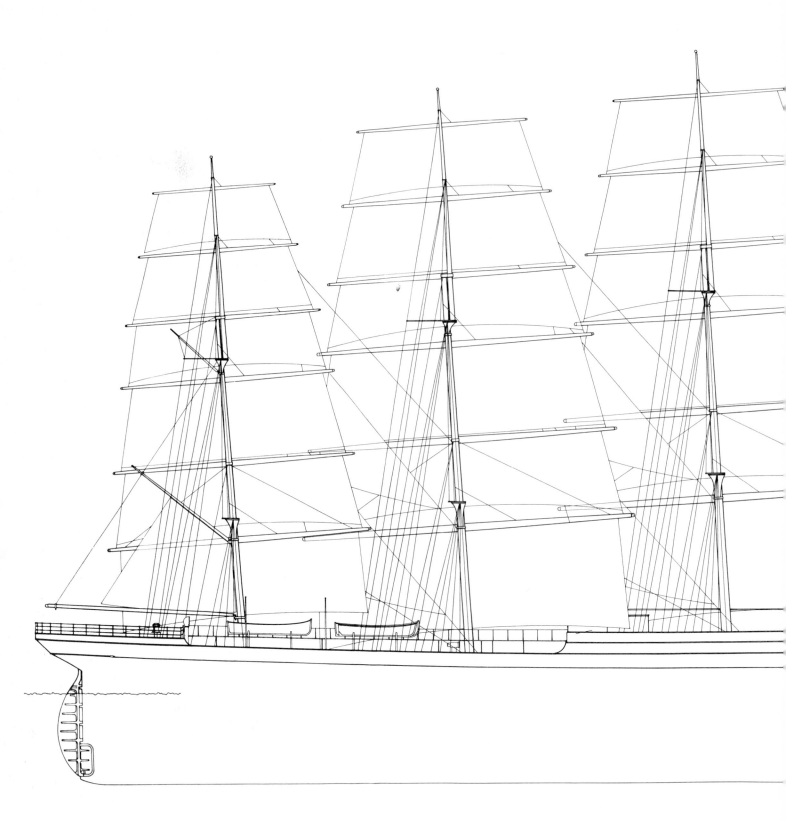

The Preussen was the world's only square-rigged five-master. The first four masts being identical, she was, in fact, a three-master with two supplementary mainmasts. The spanker has a very unusual gaff. This drawing clearly shows the cat-walks and the deck winches for the sails.

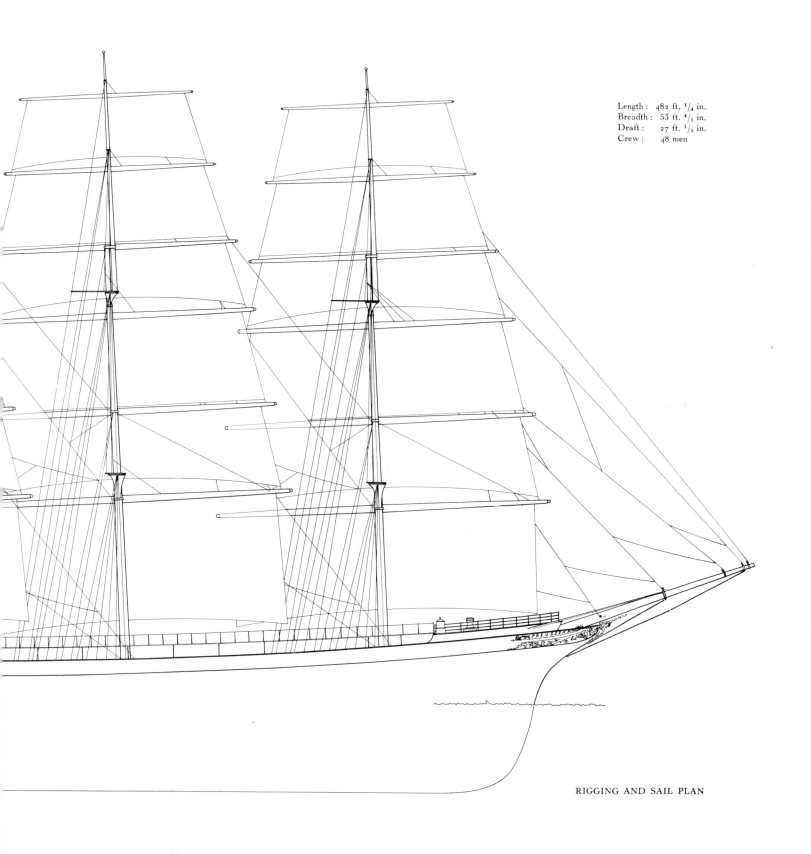

Length : 482 ft. ¹/₄ in.
Breadth : 53 ft. ⁴/₅ in.
Draft : 27 ft. ¹/₅ in.
Crew : 48 men

RIGGING AND SAIL PLAN

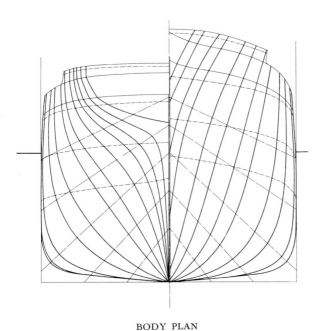

BODY PLAN

Speed was now only a secondary consideration. The first concern was the shipment of as much freight as possible at the lowest price. This hull section suggests a barge: however, the water-lines fore and aft are good, eliminating eddies.

The hull is so long that it had to be thoroughly reinforced throughout to prevent her breaking in half, a fate that often befalls some oil tankers, even today. And, like a tanker's, the deck presents a straight, uninterrupted, horizontal line.

Apart from financial considerations, *Preussen* was a complete success. She was an unusual sailing-vessel, capable of keeping to her time table almost as regularly as the cargo steamers of those days. She could maintain a speed of 16 to 17 knots for several hours at a time and even make 18 knots for one hour. The maximum efforts of the entire crew, from captain down to youngest cabin-boy, were bent on extracting the very utmost from their vessel. The captains of the *Preussen*, Boye Petersen and, subsequently, Heinrich Nissen, took a 24-hour working day for granted : nothing was spared in the merciless quest for speed.

The ship was far from easy to handle, requiring a great deal of manoeuvring space. Captains hardly dared pass another vessel in the Channel. As a matter of fact, *Preussen* as well as *Potosi* were usually towed as far as Start Point, where the Channel begins to open out. Captain Nissen, who successfully commanded the five-mast barque *Potosi* and the *Preussen* is reported to have once said : "It was always I who chose the course for the *Potosi* but sometimes the *Preussen* chose the course for me."

Just imagine what it must have been like to stand at the wheel of such a sailer, at night, in a gale, hauling 11,150 tons through the water at a speed of 16 to 17 knots or, roughly, twenty miles an hour. Including the jib-boom, the *Preussen* measured 490 ft. overall, 54 ft. beam, with a draught of 27 ft. A crew of only 48 handled 46 sails with a total area of 60,000 square feet of canvas, the smallest sail being the mizzen-royal of 650 square feet while the heavy lower sails were 3,500 square feet. One of these alone weighed well over half a ton with its gear, one square metre of sail canvas weighing more than two pounds. The mainmast measured 227 ft. from heel to truck and its circumference at deck level was nine and a half feet. The lower yards were over 100 ft. long and weighed six and a half tons apiece. They were hooped by steel bands 12 mm. thick and their centre diameter was 25 inches.

Fifteen miles of wire, ten miles of hemp and manilla rope, nearly 800 yards of cable and 1,260 blocks were needed to brace the masts and trim the sails. The winches for the rigging were worked manually, by the "Armstrong system" as sailors called it, wryly punning on the name of its inventor. Davits were worked from a steam donkey-engine on the forecastle which could also, as occasion demanded, be used to drive the rudder-chain winch. Otherwise, the vessel was steered by hand, sometimes requiring up to eight men to hold her on course in heavy weather.

Amidships, a large deck cabin served as crew's quarters. The vessel had such modern installations as a bath for the crew's use in the forepeak.

The *Preussen* successfully completed thirteen voyages and started her four-

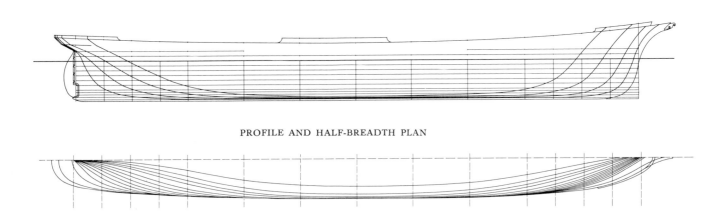

PROFILE AND HALF-BREADTH PLAN

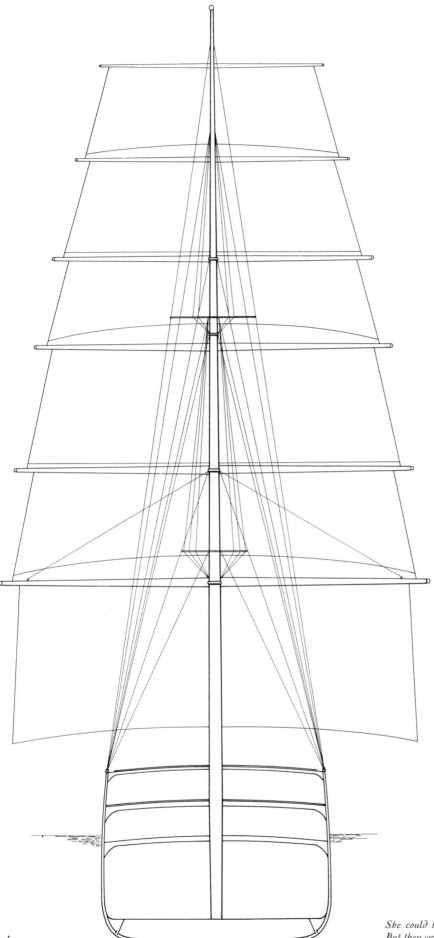

teenth from Hamburg on October 31,
1910, laden with cargo bound for Valparaiso. It was to be her last voyage.

On November 6, 1910, the *Preussen*
collided with the British steamer
Brighton off Beachy Head, on a foggy
day in the Channel. She lost her forward rigging and part of her foremast,
seriously hampering her handling.
Captain and crew strove with all their
might and seafaring skill to bring her
safely into port. All their efforts were
foiled. Just before reaching the shelter
of the habour at Dover, a gale blew up.
With the force of the wind on her top
hamper, even the three tugs could not
hold her. Tow-lines severed, at the
mercy of wind and currents, *Preussen*
drifted along the Dover mole. Despite
a last brave attempt by Captain Nissen
and all his crew to free the vessel,
she piled herself on the rocks.

At the Maritime Tribunal on March
14, 1911, at Hamburg, the following
verdict was passed on this disaster
which had aroused world-wide curiosity and speculation at the time. "On
November 6th, 1910, a collision took
place off Beachy Head, between the
five-master *Preussen* and the British
steamship *Brighton*. In attempting to
reach the port of Dover in order to
repair the damage caused by this
collision, the *Preussen* was driven
ashore by freshening south-westerly
winds to the east of Dover and was
completely destroyed. The fault of the
collision, which resulted in the total
loss of the vessel, lies entirely with
those in command of the steamship
Brighton in failing to avoid the *Preussen*
and allow her to pass and for having
attempted, at the last minute, to pass
in front of her.[1] Captain Nissen and
the officers of the *Preussen* are in no
way responsible for the collision." The
verdict added: "The measures subsequently taken cannot be criticized
and no mismanagement can be traced re-
garding the running aground of the vessel
on the afternoon of November 6th."

[1] All steam-powered vessels in all circumstances
must give way to vessels under sail (recent
reservations not being applicable to this case) and
must avoid crossing ahead of the other vessel when
there is any risk of collision. (The Translator)

*She could be compared to a "packing-case", overloaded with sails.
But they were quite easy to manoeuvre, topsails and topgallants being
divided in two and handled together by means of steam driven winches.*

HULL SECTION AT THE MAINMAST AND SAIL PLAN

Sails and more sails, nothing but small rectangles of canvas. And between the masts can be seen three-cornered staysails. Oddly enough, there are only three very small jibs, but so well designed as to be very efficient in paying off this extremely long "scow". Unhappily, even the greatest and most beautiful ships meet their destiny. Here, the Preussen, all her sails furled, is aground on the rocks. With her broken foremast, she was doomed, virtually unable to manoeuvre. The illustration above, on the left, is from the Newport News Mariners Museum, (VA.). Above, to the right, a lively painting from the Musée du Long-Cours in St.-Malo. The two photographs on the left are from the Peabody Museum in Salem (Mass.), while the illustration below, to the right, depicts the shipwreck off Dover.

Brynhilda *looks somewhat dejected under tow, with sails hanging limp and loose. But a fair wind will soon transform her into a living, winged form, quivering as she rides the seas.*

Billowing out in a steady breeze, these jibs appear strangely altered from this angle. They might be likened to white wing-feathers or spurts of white-hot flame from gas-burner jets, the bowsprit.

On the facing page, a ship's canvas, serene and stiff as it takes the wind, is symmetrically aligned in precise order, symbolizing centuries of courage, skill and science — the modern seafarers' heritage.

Below is the sea, the raging sea. High as hills, the foaming waves, ceaselessly reborn by the promiscuous wind, batter the ship's sides and roll her over until her decks are under and even the rails awash.

A true monarch of the high sea, the **Pamir,** *had all the majesty, beauty, grace and power that made her one of the world's great sailing-ships.*

APPENDIX

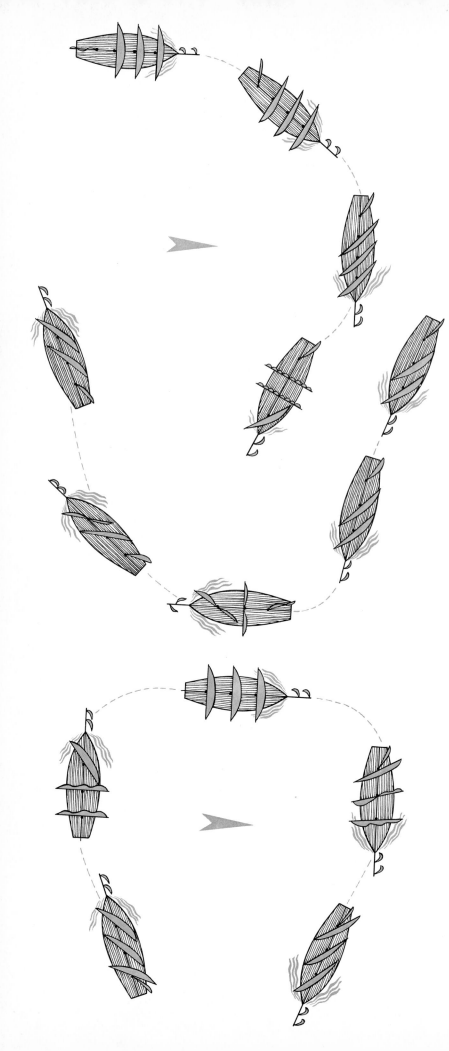

Heaving to in a square-rigged four-masted barque, when she was running before the wind.

Coming to a stop or heaving to was necessary for a sailing-vessel in order to drop anchor, to take a pilot aboard or when lowering a ship's boat, for instance at the cry of "Man overboard". When the vessel is running before the wind, it is made to "luff", the head being brought into wind. To luff a sailing-ship, the yards are progressively braced as the vessel goes about. The foreyards are then braced for "close-hauled", the sails continuing to fill, but the yards of main and mizzen-mast are squared. In this way, the after sails are blanketed, abacked with what wind there is, blown against the masts. When the sails set in this way, the vessel makes less and less forward speed until it begins to drift broadside on.

Going about, head to the wind, in a barque.

When a sailing-vessel is beating up to windward and goes about in order to catch the wind from the other quarter, it is carrying out the manoeuvre known as tacking. A square-rigged sailing-ship could only do this in moderate winds and a light sea since, at one given moment, the vessel would be head to wind. Starting by bearing off a little, the vessel would stand away slightly from the wind's eye and pick up speed. At the command of "Bout ship!", the helm was put down to leeward. As soon as the sails caught the wind from the opposite quarter, the yards of the mainmast were braced but the fore-topsail remained across the wind, assisting the ship in falling off to leeward. Later, the other yards were braced to fill the sails.

"Wearing" in a square-rigged three-master.

This manoeuvre enabled a vessel to be brought round on the other tack, stern to wind, even in heavy weather. On the command "Ready about!", the helm was put up to make the vessel fall off, running more before the wind until, still turning, she was sailing "by the lee". To help the ship round, the spanker sheets were hauled in, the main and mizzen-mast yards braced to shiver and sails neither filled nor aback. When the vessel reached the point where she was running before, the yards were squared by the braces. Then, to ease the luff onto the other tack, the spanker was braced full. Subsequently, main, mizzen and foremast sails had their sheets hauled in until the vessel was sailing close-hauled on the other course.

In full sail, a 3,000-ton four-masted barque carried all of 47,000 square feet of canvas.

The efficient use of sails depended on many factors, such as the wind speed and direction, the size and burden of the vessel, the state of the sea and the number of crew and their experience. Last, but not the least important, were the idiosyncrasies of the particular vessel, for instance the strain it put on the sails and the way it handled in high winds. As a general rule, a fully-laden ship could wear its complete suit of sails in winds up to Force 5 on the Beaufort Scale when close-hauled, sailing into wind, and up to Force 7 when she was running before.

The same rig with royals, royal staysails, mizzentop staysail and gaff topsail furled.

In certain weather conditions, these light sails were the first to be furled as they tended to make the vessel list and lose more forward speed than their actual area of canvas contributed. When the vessel was running before with the yards squared, stay-sails were also sometimes taken in, otherwise they flapped about idly and tended to make the vessel yaw off course. With a wind over the quarter, and if the canvas was stiff enough, royal-sails could be set in winds up to Force 6, a strong breeze, unless the weather showed signs of blowing up and the winds freshening.

Canvas further reduced by furling the sky-sails, flying jib and topgallant staysails.

As the wind freshened, so other upper sails were taken in. When sailing with a commanding wind, over the stern quarters, a vessel should be able to carry this canvas in a wind of Force 8 or 9 and, when beating to windward, up to Force 7. When the vessel is running before, the mizzen topsail and mizzen-topmast staysail were usually taken in. If the vessel answered the helm badly, the surface of the crossjack could also be reduced, by reefing, as illustrated in the drawing opposite. In this way, the total area of the canvas could be reduced by one third.

Rigged with topsails and lower courses.

The lower topgallants, flying jib, the middle staysail, mizzen topsail and the crossjack have been furled and the mainsail shortened. This sail arrangement was adopted when running before with a Force 9 or 10 wind or, when tacking, with a wind of Force 8. As all depended on the state of the sea with such a wind force, the vessel would probably be sailing with her decks well awash. If she was beating to windward, the vessel might also be rolling and pitching badly. It rested with the captain to take the strength of his vessel and the ability of his crew into account.

Heavy weather sails only with part of the courses and fixed topsails in "0" canvas.

Sail canvas for these large vessels was graded in numbers from 0 to 4. One square yard of grade O canvas weighed approximately two pounds and the same amount of grade 4, about half this weight. Rigged in this way, a ship would make very little headway against the wind, the seas being too heavy. Sailing with a commanding wind, the vessel could make way at a reasonable speed but would, however, be extremely difficult to handle. For this reason, the foresail was usually kept in position, although reefed, while the mainsail and crossjack would have been furled.

SURVIVORS OF THE AGE OF SAIL

THE FOLLOWING SHIPS HAVE BEEN PRESERVED EITHER AS TRAINING-SHIPS OR FLOATING-MUSEUMS

1 displ. : displacement, see note ;   2 tonn. : see note at the end of section.

Name	Type	Tonnage and Displacement	Date and place of construction	Last voyage	In Service as
Argentine					
Libertad	square-rigged three-master	3765 displ. [1]	1958 La Plata	in service	training-ship
Presidente Sarmiento	square-rigged three-master	2850 displ.	1898 U.K.	1954	floating-school
Belgium					
Mercator	barquentine	770 tonn. [2]	1932 Leith	1963	floating-school
New vessel similar to Gorch Fock in design		—	—	—	—
Brazil					
Albatros (ex Wishbone)	fore-and-aft schooner	100 displ.	1920 U.S.A.	in service	training-ship
Almirante Saldanha	four-masted topsail schooner	3325 displ.	1933 Barrow	in service	training-ship
Custdio de Mello	schooner	—	U.S.A.	—	floating-school
Bulgaria					
Assen	topsail schooner	240 displ.	1912	in service	training-ship
Burgas	topsail schooner	240 displ.	—	in service	training-ship
Kamcia	topsail schooner	240 displ.	—	in service	training-ship
Canada					
Bluenose II	fore-and-aft schooner	285 displ.	1963 Canada	in service	training-ship
Harelda	fore-and-aft schooner	30 displ.	—	in service	training-ship
St. Lawrence II	brigantine	43 displ.	1957 Canada	in service	training-ship
Chile					
Esmeralda	four-masted topsail schooner	3673 displ.	1952 Cadiz	in service	training-ship
General Baquedano	three-masted barque	2500 displ.	1898 U.K.	1951	floating-school
Columbia					
La Altrevida	ketch	—	—	in service	training-ship
Denmark					
Arken (ex Roscovite)	topsail schooner	c. 120 tonn.	1908 Saint-Malo	about 1936	floating-school
Danmark	square-rigged three-master	777 tonn.	1933 Odense	in service	training-ship
Georg Stage	square-rigged three-master	298 tonn.	1935 Frederikshavn	in service	training-ship
Jylland	square-rigged three-master	c. 3000 displ.	1860 Copenhagen	about 1890	floating-museum
Lilla Dan	topsail schooner	120 tonn.	1951 Svendborg	in service	training-ship

Name	Type	Tonnage and Displacement	Date and place of construction	Last voyage	In Service as
Dominican Republic					
Duarte (ex Nueva Tioditi)	fore-and-aft schooner	170 displ.	1943	in service	training-ship
Patria (ex Hussar, ex Seacloud, ex Angelita)	four-masted barque	3077 displ.	1931 Kiel	in service	training-ship
Finland					
Pommern (ex Mneme)	four-masted barque	2376 tonn.	1903 Glasgow	1939	floating-school and museum
Suomen Joutsen (ex Laennec, ex Oldenburg)	square-rigged three-master	2259 tonn.	1902 Saint-Nazaire	1955	floating-school
France					
Duchesse Anne, (ex Herzogin Elisabeth)	square-rigged three-master	1260 tonn.	1901 Geestemünde	1932	floating-school
La Belle Poule	topsail schooner	214 displ.	1932 Fécamp	in service	training-ship
Le Dauphin (ex Simone Marcelle)	ketch	—	1954 commissioned	—	training-ship
Le Mutin	schooner	—	—	—	
L'Etoile	topsail schooner	214 displ.	1932 Fécamp	in service	training-ship
La Zélée	—	—	—	in service	training-ship
Federal Republic of Western Germany					
Gorch Fock	three-masted barque	1780 displ.	1958 Hamburg	in service	training-ship
Nordwind	ketch	112 displ.	1944 Bremen	in service	training-ship
Passat	four-masted barque	3317 tonn.	1911 Hamburg	1957	floating-school
Schulschiff Deutschland	square-rigged three-master	1257 tonn.	1927 Geestemünde	1944	floating-school
Seute Deern (ex Pieter A. Koerts, ex Seute Deern, ex Bandi, ex Elisabeth Bandi)	three-masted barque	814 tonn.	1919 Gulfport	1944	floating-museum and restaurant
Seute Deern (ex Nona Dan)	ketch	c. 120 tonn.	1948 Svendborg	in service	training-ship
German Democratic Republic					
Wilhelm Piek	brigantine	c. 250 displ.	1948 Rostock	in service	training-ship
Greece					
Eugène Eugenides (ex Flying Clipper, ex Sunbeam II)	three-masted topsail schooner	636 tonn.	1929 Dumbarton	in service	training-ship
Indonesia					
Dewarutji	barquentine	810 displ.	1953 Hamburg	in service	training-ship
Italy					
Amerigo Vespucci	square-rigged three-master	3543 displ.	1931 Castellamare	in service	training-ship
Ebe	ketch	c. 100 displ.	1924	in service	training-ship
Giorgio Cini (ex Fantome II, ex Belem)	barquentine	562 tonn.	1896 Nantes	in service	training-ship
Palinuro (ex Jean Marc Aline, ex Comandante Louis Richard)	barquentine	c. 500 displ.	1933 France	in service	training-ship
San Giorgio	fore-and-aft schooner	c. 90 tonn.	—	—	—

Name	Type	Tonnage and Displacement	Date and place of construction	Last voyage	In Service as
Japan					
Kaiwo Maru	four-masted barque . .	2284 tonn. . .	1930 Kobe	in service	training-ship
Meiji Maru	square-rigged three-master	1010 tonn. . .	1874 U.K. as steamship —		floating-school
Nippon Maru	square-rigged four-master	2285 tonn. . .	1930 Kobe	in service	training-ship
Unyo Maru	brigantine	448 displ. . .	1909 Japan . . .	in service	floating-school
Jugoslavia					
Jadran	barquentine	720 displ. . .	1932 Kiel	in service	training-ship
Villa Velebita	brigantine	257 tonn. . .	1908 Kiel	—	floating-school
Netherlands					
Albatross (ex Alk)	schooner	93 tonn. . .	1920 Netherlands .	in service	training-ship
Pollux	three-masted barque . .	c. 600 tonn. . .	1942 Amsterdam . .	—	floating-school
Urania	schooner	38 displ. . .	1927	in service	training-ship
Norway					
Christian Radich	square-rigged three-master	677 tonn. . . .	1937 Sandefjord . .	in service	training-ship
Sørlandet	square-rigged three-master	577 tonn. . . .	1927 Kristiansand .	in service	training-ship
Statsraad Lehmkul (ex Grossherzog Friedrich August)	three-masted barque . .	1710 tonn. . .	1914 Geestemünde .	in service	training-ship
Panama					
Wandia	three-masted fore-and-aft schooner	—	—	in service	training-ship
Poland					
Dar Pomorza . . . . (ex Pomorza ex Colbert, ex Prinzess Eitel Friedrich)	square-rigged three-master	1566 tonn. . .	1910 Hamburg . . .	in service	training-ship
Henryk Rutkowski	ketch	70 tonn. . .	1944 Germany . . .	in service	training-ship
Iskra (ex Vlissingen)	three-masted fore-and-aft schooner .	560 displ. . . .	1917 Netherlands .	in service	training-ship
Janek Krasicki	fore-and-aft schooner .	75 tonn. . .	1950 Poland	in service	training-ship
Lwow (ex Chinsura)	three-masted barque . .	c. 1200 tonn. .	1869 Birkenhead . .	1929 . .	floating-school
Marius Zaruski	ketch	71 tonn. . .		in service	training-ship
Mloda Gwardia	fore-and-aft schooner .	c. 120 tonn. . .	1939	in service	training-ship
Zawisca Czarny (ex Petrea). .	three-masted fore-and-aft schooner .	173 tonn. . . .	1902 Denmark . . .	in service	training-ship
Zwe Morza	fore-and-aft schooner .	75 tonn. . .	1950 Poland	in service	training-ship
Portugal					
Don Fernando de Gloria . . .	three-masted barque . .	c. 1600 displ. .	1857 India	—	floating-school
Sagres II . . . . (ex Guanabara, ex Albert Leo Schlageter)	three-masted barque . .	1869 displ. . .	1937 Hamburg . . .	in service	training-ship
Santo Andre . . . . (ex Sagres I, ex Flora, ex Max, ex Rickmer Rickmers)	three-masted barque . .	3067 displ. . .	1896 Geestemünde .	1961 . .	floating-school

Name	Type	Tonnage and Displacement	Date and place of construction	Last voyage	In Service as

Roumania

Name	Type	Tonnage and Displacement	Date and place of construction	Last voyage	In Service as
Mircea	three-masted barque	1630 displ.	1938 Hamburg	in service	training-ship

Spain

Name	Type	Tonnage and Displacement	Date and place of construction	Last voyage	In Service as
Baleares	barquentine	607 tonn.	1919 Majorca	—	floating-school
Cruz del Sur	fore-and-aft schooner	220 tonn.	1945 Spain	in service	training-ship
Estrella Polar (ex Rømø)	three-masted topsail schooner	144 tonn.	1939 Denmark	in service	training-ship
Galatea (ex Clara Stella)	three-masted barque	800 displ.	1896 Scotland	1960	floating-school
Juan Sebastian d'Elcano	four-masted topsail schooner	3697 displ.	1927 Cadiz	in service	training-ship

Sweden

Name	Type	Tonnage and Displacement	Date and place of construction	Last voyage	In Service as
Af Chapman (ex G. D. Kennedy, ex Dunboyne)	square-rigged three-master	1428 tonn.	1888 Whitehaven	1939	floating-museum
Albatros	four-masted schooner	1063 tonn.	1942 Sweden	in service	training-ship
Elida	ketch	c. 80 tonn.	Sweden	in service	fitted out in 1958
Falken	fore-and-aft schooner	220 displ.	1946 Sweden	in service	training-ship
Gerda	brig	234 tonn.	1869 Gefle	1931	floating-museum
Gladan	fore-and-aft schooner	220 displ.	1947 Sweden	in service	training-ship
Jarramas	square-rigged three master	350 displ.	1900 Karlskrona	1939	floating-museum
Lys	ketch	—	Sweden	in service	training-ship
Najaden	square-rigged three-master	350 displ.	1897 Karlskrona	1939	floating-museum
Viking	four-masted barque	2952 tonn.	1906 Kopenhagen	1947	floating-school

United Arab Republic

Name	Type	Tonnage and Displacement	Date and place of construction	Last voyage	In Service as
El Faroukieh (ex El Kahera, ex Adriatico, ex Henny, ex Cap Finisterre)	three-masted barque	930 tonn.	1874 U.K.	before 1939	floating-school

United Kingdom

Name	Type	Tonnage and Displacement	Date and place of construction	Last voyage	In Service as
Arethusa (ex Peking)	four-masted barque	3120 tonn.	1911 Hamburg	1933	floating-school
Convoy	square-rigged three-master	—	—	—	floating-school
Cutty Sark	square-rigged three-master	963 tonn.	1869 Dumbarton	1935	floating-museum
Prince Louis II (ex Peder Most)	three-masted schooner	160 tonn.	1944 Svendborg	in service	training-ship
Victory	square-rigged three-master	—	1765 Chatham	1812	historical monument and museum
Sir Winston Churchill	three-masted schooner	c. 200 tonn.	1965 Hull	in service	training-ship
Worcester	square-rigged three-master	—	c. 1840 U.K.	—	floating-school

The United States of America

Name	Type	Tonnage and Displacement	Date and place of construction	Last voyage	In Service as
Balklutha (ex Star of Alaska, ex Pacific Queen)	square-rigged three-master	1862 tonn.	1886 Glasgow	1932	floating-museum
Black Pearl	brigantine	52 displ.	1957 Wickford	in service	training-ship
Brilliant	schooner	c. 30 displ.	1932 U.S.A.	in service	training-ship

Name	Type	Tonnage and Displacement	Date and place of construction	Last voyage	In Service as
Charles W. Morgan	square-rigged three-master	314 tonn.	1841 New Bedford	1924	floating-museum
Eagle (ex Horst Wessel)	three-masted barque	1816 displ.	1936 Hamburg	in service	training-ship
Emery Rice (ex Bay State, ex Nantucket)	three-masted barque	1261 tonn.	1876 U.S.A.	1944	floating-museum
Falls of Clyde	square-rigged four-master	1741 tonn.	1878 Glasgow	1921	floating-museum
Freedom	fore-and-aft schooner	100 displ.	1931 U.S.A.	in service	training-ship
Joseph Conrad ex Georg Stage I	square-rigged three-master	212 tonn.	1882 Kopenhagen	1939	floating-museum
L. A. Dunton	fore-and-aft schooner	—	—	—	floating-museum
Mariner	yawl	c. 30 displ.	1950 U.S.A.	in service	training-ship
Royono	yawl	c. 30 displ.	1936 U.S.A.	in service	training-ship

Uruguay

Name	Type	Tonnage and Displacement	Date and place of construction	Last voyage	In Service as
Aspirante (ex Exir-Dallen, ex Parodi, ex Trinidad, ex Gelmirez)	three-masted schooner	250 displ.	1919	—	floating-school

USSR

Name	Type	Tonnage and Displacement	Date and place of construction	Last voyage	In Service as
Krusenstern (ex Padua)	four-masted barque	3064 tonn.	1926 Geestemünde	in service	training-ship
Sjedow (ex Kommodore Johnsen, ex Magdalena Vinnen)	four-masted barque	3476 tonn.	1921 Kiel	in service	training-ship
Tovaritch (ex Gorch Fock I)	three-masted barque	1510 displ.	1933 Hamburg	in service	training-ship
Alpha	barquentine	c. 300 tonn.	1947/48 Finland	in service	training-ship
Capella	barquentine	c. 300 tonn.	1947/48 Finland	in service	training-ship
Junga	barquentine	c. 300 tonn.	1947/48 Finland	in service	training-ship
Kodor	barquentine	c. 300 tonn.	1947/48 Finland	in service	training-ship
Sextan	barquentine	c. 300 tonn.	1947/48 Finland	in service	training-ship
Tropic	barquentine	c. 300 tonn.	1947/48 Finland	in service	training-ship
Vega	barquentine	c. 300 tonn.	1947/48 Finland	in service	training-ship
Zenith	barquentine	c. 300 tonn.	1947/48 Finland	in service	training-ship
(The names of two other vessels of this type are unknown)					
Praktika	three-masted topsail schooner	300 t. displ.	1947/48 Finland	in service	training-ship
Utscheba	three-masted topsail schooner	300 t. displ.	1947/48 Finland	in service	training-ship
Zaritza	three-masted topsail schooner	300 t. displ.	1947/48 Finland	in service	training-ship
(The names of six or seven other vessels of this type are unknown)					
About 10 vessel (names unknown)	three-masted topsail schooners	c. 200 displ.	1947/48 Finland	in service	training-ship
« .... » ex Christoforo Colombo	square-rigged three-master	2787 displ.	1928 Castellamare	in service	training-ship

Note

Tonnage is indicated by displacement or gross tonnage, abbreviated as « displ. » or « tonn. ». Displacement is the amount of water, in tons, displaced by the underwater volume of a vessel. Gross tonnage is the measurement of the total cubic capacity of a vessel in tons of 100 cubic feet.

The tonnage of mercantile marine training-ships is usually shown as gross tonnage, that of warships as displacement, except in the case of Russian vessels, whose employment is not always known.

MARITIME MUSEUMS AND MUSEUMS
WITH NAVAL SECTIONS

BELGIUM

ANTWERP: NATIONAL SCHEEPVAARTMUSEUM

Here is an excellent collection of ship models : contemporary reconstructions of the East Indiaman *Barber Steyn*, a Dutch frigate from the late eighteenth century, the two-decker *Caesar* about 1806-1807, a quarter-size model of Napoleon's state vessel built in 1810, an early nineteenth century galliot, a Belgian man-of-war brig, the *Duc de Brabant*, a mid-nineteenth century barquentine, and a number of other models of sailing-vessels and steamships from the nineteenth and twentieth centuries. Also exhibited are characteristically regional types of vessels, such as Paviljoenpoon, Garnaalknots, Schokker, Steenschuit, Mosselhengst, as well as pilot boats. The museum owns a fine collection of marine paintings in oil and water-colour, lithographs, prints and sketches, as well as numerous photographs and a remarkable collection of maritime books. Its catalogue is published in several languages.

CANADA

HALIFAX, NOVA SCOTIA: MARITIME MUSEUM OF CANADA

This museum concentrates on the history of Canadian naval history and ship construction. Its exhibits include models, paintings and ship plans of sailing-vessels, fishing craft and steamships. Specialized publications are issued from time to time.

ST. JOHN, NEW BRUNSWICK: NEW BRUNSWICK MUSEUM, MARINE GALLERY

The models shown in this museum, as well as the paintings, sketches of galleons and other relics of sailing-vessels and steamships deal almost exclusively with shipping in the Maritime Provinces and the Bay of Fundy. Exhibits include the clipper *Star of the East*, the square-rigged three-master *Berteaux*, both fully rigged with sails, as well as longitudinal sections of the *Josephine Troop* and the *Howard D. Troop*. Models and sketches of regional types of fishing craft are also on view.

DENMARK

HELSINGOER: HANDELS- OG SØFARTSMUSEET PAA KRONBORG

The museum is housed in Kronborg castle which forms an ideal setting for this review of Denmark's trade and shipping from the past to the present. Apart from an admirable collection of contemporary models and paintings, the museum includes sections devoted to nautical instruments, charts, life-saving apparatus on board, navigation lights, beacons, active tonnage, naval architecture, etc. The museum includes a large library and publishes an illustrated year-book and periodicals dealing with maritime history.

FRANCE

PARIS: MUSÉE DE LA MARINE

This museum's collection embraces the whole spectrum of shipping for trade and military use. The excellent models that can be seen are Columbus' caravel, the *Santa Maria*, the 120-gun three-decker *Ocean*, the *Soleil Royal* of 1690, the *Louis XV*, the *Royale* and the impressive stern of the *Reale* of 1700 with its carvings attributed to Puget. There is also a famous collection of canvases, French harbours painted by Joseph Vernet about 1765. In the centre of the picture gallery is a model of the *Royal Louis* while, to the sides, are models of frigates and xebecs. Other models are of the *pyroscaphe* or "fire-ship" of Jouffroy d'Abbans, a very early steamship of 1782, the frigate *Le Muiron* aboard which Napoleon sailed back to France from Egypt, as well as the *Belle Poule* which carried the Emperor's remains to St. Helena. Beside the navy, merchant marine, fishing and pleasure craft are well represented as is, naturally, naval construction. Also exhibited are models and paintings of foreign vessels. The museum publishes the *Neptunia* review and a catalogue.

ST. MALO: MUSÉE INTERNATIONAL DU LONG-COURS

Opened in 1966, this museum is still in the course of construction and will be devoted to the sailing-ship tradition, concentrating particularly on such themes as the history of seafaring from Magellan to Beauchesne, questions of technique and economy and life aboard vessels under sail.

GERMANY

HAMBURG: ALTONAER MUSEUM

Two important rooms trace the development of the North Sea fisheries, wooden sailing-ship construction and the evolution of merchant shipping in the region of the Lower Elbe. Apart from numerous interesting models, the museum is remarkable for its oil-paintings and water-colours of ships.

The exhibits also include navigational instruments, ship's carpenters' tools and sail makers' implements. The library contains photographs and ship plans as well as a fine collection of books on maritime subjects. There is also a special collection of approximately 40 small models of galleons and early sailing-vessels. This museum publishes a year-book and two catalogues, dealing respectively with the fishing and navigation sections.

HAMBURG: MUSEUM FÜR HAMBURGISCHE GESCHICHTE

One part of this museum is devoted to the history of Hamburg's shipping and has approximately 80 models, including some 20 eighteenth and nineteenth century ships and a number of steamships of various types. Interesting paintings and photographs are also on show. A catalogue is published.

HOLLAND

AMSTERDAM: NEDERLANDSCH HISTORISCH SCHEEPVAART MUSEUM

Visitors to this museum can see approximately 300 models of warships, merchant vessels, trawlers and boats for inland waterways, almost all of these representing Dutch ships from the seventeenth, eighteenth and nineteenth centuries, 200 of them being rigged. In addition, there are approximately 90 sections of vessels from the eighteenth and nineteenth centuries. The museum has a large library as well as an interesting collection of ship plans, paintings and photographs of historic vessels. A catalogue is available.

ROTTERDAM: MARITIEM MUSEUM PRINS HENDRIK

An important collection features models of sailing-vessels of the seventeenth and eighteenth centuries, of steamships and foreign vessels, mainly from the Far East, as well as numerous sections. Also exhibited in this museum are approximately 2,000 ship plans, paintings, prints, sketches, nautical instruments, globes and charts, etc.

NORWAY

BERGEN: BERGENS SJÖFARTSMUSEUM

Here, also, can be seen models of trawlers and merchant vessels as well as pictures of galleons, paintings, sketches and plans of different types of vessels and Norwegian open-boats. A year-book and a catalogue are published.

OSLO: NORSK SJÖFARTSMUSEUM

Models of vessels propelled by oar, sail and motor and a collection of trawlers from all regions in Norway are displayed here. Sketches of galleons and details of navigation equipment are exhibited alongside numerous paintings and drawings of vessels of all types. Various sections feature polar expeditions, whale fishing, fishing in general, lighthouses, life saving equipment and the archives include drawings, ship plans and historic photographs. The museum publishes a year-book and catalogues.

SWEDEN

GÖTEBORG: GÖTEBORG SJÖFARTSMUSEUM

A large collection of models, paintings, etc., trace the evolution of Swedish naval construction and navigation from the earliest times to the present day. Fishing, lighthouses, harbour installations and oceanography are also represented. A year-book, booklets and a catalogue are pubished.

STOCKHOLM : STATENS SJÖHISTORISKA MUSEUM

Here is the history of the Swedish navy, initiated by Admiral Chapman (1721-1805) at Karlskrona. The merchant marine is represented by models, paintings and sketches. This museum publishes a year-book, occasional other pieces of literature and a catalogue.

UNITED KINGDOM

EDINBURGH : ROYAL SCOTTISH MUSEUM

The technological section contains a remarkable collection of models of warships and merchant vessels from Roman to modern times. Visitors can admire reconstructions of some of the oldest Scottish men-of-war such as the *Yellow Carvel*, dating from 1480, and the *Great Michael* from 1511. Old English types of vessels such as hoys and brigs are also displayed, many rigged with sails. Among contemporary models there are some excellent examples such as the *D'Bataviase Eeuw*, a Dutch East Indiaman of 1719, a 120-cannon ship built in 1794 and a sloop, fully rigged as of the 1830's.

The museum also has a series of models made by French prisoners-of-war, the examples of fishing craft and coasting vessels being particularly interesting, many of them actually having planked frames and fitted out with their exact gear in miniature. Various types of Scottish vessels can be seen, many of which have long since disappeared from the seas.

GLASGOW : ART GALLERIES AND MUSEUM

This collection of ship models covers the period from prehistoric dug-outs to the large steamers, merchant vessels and warships of modern times. Here, also, are eighteenth and nineteenth century sailing-ship models, mostly built by French prisoners-of-war. One of the most treasured is the Admiralty mock-up of *H.M.S. Oxford*, about 1727. Steamship models range from the paddle-steamer *Comet*, built in 1815, to the liner *Empress of Britain*, while the collection of warships covers the period from 1866 to 1942 and includes the troop carrier *Malabar* and the battle-cruiser *Howe*. Also shown are pleasure steamers from the Firth of Clyde as well as the 25,500-ton motor boat *Stirling Castle* and the 11,063-ton cargo-boat *Essex*.

LONDON, GREENWICH : NATIONAL MARITIME MUSEUM

Known the world over is this rich collection of naval treasures, paintings, models and a wide variety of exhibits. The models include a series from naval shipyards of the seventeenth and eighteenth centuries, Admiralty mock-ups and scale models of the nineteenth and twentieth centuries, as well as Royal Yachts from the seventeenth and eighteenth centuries and steam yachts from the Victorian era, British and foreign merchant vessels from eighteenth century barques to nineteenth century clippers, as well as a number of twentieth century merchantmen. Models of foreign warships, construction models of eighteenth century British vessels, as well as models of hoys, cutters and landing craft, eighteenth and nineteenth century lightships and many more are also included. Fishing vessels and all types of barges are to be found among the exhibits. In addition, the museum is proud of its complete series of Admiralty designs and plans of all types of vessels built from the beginning of the eighteenth century until 1837, comprising some 4,000 drawings. There is a small collection of plans of nineteenth century merchant vessels as well as sets of plans relating to the various types of coastal vessels dating from the end of the era of sail. The old clipper *Cutty Sark*, belonging to the museum, features a highly interesting collection of figure-heads. The library contains over 10,000 manuscripts, a collection of seafaring books and a complete card-index of historical ship photographs.

LONDON : THE SCIENCE MUSEUM

The shipping section of this famous museum contains a large collection of contemporary models of sailing men-of-war from the seventeenth, eighteenth and nineteenth centuries, many fully rigged, as well as a special collection of models of steamships, motor boats and many smaller craft of all kinds from every part of the world. The museum has published the following booklets : *Sailing-Ships*, Volume I and II, *British Fishery-Boats and Coastal Craft* and *Merchant Steamers and Motor-Ships*.

SUNDERLAND : PUBLIC MUSEUM

Mainly featuring models of vessels built in Sunderland, including sailing-vessels, steamships, warships, various types of small craft, trawlers, etc., the museum also displays a dug-out found in the River Wear. Models of ship engines and nautical instruments are on view and the museum possesses some fine paintings, a large number of prints and photographs of vessels built in the harbour and shipyards around this region.

WHITBY : WHITBY MUSEUM

Approximately 120 models of vessels of all sizes can be seen in this collection. Among the shipyard mock-ups are the steamships *Whitehall*, *Beemah*, *Normanby*, *Laarpool*, *Bagdale* and *Arndale*. Visitors can see scale models of the *Golden Hind*, *H.M.S. Endeavour*, *H.M.S. Resolution*, the clipper *Cutty Sark*, the 1832 emigrant ship *Columbus* and the last sailing-vessel built in Whitby, the *Monkshaven*.

This museum also exhibits bone models of 50, 64, 74 and 100 cannon vessels made by prisoners-of-war. A collection of small craft features trawlers, colliers and lifeboats, Newfoundland schooners and various other types from this area.

U.S.A.

MYSTIC, CONNECTICUT : MARINE HISTORICAL ASSOCIATION INC.

A fine collection of models of rigged sailing-vessels and steamships as well as prints, paintings and sections are featured in this museum. It also owns the Breugle collection of works by the famous French painter Roux, from Marseilles. In addition, there are plans and sections of American seal-fishing vessels and ships built in Connecticut. Among others belonging to this museum are the original whaler *Charles W. Morgan* and the famous training-ship *Joseph Conrad*.

NEW BEDFORD, MASSACHUSETTS : OLD DARTMOUTH HISTORICAL SOCIETY AND JONATHAN BOURNE WHALING MUSEUM

A fine collection of material has been assembled on the whaling industry of New England, including models, nautical mementos, fishing tackle, log-books, bone carvings and various other objects fashioned or collected by the American whale fishermen. Among the rigged models are an English cutter and a schooner-rigged clipper. In a special room is a model of the whaler *Lagoda*, the largest ship-model in the world.

NEWPORT NEWS, VIRGINIA : THE MARINERS MUSEUM

This important museum contains a vast and varied collection of naval material from all over the world : engravings and paintings of ports, sailing vessels and steamships, longitudinal sections, rigged models, rescue organization, navigation lights, anchors, original small craft and all types of sea relics. Visitors to the museum can also see a collection of models of Indian canoes and visit the vast library of maritime documents. The reference library includes one of the largest collections of photographs of ships from all over the world. The museum issues a catalogue and other publications.

SALEM, MASSACHUSETTS : PEABODY MUSEUM

Principally concerned with sailing-vessels built in Salem and New England, the Peabody Museum includes numerous longitudinal sections of trawlers and merchant ships. In addition, a number of ship plans and a large collection of historical ship photographs are on display. Also to be seen are paintings by the famous French artist, Roux, whale-fishing equipment, models, navigation instruments and small reproductions of ancient galleons. The museum occasionally publishes specialized literature as well as a quarterly review entitled *The American Neptune*.

SAN FRANCISCO, CALIFORNIA : SAN FRANCISCO MARITIME MUSEUM

The accent is on the tradition and history of modern seafaring, particularly in the Pacific. Here can be seen models of schooners and square-rigged sailing-vessels, including the fully rigged five-master *Preussen*, built in Hamburg. The museum also has paintings, prints, navigation instruments, plans and architects' drawings of ships on view, and includes an excellent nautical library with a large collection of photographs. Of especial interest to visitors is the historic, iron-hulled, fully-rigged *Balclutha*, completely restored to its original state and lying in San Francisco harbour, close to the museum. The Museum publishes *Sea Letter*, a review.

SEARSPORT, MAINE : PENOBSCOT MARINE MUSEUM

Outstanding for its small but magnificent collection of ship paintings by the French artist, Roux, and other masters, this museum also has models, charts and navigation instruments used by vessels from Maine on display. The museum occasionally publishes various interesting printed material.

WASHINGTON, D.C. : UNITED STATES NATIONAL MUSEUM (SMITHSONIAN INSTITUTE)

The navigation section exhibits a large collection of American-type vessels, including both originals and longitudinal sections of small boats, as well as shipyard mock-ups and rigged models. The collection primarily features small craft, fishing schooners, pilot boats and a few models of clippers. In addition can be seen numerous plans and drawings of American merchant sailing-ships. *The National Watercraft Collection* catalogues the riches of this collection in great detail.

ACKNOWLEDGEMENTS

The publishers extend their warmest thanks to the Curators of museums and libraries and the Collectors who have helped in the preparation of this work. Special thanks go to : The Academy of Sciences, Lisbon : pages 12, 14, 15, 26 ; Graphische Sammlung Albertina, Vienna : pages 17 above on the right, 18 below ; Altonaer Museum, Hamburg : pages 238, 239, 240, 244, 245, 248 above, 250, 251, 253 ; Bibliothek der Akademie der Bildenden Künste, Vienna : pages 168, 169, 172-173 ; Bibliothèque Nationale, Paris : pages 10, 13, 25, 28, 29, 35, 62, 63, 88, 89, 92, 93, 94, 95, 103, 109, 116, 117, 122, 123, 124, 142, 147, 165, 188 above, 188 below on the left ; Bibliothèque Royale, Bruxelles : page 38 ; British Museum, London : pages 47 above, 49 below ; Dixson Galleries, Sydney : pages 128 below, 129 below on the left ; Frans Hals Museum, Haarlem : page 54 ; Helmut Grubbe, Lübeck-Travemünde : pages 235, 248 below, 249, 254, 262, 263, 264 ; Laffont Publications, Paris : page 181 above, and below on the right ; The Masters and Fellows of Magdalene College, Cambridge : page 41 ; The Mariners Museum, Newport News : pages 110, 111, 151, 204, 205, 215 above, 260 above on the left ; Jean Meissonnier, Marseilles : pages 143, 144, 145, 146 ; Ministère de la guerre, Paris : page 36 ; Mitchell Library, Sydney : page 129 below on the right ; Musée des Arts Africains et Océaniens, Paris : pages 180, 188 below on the right, 189 ; Musée des Beaux-Arts, Marseilles : pages 80, 98 below, 99 ; Musée international du long-cours, St.-Malo : cover and pages 241, 242, 243, 246, 247, 260 above on the right ; Musée du Louvre, Paris : pages 40, 97 above, 98 above, 102, 127 ; Musée de la Marine, Paris : pages 71, 90 below, 91 below, 97 below, 119, 125, 162 below ; Musée du Havre, Le Havre : pages 170, 171 ; Museo de Arte Cataluna, Barcelona : page 17 on the left ; Museo Correr, Venice : page 11 ; Museu Nacional de Arte Antiga, Lisbon : page 27 above ; National Archives, Washington : pages 152, 158 ; National Maritime Museum, Greenwich : pages 30, 43, 44, 45, 48, 49 above, 50, 90 above, 91 above, 101, 104, 105, 114, 115, 128 above, 129 above, 136, 137, 181 below on the left, 197, 260 below on the right ; Peabody Museum, Salem : pages 140, 148, 162 above, 163, 174, 177, 192, 195, 209, 211, 214, 215, 218, 219, 222, 224, 225, 236, 237, 260 below on the left, 261 ; Prins Hendrik Museum, Rotterdam : pages 24, 86 ; Rijksmuseum, Amsterdam : pages 47 below, 55, 107 ; Scheepvaart Museum, Amsterdam : pages 37, 64, 72, 120-121 ; Science Museum, London : pages 59, 164, 196 ; Service historique de la Marine, Paris : pages 116-117 above ; Service hydrographique de la Marine, Paris : pages 60, 61, 73, 74, 75, 76, 77, 78, 79 ; Staatliche Kunstsammlungen, Dresden : page 17 below on the right ; Staatliche Museen, Berlin-Dahlem : page 18 above ; Statens Sjöhistoriska Museum, Wasavarvet, Stockholm : page 69 ; Yale University, The Beinecke Rare Books and Manuscript Library, New Haven : page 27 below.

The plans of the eight monographs were drawn by Uli Kohler, from documents and information provided by the Prins Hendrik Museum, Rotterdam, Statens Sjöhistoriska Museum, Wasavarvet, Stockholm, Percivall Marshall, London, National Archives, Washington, Association des Amis des Musées de la Marine, Paris and captain Helmut Grubbe, Lübeck-Travemünde.

PHOTOGRAPHY

Graphische Sammlung Albertina, Vienna : pages 17 above, 18 below ; Alinari, Florence : page 11 ; Altonaer Museum, Hamburg : pages 238, 239, 240, 244, 245, 248 above, 250, 251, 253 ; Amplicaciones y Reproducciones MAS, Barcelone : page 17 on the left ; Bibliothèque Nationale, Paris : pages 13, 25, 63, 89, 92 above and below, 188 above ; Bibliothèque Royale, Bruxelles : page 38 ; British Museum, London : pages 47 above, 49 below ; Yves Debraine, Lausanne : pages 80, 98 below, 99 ; Dixson Galleries, Sydney : pages 128 below on the left, 129 below on the left ; Antonio Pereira Forjaz, Lisbon : pages 12, 14, 15 ; Frans Hals Museum, Haarlem : page 54 ; Giraudon, Paris : page 36 ; Helmut Grubbe, Lübeck-Travemünde : pages 235, 248 below, 249, 254, 262, 263, 264 ; Helmy's, Le Havre : pages 170, 171 ; Mel Jos, Marseilles : pages 143, 144, 145, 146 ; Laffont Publications, Paris : pages 181 above on the right, 181 below on the right and on the left ; Magdalene College, Cambridge : page 41 ; The Mariners Museum, Newport News : pages 110, 111, 151, 204, 205, 215 above, 260 above on the left ; Erwin Meyer K.G., Vienna : pages 168, 169, 172-173 ; Mitchell Library, Sydney : page 129 ; Musée du Louvre, Paris : page 98 above ; Museu Nacional de Arte Antiga, Lisbon : page 27 above ; National Archives, Washington : pages 152, 158 ; National Maritime Museum, Greenwich : pages 30, 43, 44, 45, 48, 49 above, 50, 90 above, 91 above, 102, 104, 105, 114, 115, 128 above, 129 above, 136, 137, 197, 199, 201, 215 on the left, 260 below on the right ; Peabody Museum, Salem : pages 140, 148, 162 above, 163, 174, 177, 192, 195, 209, 211, 214, 215 below on the right, 218, 219, 222, 224, 225, 234, 236, 237, 260 in the middle on the left, 260 below on the left, 261 ; Jean-Claude Philippot, St.-Malo : pages 241, 242, 243, 246, 247, 260 above on the right and cover ; Prins Hendrik Museum, Rotterdam : pages 24, 86 ; Rijksmuseum, Amsterdam : pages 47 below, 55, 107 ; Scheepvaart Museum, Amsterdam : pages 37, 64, 72, 120-121 ; Science Museum, London : pages 59, 164, 196 ; Sophocolor, Paris : pages 40, 101 ; Horacio de Sousa Novais, Lisbon : page 26 ; Staatliche Kunstsammlungen, Dresden : page 17 below on the right ; Staatliche Museen, Berlin-Dahlem : page 18 above ; Statens Sjöhistoriska Museum Wasavarvet, Stockholm : page 69 ; Studio Henri, Paris : pages 10, 28, 29, 35, 60, 61, 62, 71, 73, 74, 75, 76, 77, 78, 79, 88, 90 below, 91 below, 92 in the middle, 93, 94, 95, 97, 103, 109, 116, 117, 119, 120, 122, 123, 124, 125, 127, 142, 147, 162 below, 165, 180, 188 below, 189 ; Yale University, New Haven : page 27 below.

PRODUCTION EDITA S.A., LAUSANNE

The first edition of
this book was designed and produced in 1967
by the Edita staff composed of
Ami Guichard, Joseph Jobé, Charles Riesen,
Ursula Claren and Max Thommen

Offset printed by
GEA, Milan
Bound by Maurice Busenhart, Lausanne